THE FUTURE OF HUMANITY

Fiction has never been this close to reality

AUGUSTO CURY

Translation:
Marcos Cristovam de Paula

Copyright © 2024 Dr Augusto Cury.

All rights reserved. This book or any portion thereof may not be reproduced or used in any manner whatsoever without the express written permission of the publisher except for the use of brief quotations in a book review.

ISBN: 978-1-965965-11-5 (Paperback)

DEDICATION

I offer this book to _____.
The greatest adventure of a human being is to travel. And the greatest journey one can undertake is the journey within oneself.
And reading a book is the most exciting way to travel, for a book reveals that life is the greatest of all books.
But it is of no use for those who cannot read between the lines And discover what the words did not say.
Deep down, a reader is the author of their own story…

___/__/_____

ACKNOWLEDGEMENTS

I'd like to thank each and every one of the patients I have met throughout my journey as psychiatrist and psychology researcher. They have taught me to see through the eyes of the heart, to discover the fascinating world hidden within the valleys of losses and the cliffs of emotional pain. They are living pearls in the theater of existence. I dedicate this work of fiction to them and to everyone who has been mutilated by life. In some way, all of them have been portrayed in the pages of this book.

Table of Contents

Preface 1

Chapter 1 – The Challenge 5

Chapter 2 – The Search (Or the Second Challenge) 11

Chapter 3 – The Discovery 19

Chapter 4 – The Turn Over (Or an Unexpected Turn of Events) 27

Chapter 5 – Traveling Within 35

Chapter 6 – Rising From the Ashes 45

Chapter 7 – Old Philosophy and Teen Psychiatry 55

Chapter 8 – The Worst Part 61

Chapter 9 – An Illustrious Visitor 71

Chapter 10 – A Spectacular Performance 81

Chapter 11 – The Principle of Co-Responsibility 91

Chapter 12 – The Reencounter 105

Chapter 13 – The Student's Boldness 115

Chapter 14 – Turning Things Upside Down 125

Chapter 15 135

Chapter 16 141

Chapter 17 149

Chapter 18 165

Chapter 19 173

Chapter 20 183

Chapter 21 193

Chapter 22 213

Chapter 23 227

Chapter 24 237

Chapter 25 243

Chapter 26 251

Chapter 27 261

Chapter 28 267

Preface

A brilliant and demanding doctor received a book called *The Future of Mankind* as a gift from a colleague who was also a doctor. He skeptically started reading it, and little by little was getting immersed in it, breathing in the words and getting involved in the character's dramas. While reading, he could see himself in those conflicts, taking part in their hardships and joy, crying and laughing with them. A few days later, due to a stroke, he suffered a brain hemorrhage and fell into a coma. Regaining consciousness for a brief moment, he quoted parts of *The Future of Mankind*. And, despite being an atheist, he spoke of God in a way he had never done before. And then he closed his eyes one last time.

One day, I was touring the Douro River Valley. Having traveled 120 miles, in that beautiful region where Port wine is produced, I stopped at a small roadside restaurant. After ordering a delicious codfish, the young owner – who did not know who I was – told me he was not fond of reading, but had recently read a book that made him rethink his life story. It was *The Future of Mankind*.

It gladdens me that some members of the technical committee of the Brazilian soccer team, along with some of the players, have read *The Future of Mankind*. During my chats with the technical committee, we talked about how everyone wants the perfume of the flowers, yet few wish to get their hands dirty to cultivate them. Everyone wants to win, especially in sports, yet no one deserves it without discipline or knowing how to use their defeats to conquer it. A human being does not reveal their dignity amidst an oasis of applause, but in the desert of boos. I have mentioned that some celebrities, including soccer players, surrender themselves to depression when they leave the media spotlight and discover that they never were gods, but simple humans that will one day go by unnoticed.

These stories and so many others experienced through the reading of this book make me emotional. I was in tears writing their narrative. I felt as if I was leaving a piece of me in each paragraph, rebuilding real stories of fascinating people I have met along my journey as a medicine student and, later on, as a psychiatrist, psychotherapist and, especially, as a researcher of the most complex of worlds: the human mind.

Falcon, one of the main characters of this novel, shows that the human mind shelters an even bigger and more complex universe than the one restricted to the physical world. Falcon is a very clever philosopher who develops a severe psychosis. While he tries to get back on his feet, he becomes irreverent and starts singing and giving speeches in inappropriate places, talking to flowers and hugging trees. He is a free being, he does what he loves to do, and he knows that there are simple yet irreplaceable riches, more valuable than mountains of gold. He has nothing, yet he has much; unlike the ones who have much, when, actually, they have so little.

In *The Future of Mankind*, I use the anatomy class of a medicine school to represent the world we are building. The plot starts with astonished students who standing in front of naked corpses that are lying on white marble countertops. Who are those people? Which tears have they shed? Which adventures have they lived? What are their stories? No one seems to care. But one student, Marco Polo, raises his hand and asks. He wants to know their names. According to that cold-hearted professor, those were homeless people – no story, no identity. Marco Polo disagrees and becomes the laughing stock of the master and his classmates. Humiliated, and instead of giving up, he decided to venture into a fascinating investigation about those people's past, just as his Venetian namesake would have done. With Falcon's help, he meets amazing characters.

This book reveals that, just like those corpses in the anatomy class, we are losing our humanity, becoming mere consumers, just like a credit card or passport number. This is unsettling! The loss of humanity corrodes our emotional and intellectual health without us even realizing it. It shatters the art of thinking and our ability to notice the pain of others, it makes us punitive and self-punitive beings.

Young people and adults, intellectuals and students, psychotherapists and patients have traveled Falcon and Marco Polo's journey and seen the human mind through different perspectives, realizing that there is a treasure buried inside the suffering people. A beggar and a doctor, a psychotic and a psychiatrist, together in search of a better world, challenging the social standards and revealing that, if it is impossible to fix the past, we can at least build the future if we act in the present. We must be sellers of dreams. We are part of both the problem and the solution. We will be either victims of the future or protagonists of our stories. The future of mankind has already begun.

Augusto Cury

CHAPTER 1

The Challenge

Anxiety was flowing inside some young people. The greatest dream was being performed in the theater of their emotions. Filled with euphoria, they ran like children through the hallways of the medical school.

Their eyes stared at the walls, captivated by the strange and beautiful images portraying details of the thorax and muscles. The images of naked dissected bodies revealed that, on the inside, human beings were more similar than they had imagined. A photograph of a brain, full of grooves like streams that carve the land, would indicate the vital center of our intelligence and our madness.

The great day had arrived. The day they had expected and feared the most. The new students would have their first anatomy class. They would find out the secrets of science's most complex object: the human organism. They waited, impatiently, outside of the laboratory for their masters; a mysterious atmosphere filled the air.

They had no idea of what awaited them. They wanted to be heroes of life, relieve pain and prolong existence, but medicine's insensitive curriculum would shock them, without any preparation, with the grotesque image of death. The dream of being heroes of life would take a harsh blow. They would be faced with naked bodies, displayed sequentially like animals.

The anatomy professors and technicians finally arrived. Words were subtracted and a cold silence embraced the group. The professors entered the large laboratory and invited the sixty students to come in. They slowly squeezed through the narrow doors.

Like spectators at a show, the tension was rising and it searched for organs to occupy, triggering psychosomatic symptoms. Some students felt palpitations, others were breathless and there were others who were sweating.

As they entered the lab, an emotional shock echoed within the core of the young audience. The students saw twelve completely naked cadavers, lying rigidly with their faces and chests turned to the ceiling. Each one was extended across a white marble table.

The smell of formalin, used to preserve the bodies, was almost unbearable. Wide-eyed with astonishment, the students contemplated the opaque and inert eyes of the cadavers. Most of them were middle-aged but among them was the body of an old man with lackluster skin and a kind face.

The tables were six feet apart from each other. Each group of five students would be responsible for dissecting and studying a cadaver during the year. They would have to pull the skin back, separate the muscles and find the trajectory of nerves and arteries. They would have to open the thorax and the abdomen and, precisely, know the color, size and location of each internal organ. The young students should be artisans who would cut into the most beautiful of masterpieces.

But no one wanted to dissect them at that moment. Everyone was still under the impact of that image. Permeated by existential conflicts while facing the naked portrait of human life, the students asked themselves: "Who are we?", "What are we?", "What do we become in the face of the chaos of death?", "What is the meaning of human existence?" These are simple, yet intriguing questions that have always disturbed Mankind. These questions started a drama on the stage of the intelligence of those young spectators.

The atmosphere brought a sudden and uncontrollable emotional blow. Some of the more sensitive students tried to leave the room abruptly. They were teary-eyed, frightened and apprehensive. Those were not relatives or friends who were lying there, but they could see in those bodies the mirror of the human existence. They noticed that life is so vast, yet so ephemeral, so complex yet so fragile. While some students were trying to leave the room, others wanted to get in. The turmoil increased. No one knew what to do.

In contrast to the students' conflicts, the professors and technicians stood at the back of the room. Some of them looked at each other and laughed at the audience's despair. "Freshmen!" they thought arrogantly. In the past, they had also been anxious, but over the years they had lost their sensitivity, obstructed their capability of asking and searching for answers. They smothered their conflicts and became technicians of life.

This famous medical school's curriculum had no philosophy or psychology classes to prepare students to face the dilemma of life and death, the paradox between the will to maintain life and the defeat of witnessing one's last breath. Dreams were broken and passion for life was crushed. The damage caused in the unconscious mind of the future doctors was intense. Trained to be logical and objective, they had not yet developed the skills to deal with the field of emotions.

Patients gradually became just ill organs, instead of unique human beings, who needed to be submitted to examinations and not talked to. Thus, the most beautiful and important of sciences was submitted to the prison of the market economy. Hippocrates, the father of medicine, would turn over in his grave if he knew this. Trying to control the initial impact,

Dr. George, head of the anatomy department, asked for silence, called them back in and asked them to stand in a circle around the room.

He began his class ignoring the emotional chaos that his students were going through, and completely disregarded their anguish. With an imposing voice and eloquent gestures, he quieted down the freshmen's agitation. The professor began by presenting his credentials. He had first specialized in gastrointestinal surgery. Later, he became a specialist in anatomy and received his doctorate from Harvard, being internationally recognized. He had published over fifty articles in scientific journals and was a notable scientist in his field.

Hiding behind his resume, he introduced his discipline's program. After the introduction, he immediately began to reveal a few techniques for dissecting the skin, muscles, arteries and nerves. Everything was progressing normally, just like every other year, until one student suddenly raised his hand. His name was Marco Polo.

Dr. George would not like being interrupted. He was not fond of debates. Each student would have to ponder on their doubts until the end of the class and then ask him or one of the other assisting professors and technicians. He ignored Marco Polo's gesture. A few of his classmates became even more apprehensive. So as not to make a fool of himself, the young student lowered his hand.

Marco Polo was an intrepid and determined young man. He could not elaborate the whirlwind of thoughts that went through the theater of his mind during the anatomy class. However, he was an observer and was not afraid of expressing his ideas. Although immature, he exercised an important characteristic of the most brilliant thinkers throughout history: great ideas emerge from observing small details.

Five minutes after hearing about techniques and anatomical parts, Marco Polo could no longer withhold his anxiety. He was sweating. Once again, he raised his hand. The professor, irritated with his boldness, explained that all doubts should be clarified at the end of each class but he would make an exception. With a gesture he indicated that Marco Polo could speak, as if he were doing him a huge favor.

With crystal clear sincerity, Marco Polo asked:

"What are the names of the people we are about to dissect?"

Dr. George took a hit with that question. He looked towards the professors who assisted him, shook his head and mumbled, "There's always a stupid one in each class." With a deep voice, he said:

"These bodies have no names!"

Hearing such a harsh reply, the other students left their anxiety behind and began laughing timidly. Embarrassed, Marco Polo looked at the cadavers and commented:

"How can they not have names? Didn't they cry, love, have dreams, friends or a story?" The audience was silent. The professor was clearly annoyed. He felt challenged, so he publicly mocked his student:

"Listen young man, there are only lifeless bodies here, no story or anything. No one breathes or speaks. You are here to study anatomy. There are many mediocre doctors in society because they didn't dedicate enough time to this subject. If you do not wish to become one of them, I advise you to stop philosophizing and interrupting my class."

The students' chuckles started getting louder. They thought Marco Polo had been taught a lesson that would paralyze him. Listening to the unrestrained laughter, the professor felt victorious but Marco Polo still had the nerve to reply:

"How can we penetrate someone's body without knowing anything about their personality? This is an intrusion!"

And to needle his professor he decided to really philosophize:

"A man without a story is like a book without words."

The audience was surprised with the depth of the sentence. Dr. George aggressively interrupted him:

"Let's not dwell on cheap philosophy. If you wish to be a detective who investigates the identity of the dead, you have chosen the wrong school. You should try the police academy." Marco Polo's classmates mocked him this time. Some of them uttered catcalls as if they were in a stadium match. Marco Polo observed the scene and was shaken, not so much because of the professor's aggressiveness, but especially because of the complexity of the human mind. Just a few minutes earlier, his classmates had been in a room of terror and now were in a circus and he was the clown. He began to understand that pain and laughter, madness and sanity are not very far apart.

The professor ended the subject by saying:

"These cadavers have no stories. They are beggars, indigents, with no identity or family. They die in the streets and hospitals and no one claims their existence. It's not up to us to claim them."

Besides publicly humiliating his intrepid student, he sarcastically challenged him. He stared at the young man and said:

"If you wish to try to identify them, go to the department's office for information. If any of these indigents has an interesting story, please let us know so we can hear it." Marco Polo remained silent.

"Congratulations. You really showed the boy," one of the assisting professors whispered to his boss.

"You are a specialist at putting freshmen in their place," said another.

Dr. George smiled; however, his emotions were not a placid lake, but a tormented sea. A student had never brought up such questions in the anatomy lab before.

Marco Polo left the class with the impression that those who wish to think have a price to pay. It would be more comfortable to be silent, follow the scripted program and be just another student in the crowd. However, the comfort of being silent would generate a debt to his conscience that could not be paid... He would have to make a choice.

CHAPTER 2

The Search
(Or the Second Challenge)

Marco Polo could not get over the way he had been treated by his professor. He wondered if his questions were pertinent or foolish. "They cannot be foolish. Each human being is a world", he thought to himself. Many people love routine; others cannot live without adventure. That young man belonged to the latter group: he hated routine. Dr. George's last sentence provoked his intelligence and he could not get it out of his mind. It had become an obsessive challenge.

The next day he went to check the papers that recorded the admittance of the cadavers. He was disappointed because there was no record of names, activities or relatives. After going over several documents, he only found vague information about one of the bodies. The information had been written down by one of the social workers at the medical school hospital.

She reported that the old man had a bizarre nickname - "Poet of Life." She had written down on his medical chart: "A beggar named Falcon, who lived in the city park, identified the body. He was unable to express himself because he clearly had a serious and incapacitating mental illness. Therefore, Falcon gave no details about the deceased; he only said that he was his friend and that he was called "Poet of Life." These vague words stirred Marco Polo's imagination. "Who could he be? Why did that dead beggar have the strange nickname *Poet of Life*?" He looked for the social worker for more information.

He found her talking to a psychologist. He introduced himself and asked her how he could find that Falcon she had mentioned in her report, because he would like to interview him. When asked why he wanted such information, he told them, to their amazement, that he wanted to discover the story of one of the cadavers in the anatomy lab. The social worker discouraged him.

"I remember this Falcon. I tried to get him to talk for more than fifteen minutes but the poor man was insane and his personality was completely destroyed. He was unable to maintain a rational dialogue. You'll only be wasting your time if you actually get to find him." The psychologist, showing authoritarian *psychologism*, went further.

"Most of the cadavers in the anatomy room have history of serious mental disease. They had no documents or culture and they could barely carry a conversation. They lived by instinct at the margins of society roaming the streets like animals."

Marco Polo got angry at their attitude. They had been even more incisive than his anatomy professor. It was as if the cadavers had been mounted from anatomical parts without the right to a unique story. Outraged, he confronted them:

"I do not agree with you. Don't these beggars have complex personalities or are we the ones who are incapable of understanding them?"

The psychologist, losing her patience with his petulance replied:

"You have just begun studying medicine and you already think you are a professor?"

Marco Polo left it at that and went away feeling frustrated.

The social worker commented to the psychologist:

"Don't worry. This romantic fever will go away over time."

The young man spent the following days searching for Falcon at the park. The park was as large as New York City's Central Park, with streets, woods, benches and open areas.

Due to the park's dimensions, as well as the increase in homelessness, because of the financial crisis, and the fact that beggars are frequently nomadic, the task of finding Falcon was really difficult.

He conducted his investigation by trial and error. He would approach any beggar he could find. Some of them had no idea of what he was talking about, others pretended to be deaf, and a few of them gave him some attention, but said that they had never heard of Falcon. One of them just laughed and hopped around imitating a bird in flight.

Sometimes, he had the impression that some of them knew Falcon, but their conversation would not progress. He could never talk to them for more than a minute. He began to think that the others were right and he had been wrong. He considered ending his "Indiana Jones" quest for society's outcasts. However, every time he saw his professor, he felt he was being taunted.

His classmates teased him, "Where's the beggar's story?". Some of the funnier and disrespectful students would point at a cadaver and say something like: "This was Julius Caesar, the Emperor of Rome!" and everyone laughed. The cadavers no longer shocked the class. What used to be abnormal now became normal.

Marco Polo observed all these phenomena. He did not understand, but he registered them. He began to realize that human beings adapt to everything, even chaos. Humiliation only fueled his challenge. He was disturbed by the idea of giving up.

A month after his first anatomy class, he decided to try one more time. Once again, he went to the enormous park, walked all over the place talking to a few beggars, but he did not get the answers he was looking for. Two of them were sitting on the same bench, mumbling to each other when Marco Polo asked them, but they remained silent about Falcon.

Suddenly, fifty yards ahead, he saw a beggar approaching the passersby. He was trying to get some money for his evening meal. He had a long white beard. His hair was tousled like Einstein's, mocking the world, but it really looked like he mocked bathing. His skin was dry, lackluster, dehydrated and scarred by time. He wore a black coat mended with white strips. He had a rancid smell.

Marco Polo approached him, gave him some change and asked him if he knew Falcon. The beggar looked at him, took the money and pretended not to have heard. Marco Polo asked him again. This time, the beggar raised his finger to his lips and said:

"Quiet! The princess is arriving."

The young man looked around and saw nothing. But the beggar was still alert. He got up and, completely mesmerized, began to follow a butterfly with his eyes. He raised his hands and started swaying, imitating its dance. It flew up to the trees and came back down landing softly on his hand. Astonished, Marco Polo could not say whether it had been a coincidence or an instinctive and inexplicable attraction. The beggar sighed and contemplated it. He seemed to be as free as the butterfly. Then, he blew it softly and said: "Goodbye, princess! You charm this place, but go your way and watch out for predators." Marco Polo was intrigued with his words and asked for a third time:

"Do you know Falcon?"

The beggar gazed at him and replied, "For many years I've been asking myself who I am. The more I ask myself, the less I know who I am. What I think I am is not what I am."

Marco Polo was confused. He understood nothing, but was ecstatic with the possibility of that man being Falcon. He introduced himself and inquired about the "Poet of Life". He had not realized that his anxiety had shut off the wanderer. To make things worse, he naively said:

"I'd like this information because the Poet is lying in the anatomy lab of the medical school I attend, and my classmates and I will be dissecting him. I'd like to know something about his life."

The beggar was astonished with this information. Marco Polo realized that he had been cold and aggressive and he quickly tried to appease him by adding:

"Even after his death, the Poet will be useful for the training of doctors and consequently, for Mankind."

With tearful eyes, the indigent seemed to have been transported to another world. Like a time traveler, he stared vacantly into space. Marco Polo insisted and asked him if he was Falcon. The beggar gave no answer. He just got up and left in complete silence.

The young student just sat on the bench, paralyzed in his intelligence. He felt as if he was the miserable one in this story. He had plenty and nothing at the same time. He was unable to determine his feelings and felt incapable of understanding the world of these wanderers who roam aimlessly through life. He came back the next day and could not find the beggar. He was dismayed.

Three days later, he found him again. This time the student was more careful. He delicately sat on the bench without speaking. He would glance at the beggar, who seemed to ignore him.

"Please sir, tell me if you are Falcon."

After insisting once again, the beggar turned to him and asked:

"Who are you?"

Marco Polo introduced himself by saying his name, address, where he studied, among other things.

"I'm not asking you what you do; I'm asking you who you are. What is your essence, what is behind your social makeup?"

Marco Polo felt a knot in his throat. The beggar's intelligent reasoning had caught him by surprise. "This beggar is not demented, on the contrary. On our first meeting he used the word predator, and now he talks about social makeup", he analyzed. He did not know what to answer. So the beggar said:

"If you are so slow to tell me who you are, how dare you ask who I am?"

The young man was shocked again, so he insisted:

"You knew the "Poet". Who was he? Why was he called the *Poet*?"

"You perfumed boys, who wear nice clothes and live on the surface of existence… who do you think you are to study the Poet of Life? You can cut his body but you will never penetrate his soul."

These words shook Marco Polo. It was brilliant reasoning, albeit offensive. He was convinced that this beggar was actually the Falcon.

Then the beggar became dead silent. He raised his arms, closed his eyes and listened carefully to the serenity of the wind blowing through the nearby trees. He took a deep breath and said to himself:

"What a wonderful breeze!"

Dumbfounded, Marco Polo insisted: "Tell me about your friend".

Falcon did not like his tone and said:

"Do not give me orders, kid! Do not control me! I'm not in your world! I'm free!"

"Forgive me for my insistence".

"I will only continue this conversation if you answer one question."

Confident that a beggar would not ask anything complex, Marco Polo immediately replied that he would be glad to answer any question.

"What is the difference between a *poet* and a *poet of life*?" He asked, while looking deeply into Marco Polo's eyes.

The young man realized that he had been tricked. He had underestimated the beggar's intelligence. He ran his hands over his face, lowered his head and, after thinking about it for a long time, admitted:

"Forgive me sir, but I don't know the answer."

"A poet writes poetry; a poet of life lives as if life were a poem. My friend was a Poet of Life."

Marco Polo was about to ask another question when Falcon interrupted him and said:

"Be honest. You didn't answer the question so the conversation is over."

Marco Polo just sat on the bench. He thought he was so smart, but he had just been confronted with his stupidity and arrogance. Despite being disappointed with himself, he was euphoric with Falcon's intelligence.

Falcon got up as if nothing had happened and began to walk away. He hugged a tree and kissed it. He then knelt before a flower and appeared to want to penetrate its entrails. He mumbled a few words as if he were saying a prayer or complimenting the flower.

"See you tomorrow", said Marco Polo stubbornly and with a quivering voice, trying to maintain some kind of link.

Falcon stood up and remarked:

"Time does not exist, kid. The flame of life might be extinguished by tomorrow".

He then left without saying goodbye. He opened his arms and moved around as if he were dancing. With a vibrant voice he began to sing Louis Armstrong's *What a Wonderful World*.

I see trees so green, red roses too
I see them bloom for me and you
And I think to myself... What a wonderful world.

I see skies so blue and clouds so white.
The bright blessed day, the dark sacred night.
And I think to myself... What a wonderful world.

Marco Polo's intellectual world was not at peace, he had just gone through a whirlwind. Deeply intrigued he thought to himself, "Who is this man who hides under the skin of a panhandler? Who is this beggar who seems to have so much, but owns so little?"

CHAPTER 3

The Discovery

The young student went back to his dorm and began an introspection process. His father, Rudolph, had always admired Marco Polo, one of history's greatest adventurers. The Venetian traveler was only 17 years old when, in 1271, he left beautiful Venice and went to Asia with his father and uncle. His incredible odyssey lasted for 24 years.

They took giant risks, navigated through rivers and seas, walked through deserts, climbed mountains and stepped on lands never before explored by a European. Their adventure revealed a fascinating world, which had never been described before. His book,

"*The Description of the World*", influenced map-making in 1450 and is now on display at the *Biblioteca Nazionale Marziana*, in Venice.

Rudolph was an avid admirer of Marco Polo's adventurous courage and, therefore, named his son after him. As the boy grew, Rudolph would excitedly describe the adventures of the Italian adventurer to young Marco Polo. His father would tell him, with doses of fiction, the Venetian navigator's dreams, his unfaltering courage and his uncontrollable motivation to discover new worlds and explore new cultures, customs and culinary. The boy absorbed his father's every word.

Among his many discoveries, Marco Polo brought the pasta, invented by the Chinese, to Italy. Yet Italian people, with their unique culinary ability, perfected it. Rudolph, a lover of good pasta, would make a toast to Marco Polo every time he ate spaghetti. His father always repeated a phrase that echoed in young Marco Polo's mind, "Son, adventurers show off their achievements and all the others applaud them. Never be commonplace person."

Now he was a medical student. He wanted to understand the mysteries of the human body. However, since life has unpredictable turns, he was faced with a greater challenge: to understand the complicated world of the human mind.

As if this torturing challenge were not enough, the personality he was trying to understand was of a human being who lived at the outer edges of society. For that reason he was labeled as crazy, impenetrable and as someone who had a despicable existential story. He felt that he would not be able to go deep into Falcon's universe, because they lived in distinct environments and cultures. He constantly thought, "How can I do this? What tools should I use? Which measures can I take without characterizing an invasion? "Certainly the 13th century Marco Polo would also be disturbed by this adventure."

He would need to be bold and creative to travel through the intangible soil of the human soul and walk through the indecipherable territory of emotions. After traveling through his thoughts and taking notes of the facts that had happened, he had an idea. It was an unusual idea to break the barriers and the distance between the thinking beggar and himself: "I need to become one of them", he thought.

The following morning, a sunny Saturday, he went into the bathroom and spread garlic paste and a rotten turnip on his arms and chest. He took some hair gel, mixed it with garlic paste and spread it on his disheveled hair. He looked like a monster or someone who had just received an electric shock, but he would try anything to be successful. After all, he could no longer take being mocked by his classmates.

He then went to his room, ripped a bright red shirt and put it on. He put on a pair of stained and faded black jeans he had bought at a thrift store. He put on a patched-up black coat, also bought at the same place. His friends were startled when they saw him walk into the living room. Marco Polo looked more like an alien than a beggar. They all fell over laughing. His day had started badly. He could not explain anything to his friends, they would not understand. He left his ecstatic friends behind.

He smelled so bad that no one could walk by him without holding their nose. The eccentric young man astonished the adults but amused children. He had never called so much attention to himself before. As he came closer to the park, people would point out and mock him. He became angry with "normal people" and felt like confronting them. "Being a beggar must be a hard life", he thought. But his goal impelled him, it was his priority and he was convinced that Falcon would approach him.

After searching for about half an hour, he found Falcon and sat next to him. He remained completely silent trying to impress him. Falcon moved away unable to stand the smell. He furtively gazed at Marco Polo from head to toe and moved away a little further. Each of them was whistling and looking at opposite directions. Suddenly, their eyes met. When Marco Polo thought that he had made an impression, Falcon shouted out: "Man, you're really ugly!", and fell over laughing.

The park became silent with the sound of his laughter. Marco Polo blushed, not knowing whether to laugh or run. He chose to laugh. He laughed a lot. He laughed so as not to cry. It was the first time he had laughed at his own foolishness. He was an intelligent and intrepid young man but he was strict and did not have a great sense of humor. Laughing at himself was a relief. The passersby gathered around wanting to take part in their joy. Marco Polo pointed to the audience and laughed even louder. The audience also began to laugh and no one knew why. They laughed for no reason at all and they laughed at each other. It was laughter therapy, both illogical and simple.

The show was over moments later. Everyone became silent and the audience silently dispersed. As they dispersed, they threw coins. Falcon said:

"My God, how needy normal people are. How easy it is to entertain them. Even a novice clown becomes an attraction."

Marco Polo frowned and wondered if the comment had been directed to him. But he decided to stick to his plan: he took his bag and gave the beggar some food and a box of chocolates. He thought that after the circus and the gifts he had won Falcon over. But he was wrong. The beggar looked at the young man and said something painfully unforgettable:

"Your food quenches my hunger, but it does not buy my freedom."

"I don't wish to buy your freedom", Marco Polo answered immediately.

"Be honest. You want me to talk and give you information. Those who sell their freedom were never worthy of it."

Marco Polo scratched his head and asked himself once again, "Who is this person so quick to answer and with such nimble ideas?"

He could see the flaws in his plan to win over such an unusual man. Deep down, he wanted to buy something that was priceless. He would need to use the strategy of honesty. Recognizing his mistake, he said:

"Please forgive my second intentions. I really wanted my presents to open the windows of your mind".

Falcon's voice sweetened and became more affectionate with the young man's humility. "Kid, your namesake was a pioneer but you will never be one of us. You can put on makeup, wear ripped clothes and smell bad, but you will still be you. In your world, you believe that the packaging changes the value of the content. In my world that is foolishness.

You will continue to be a prisoner".

Marco Polo was astonished:

"Prisoner of what? I am free!"

Falcon replied:

"You're a prisoner of the system. You think you're free. Your feet are free to walk and your mouth is free to speak. But are you free to think?" Marco Polo thought for a minute and said:

"I think so."

"Ok, so answer me honestly: Do you suffer because of the future, I mean, are you tormented by things that haven't happened yet?" "Yes", Marco Polo sadly replied.

"Do you have unnecessary needs?"

"Yes."

"Do you suffer when someone criticizes you? Are you worried about what others think of you?" "Yes."

Falcon became silent while Marco Polo thought about this. He recalled how the opinion of his professor and classmates had tormented him. The discrimination he had suffered had been duly noted, generating a conflict. He had lost sleep several times. He had allowed the outside garbage to break into his emotions. He wondered what he was doing at that park. Winning Falcon over had been motivated by the pain of discrimination and not by what he really represented. He started to reconsider his motivations.

"I'm not as free as I thought", he admitted honestly.

Falcon continued and for the first time called him by his name:

"Marco Polo, the world you live in is a theater. People are usually acting. They observe each other all the time, expecting predictable behavior. They observe their gestures, clothing and words. Freedom is utopian. Spontaneity is dead."

Marco Polo never imagined that he would find wisdom in a ragged man. He recalled his first anatomy class, his professor's, the psychologist's and the social worker's prejudiced words. He realized how superficial we are when we judge people who are different. He understood his own superficiality.

He understood that many beggars might be mentally ill and unable to express great ideas, but all of them have a great story. Besides, he began to find out that certain homeless people, such as Falcon, and probably certain mentally ill people, had a wisdom that intellectuals could not reach. He became convinced that each human being is a box full of secrets to be explored.

We exclude them because we do not understand them. From that moment on, Marco Polo became fascinated with the human mind. It gradually awakened in him the desire to become specialized in the most enigmatic and complex of medical specialties: psychiatry. He had been inspired by the ideas of the thinker of the streets. Marco Polo remained silent for a few minutes questioning his own freedom. Falcon leaned back on the bench. Revealing his anxiety and his known incapacity of staying quiet, the young man decided to provoke Falcon.

"Could it be that because you were unsuccessful within the system that you condemn, you have alienated it? Perhaps you're a socially frustrated person who is internally tied."

Marco Polo had been insightful in his argumentation, but after he had said such words, he felt that he had risked destroying his relationship with Falcon. He recalled that he had created problems with Dr. George because of his own impetuosity. The doctor had humiliated him in public for much less. He felt that he might have shaken their relationship, but was surprised when Falcon's eyes lit up and his grin indicated that he had enjoyed being provoked.

"You are a thinking person... There's still hope for you, kid." The beggar lucidly replied and, without giving any details, said: "I was drastically wounded and banished by the system. The pain I experienced could have either destroyed me or uplifted me. I decided to allow it to uplift me. Tormented, I left without an address to find an address within myself..."

Falcon became silent and gave no further details of his life. Marco Polo did not wish to pry any further. His brief words were profound and intense. He left in silent reflection. The philosopher of the streets was becoming a master to the young member of the social elite. The young man admired the beggar and the beggar became enchanted with the young man. They became friends. Both lived in distinct worlds, but they were brought together by the universal language of sensitivity and the art of thinking. A fascinating story would unfold.

CHAPTER 4

The Turn Over
(Or an Unexpected Turn of Events)

The discovery of the rich and profound world hidden under the rubble of Falcon's poverty seemed insane in modern societies that overvalue technology and lessen wisdom. This discovery astonished Marco Polo.

He was still doubtful about wearing his normal clothes for their next meeting, so once again he wore his rags, but this time he tried to be more discreet and less fetid. His hair was still looked like it had taken an electrical shock. He was not cut out to be a wanderer. Goodnatured, Falcon did not rebuke him. Marco Polo was no longer a trespasser. The master of the streets just went on living without paying much attention to him.

He observed the passersby and laughed. Marco Polo made an effort to understand but he had no idea of what was going on. Falcon amused himself by imagining what people were thinking and allowed the young man to take part in the game. He wanted to teach the boy a lesson. "You see that anxious guy with a crooked tie, walking in a hurry over there? Look at how he frowns. He's probably thinking, 'I cannot stand my boss!

I'm going to quit!' Poor guy; he has probably been saying the same thing for years."

Marco Polo smiled analytically. He thought, "It has always been the normal people who mocked the quirks of those who have been marginalized. They talk to themselves, gesticulate and are peculiar. I had no idea that some of them see organized society as a circus." Falcon pointed to someone else.

"You see that woman all dressed up trying to balance herself on those high heels? Look at her. She almost fell. What a strange thing. No one ever looks at those high heels, but she still uses them. She's probably wondering, 'I wonder who's admiring me?'".

He turned to the young man and asked him:

"Who's admiring that woman?"

"I don't know", said Marco Polo.

"Just both of us you silly! She spent more than an hour suffering in front of the mirror so that two fools like us could observe her," he said jokingly and added, "If you don't have fun in life, life will fight back."

Marco Polo understood the message and decided to play along. He noticed a man who was apparently very famous; he was probably an actor or rock star. He was surrounded by bodyguards and was followed by a few reporters who were trying to interview him. He aggressively ignored the press.

"He's probably thinking, 'I'm the hero of this town!'"

Marco Polo had nothing else to say about the man and realized that Falcon had not appreciated his phrase. "You chose the wrong character. He's no fun. All he thinks about is his fame and he doesn't care about others. He dies a little every day, but he thinks he's above the mortals. The media has created him and the media hates him."

Disturbed, Marco Polo asked:

"Who should I have chosen?"

"You could have chosen that reporter who is trying to interview him. She is fuming inside. She's probably thinking, 'I can't believe that I make so little to interview such a shallow guy.'"

Marco Polo took a moment to think about these words and Falcon added:

"Journalists are interesting professionals. They're like bacteria that criticize the system, but they depend on it to survive."

While Falcon and Marco Polo were having fun, something abruptly interrupted the moment. A 15-year-old drug user took advantage of being in the crowd and snatched an elderly woman's purse. He pushed her down so that she would not recognize him. She fell, hurting her knees and mouth, while the young thief fled.

The woman cried out, "My purse! Someone stole my purse!" Because of the turmoil, the passersby were unable to identify the thief. Two police officers, standing 30 feet ahead, heard the shouts and ran trying to catch the thief.

When the thief realized that he was being chased, the frightened kid threw the purse onto Falcon's lap. Falcon got up to try to find its owner. As the police officers approached him, they saw the purse and assumed that a beggar could not be its owner. They grabbed him.

Marco Polo begged for the police officer's attention. He tried to explain, in vain, what they did not want to understand. One of the officers walked over to the elderly woman and asked her if the purse belonged to her. Faced with the positive response and seeing her bleeding knees and lips, the officer came back indignantly. A small crowd, thirsty for revenge, followed him in order to watch him arrest the "violent beggar".

Falcon was relatively calm. He knew that no argument would be convincing enough. It was a tense moment. Once again, he would be the target of police officers that hate vagrants. Some people shouted out that he ought to be lynched. The aggressiveness was generating more aggressiveness, revealing the inextinguishable cycle of violence. Modern societies are living in insane times where serenity is a luxurious article.

Surrounded by the shouting crowd, the police officers barely spoke the beggar's rights and handcuffed him. What rights does a ragged man have? What kind of lawyer would have the motivation to defend him? Who would believe in his innocence? Marco Polo tried to defend him in vain and desperation took over him with all that injustice.

Falcon suddenly tried to pull something out of his pocket. The police officers thought that it was a gun. They beat him and threw him down by pressing their knees on his neck. But it was only a metal tube and not a weapon.

Seeing his friend fallen and wounded, Marco Polo made an unexpected choice. He shouted out: "I did it! I was the one who snatched the purse! He is innocent!" The police officers were then confused and the crowd became silent.

Disturbed, Falcon shouted: "No! I did it. I stole it."

No one understood anything. The police officers were astonished. They had never seen such a turn of events. Marco Polo was even more incisive.

"Dad, you're an old man. You've protected me my whole life. You don't even have the strength to walk. How could you steal the purse? I stole it and put it on your lap. Don't take the blame for me!"

Without apologizing to Falcon, the police officers simply removed his handcuffs, placed them on Marco Polo and led him to the squad car followed by a procession of people that shouted: "Thief! Kill the thief!"

As they approached the car, Falcon opened the metal tube and a silk red rose popped out of it. He was going to give it to the police officers as a sign of peace, but now he had found someone more worthy of receiving it, his young friend. Falcon had always been friendly to children. A little boy, who every now and then brought him food at the park, had given him the tube as a gift.

The beggar's eyes penetrated the young man's eyes. His silence shouted his gratitude but he was concerned about the consequences of Marco Polo's actions. Marco Polo got into the car and left. He had never been inside a police station before. He could not plead innocence after he had confessed the crime. During his interrogation, Marco Polo's argumentation ability became useless. Everyone felt indignation at a criminal who had robbed and hurt a fragile elderly lady.

The police chief asked him if he had ever attended school or held a job. Marco Polo told him he was a medical student. The police chief and the clerk burst out laughing.

"That's all we need, a clown in the PD." Then he shouted, "I'm not here to joke around, kid. What do you do?" "I've already told you. I'm a medical student", Marco Polo insisted.

"A beggar is a future doctor?! If you're going to be a doctor with hair like that then I'm Marilyn Monroe." Still laughing a lot, the clerk opened the door, inviting several people to come in and introduced them to the intellectual beggar. They all clapped, mocked him and jeered.

Marco Polo began to understand what it meant to be an excluded person and the dangers of living outside of the social standard. Yet by now he was calloused. With his strange hairdo and his ragged clothing, it was impossible to be taken seriously.

The chief knew that most beggars were psychiatric patients. He thought that Marco Polo might be delirious. Disrespectfully he mumbled to the others, "I can't stand these vermin." Then he came closer and shouted: "Tell me who you are, you degenerate! If you are a future doctor, let me see your student card."

Marco Polo gulped. He did not have his ID or student card on him at the moment.

"I forgot it at home."

"So you forgot it at home, huh?" – The police chief had set the stage and wanted to continue the show.

"Very well, so describe the human body to me. Teach me what you have learned in class, you megalomaniac." – Everyone enjoyed watching the chief's display of wit.

"You're the man", they said wanting to exalt his ego. The officer ran his hand over his big head.

They had messed with a hornet's nest. They were unaware of the trap they had fallen into. Marco Polo had to be an excellent student to be able to pass his exams, since he was persecuted in his anatomy classes. He stared at everyone present and, confidently, began to describe the intricate muscles of the forearm. Everyone started to look at one another. Then he began to describe the trajectory of the radial nerve and he astonished them with his description of the heart's atria and ventricles. He talked about the aortic artery, its branches and sub-branches. He also pointed out how many bones the human skeleton has.

After he had won over his audience, he decided to subtly make fun of the police chief: "Judging by the size of your enormous cranium, you certainly have a privileged brain." He picked up a sheet of paper lying on the table, folded it, asked for permission to measure his forehead and made a scene:

"I'd say that you probably have about 90 billion neurons."

The officer had had an inferiority complex since childhood because of his large head. He had been made fun of by his classmates who called him Big Head. As he grew, he tried to compensate his low self-esteem by being aggressive and authoritarian. He used to impose his ideas instead of exposing them. But he felt to be an intellectual because of Marco Polo's apparently favorable description.

He was unaware that Marco Polo had jokingly reduced the number of his neurons. A normal brain has more than 100 billion neurons and Marco Polo had called him "big brain" in front of his friends.

"No one has ever called me Big Brain before".

Pleased, he ran his hands over his head again feeling relief for first time. With the young man's vast knowledge of anatomy and feeling praised by his words, he changed the tone of the interrogation.

"This young man behaves in a strange way, but he seems like a good person," he thought to himself. Besides, he might really be an eccentric medical student, and the officer feared he might be sued for abuse of authority.

He asked Marco Polo why he was dressed that way and listened to his explanations. He did not know what to do after he heard such a strange story, so he left the young man in a room until he could put the facts in order.

An hour later, a witness appeared to testify. He was a salesman in a neighborhood store. While he was walking through the park, he saw the thief toss the purse onto the old beggar's lap.

He also told the police officer that the beggar could usually be seen at the park and was known for his intelligence and bizarreness. He told them how Marco Polo had protected the old man and before the detective could ask him, he said that he had not said anything earlier because the whole situation was a mess. He had been afraid of clarifying the facts at the park, yet moved by the young man's attitude he came forward to testify.

The officer rubbed his neck, blinked and took a deep breath. He was trying to figure out if this was just a dream or reality. He was so perplexed as to say: "I've never heard of an intelligent indigent, I've never heard of anyone taking the blame for someone else, and I've never seen a medical student who is also a beggar. This is too much for me. It's the kind of stuff crazy people do."

"Or of people who love each other." The salesman added.

Aware that he had been authoritarian with Marco Polo, he called him to the side and tried to justify the unjustifiable: his discriminatory attitude. He said that he could never have imagined that under the skin of a vagrant, there would be a young man of the elite. He also took the opportunity to make sure whether Marco Polo really thought that his brain had billions of neurons.

"You have a head of a genius. Freud would surely envy you", Marco Polo replied.

The officer felt like a million bucks, but Marco Polo was dismayed and disappointed as he left the precinct. He had experienced how severe justice is to the weak and fragile to those who are strong...

Despite all he went through, he was humming as he left. After all, his master had taught him to have fun with life and not fight with it.

CHAPTER 5

Traveling Within

Marco Polo met his friend again the following day. He was wearing his normal clothes. However, day-by-day, he was more and more convinced that those who are normal were more ill than he had ever realized.

This time, Falcon was expecting him.

"It's been a while since I've worried about anyone."

"You were worried about me?" Marco Polo asked both surprised and pleased.

"Have you forgotten that I now have a hard-headed son?" he joked.

The situation that they had both been involved in was so unusual that Marco Polo was able to get the old sage to talk about his world. Falcon had been like a vault. The young man was only able to get him to speak because he had won over his soul. They sat down and had a long conversation.

Marco Polo was astonished with Falcon's revelations of the Poet of Life. He said that the Poet of Life knew how to turn simple things into spectacles in his eyes. He would turn the break of dawn into a moment of meditation. He would compare the morning dew to anonymous pearls that appear for an instant and then dissipate, but only those who were sensitive could notice them. He would say farewell to the moon as if to a friend. He would sing when the drops of rain moistened the earth. He had been passionate about life, nature and the Author of existence. The young man absorbed the old man's words as water is soaked up in the desert sand. Marco Polo felt that those who were at the margin of society had a lot of hardships, but at least some of them, experienced more adventures. Society had become a tedious place, without poetry or sensitivity. Falcon had a peculiar way of expressing himself. He spoke as if he was looking at an invisible audience and not directly to Marco Polo. When he wanted to, he was a man full of details and who dissected feelings. He had an impressive ability to create clever phrases.

Falcon also said that the Poet of Life was a hard critic of the social system. He had felt that there were too many people trying to conquer the external world but not their internal one. They purchased adulators but not friends; designer clothes but not comfort. They put locks on their doors, but had no emotional protection. "They beg for the bread of tranquility. They are worse off than we are, my friends", he would tell me and to those who gathered to drink from his intelligence.

"He used to proclaim that rich are those who extract a lot from little, and free are those who are not afraid of being who they are". He'd try to console the vagrants by telling them that they were rich and free. Some of them did not understand his words, but he would say that, anyway."

A beggar approached them and asked Falcon for some food. All that Falcon had was some change, but he gave it to him and told him to go in peace.

"You gave him all your money. Won't you get hungry tonight?"

"Maybe… but there's a hunger I've already quenched: the hunger for relieving someone else's pain."

Marco Polo was speechless. After a moment of silence, Falcon gazed again at his invisible audience and asked: "Do you go through the valleys of pain?" Marco Polo pondered, "Sometimes I do."

"Don't be intimidated. The Poet and I used to say that no one is exempt of suffering, neither in my world nor in yours. Some people are less imprisoned than others. We are all hostages of some period of the past."

Falcon did not say anything about the shackles of his own past and Marco Polo did not dare to ask him. He continued to describe the Poet: he said that when his friend felt hunger, he did not beg for money, he made men travel.

"To travel?"

"Yes. Travel into themselves."

"What do you mean?"

Falcon stood on a bench and repeated something that his friend used to do. He asked the crowd to gather around him and in a loud voice recited a poem to nature. The admiring passersby stood in a semicircle. He pointed at a beautiful bird and led the crowd to travel on its wings. "Birds are wiser than men. They face nocturnal storms, they fall out of their nests, they suffer losses and dilacerate their stories. But when morning comes, despite having every reason to be sad and to complain, they sing thanking to God for another day. And what about you, bearers of noble intelligence, what do you do with your losses?"

Then, he placed his tattered hat in front of him. He was silent and sat next to Marco Polo who was astounded. The listeners were ecstatic and gave him some money.

"Did you receive a lot of handouts?" Marco Polo asked.

"I did not receive handouts. They paid me for the journey I provided them, and it came out cheap." That was too much for Marco Polo's mind. Each of Falcon's phrases astonished him. After the crowd had dispersed, several hungry beggars came closer and Falcon distributed the money among them. This was a common ritual.

"Did you give them all the money?"

"In my world, the stronger serve the weaker ones. In your world, the weaker ones serve the stronger. Which one is fairer?"

Marco Polo felt a lump in his throat. He felt that a reply was unnecessary. After this fact, Falcon began to talk about the Poet's social identity. Marco Polo had been waiting for this for weeks.

Falcon told him that the Poet had been a renowned doctor. He was in love with his wife and they had two children who enchanted them. He loved them to the limit of his understanding. He used to kiss them every day. Rarely had a father been so present and affectionate. However, the "bird" faced the most dramatic nocturnal storm.

The Poet's nest came crashing down. He and his family were traveling by car. It was raining hard. While he was passing another car, he lost control and had a serious accident. His whole family was gone. One of his children had not died immediately and was in a coma for a prolonged time. The Poet had also been in a coma, but only for a few days.

When he awoke from his coma, the world came crashing down on him. He was tormented day and night with negative ideas that supported his feelings of guilt and crushed his tranquility. As a consequence, he had a series of depressive crisis. Nothing could console him.

"Didn't he seek treatment, didn't he take antidepressants?" Marco Polo asked and, to his surprise, Falcon said: "Antidepressants treat the pain of depression but don't cure the feelings of guilt or treat the anguish of loneliness..." "Didn't anyone talk to him? Wasn't he in therapy?"

"He was thirsty for understanding, for internalization and not for advice and cold techniques. Very few people have the maturity to understand the drama of someone who has lost everything. What psychological theory and technique could rescue hope from chaos? The therapists had the theory, but they lacked wisdom."

Such words echoed within young Marco Polo and broadened the scope of his intelligence. He wanted to take more detailed notes of the talks he had with his master. Encouraged by his dialogues he also began to take notes and reflect on the behavior of those gathered around him. Little by little, he learned how to be a prospector of the indecipherable world of the human mind. The conversation continued and the young man asked:

"Was the Poet ever admitted to a psychiatric hospital?"

"He would isolate himself for days in his room, in order to organize his ideas and find meaning for his life, but his psychiatrists interpreted this isolation as a sign that his depressive crisis was becoming worse, so they had him committed. At the hospital, the medication numbed his feelings. He was unable to think, reflect or nourish his lucidity. Thus, he became even more depressed and refused to eat or maintain any social contact, so they started electroshock therapy on him. He did not show any sign of improvement."

"But how did he end up on the streets?"

Falcon told him that, when the Poet heard that his son's heart had failed and he had died in the ICU after six months in a coma, he became despaired. It was the fatal blow and they had him committed once again.

"If only he had been embraced, listened to and supported, perhaps he would have endured his chaos. But he was treated only as a mental patient. The pain became unbearable. He did not try to kill himself, he did not give up on living, but he left the hospital to wander the world.

Falcon told him that, just as himself, the Poet had become a wanderer without an address because he was searching for a home within himself to be able to rest – a place of comfort within the rubble of his loss. He wanted to find a reason to continue breathing physically and oxygenating his emotions.

"How did he adapt to an inhospitable environment? Didn't his crises worsen once he was out in the world?"

"In the streets, the Poet found wretches such as himself. He got to know those who were misunderstood, those who had been mutilated by guilt, those who were afflicted by psychosis and those considered to be the system's refuse. By helping all those people, gave him fortitude."

Then he pointed to an indigent woman in the distance. Her name was Barbara, and Falcon said she had lost her parents, her security and her stability. She became an alcoholic and homeless. He then pointed to other people.

"James was rich, but he lost everything: money, privilege, hope, self-confidence and his capacity to fight. He used to have social status and glamour, but lost his glory and friends. Unable to bear anonymity, he abandoned himself. That one over there, in a black coat, is Thomas. He used to be a brilliant journalist. However, alcoholism and depressive crises robbed him of his job, his wife, his possessions and his serenity."

Next, he pointed at two other people: "John and Adolph are psychotic, delirious, and are tormented by frightening images. Both used to be college professors. They got tired of their crises and of being committed. So, they turned the world into a broader place to escape their ghosts."

He then pointed to an extremely thin woman – Joanna had been a model when she was in her teens. She gained weight, lost her shape, external beauty and social admiration. She was discarded, became disheartened and anorexic. Her foster parents died and she was all alone. She was admitted to several hospitals, until she decided to find a place where no one cared about looks.

"Your society uses people and then discards them as objects. Be careful, young man! Applause never lasts."

Marco Polo was impressed. All of those people had very rich stories, but they went unnoticed to the prejudiced gaze of the passersby. "No one would have the courage to completely abandon their social comfort, unless their life had been dilacerated. This is a very strong reason", he pondered.

Falcon took a deep breath and then told Marco Polo about how he met his friend. He said that the Poet had cried many times along the road. Night after night he had cried in the parks and dark alleys asking: "Why? Where are you, my children?" It was at one of these parks that Falcon found him in tears.

The tears brought them closer. No one said a word. They cried together, because of their own stories. Neither one needed to introduce himself nor give their credentials.

"I understood him without having to listen to him and he understood me without having to listen to me. From those tears a great friendship was born", he completed by slowly breathing. "The Poet felt that helping those who had been abandoned was paying homage to his children and wife. He gradually rescued his faith in God. He became aware of the Creator's signature in the delirium of a psychotic, in the despair of someone depressed, in the scent of a flower and in a child's smile."

Marco Polo could hear his own breathing while he listened to Falcon's words.

"Thus, the Poet got out of his cocoon and rose from the ruins. He turned his loss into a sharp blade to lapidate his intelligence, something rare both in your world and in mine. His longing was never healed, but his loss no longer asphyxiated him. So, he could mention his wife and children cheerfully without feeling guilt, during the long conversations with the excluded ones. His wife and children were alive in the only place where they could never die, within him."

"Were you helped by him?"

Marco Polo's question echoed within Falcon. The strong man fell apart, became sad and held back his tears. He was silent.

Marco Polo read his silence and realized that Falcon not only had lost his friend but, perhaps, his whole family. He tenderly touched Falcon's shoulder as a sign of understanding. He got up to leave; it was not time to talk anymore.

While he walked home, he knew that his friend was walking along the avenues of his past. Ragged clothes, broken hearts and open wounds, a story of secrets that had been reconstituted and became a brilliant poem.

"It's a pity that I didn't get to know the Poet", he thought. He wondered if he was not missing the opportunity of getting to know other Poets, other interesting people who came into his life, whom he only knew superficially.

In particular, he thought of his father who lived in a faraway town. His father, Rudolph, had always been misunderstood because of his social idealism and for not being concerned with the future.

Up to his pre-teen years, Marco Polo had admired his father and had been influenced by his storytelling ability. However, as he grew, the conflicts between his mother, Elisabeth, who was ambitious, and his father, who was laid back, increased. She ended up exerting greater influence over her son in the years before he went to college.

Elisabeth loved her husband, but she frequently criticized him to Marco Polo, saying that his father should dream less and earn more money. Siding with his mother, Marco Polo had his own share of conflicts with his father to the point that Marco Polo felt that his father was a failure, alienated, and a person who was not well resolved.

Now that his personality was formed and more mature and he also had a better critical conscience, he needed to judge his father less and understand him more. His contact with Falcon had made him see the world through different angles, ones he had never seen before. He had to go beyond the appearance. He needed to find the subtle traces that composed the painting of his father's behavior.

When he got home, he wrote his father a letter:

Father,

Please forgive my rash attitudes. I know that I have hurt you with my precipitated criticism. I have wasted so much time judging you. I feel that I don't know who you are on the inside, even though we lived together in the same small space for so many years. We were strangers living in the same house. I'd like to find out who you are, what were the tears you didn't shed, which were the saddest days in your story, and what were the challenges you never had the courage to tell me?! Father, if I could go back in time, I would not only ask you to tell me beautiful stories but would especially ask you to tell me your own story, to tell me what your projects are, your dreams and your failures. I'm sure it's a fascinating story. I have many flaws, but I'd like to have a new chance of being your friend.

Rudolph was deeply moved when he received this letter. He did not know what his son was going through, but he became aware that he himself didn't know him either. He could have played more, talked more, and had more carefree moments with him. Now, separated by the physical distance, they began to write each other, to get closer and to admire each other.

Marco Polo understood that most people would one day need to pick up the pieces and rewrite their story. However, he learned that the reconstruction of social relationships was not an easy task; it demanded boldness. As Marco Polo took notes about his last meeting with the beggar-philosopher, he ended his notes with: "Many of those who have a permanent address go through existence without ever walking along the avenues of their own being. They are foreigners to themselves and therefore, are incapable of correcting their routes and overcoming their madness."

CHAPTER 6

Rising From the Ashes

Marco Polo arrived at the park at 3:00 PM. He'd had a tiring day, but meeting Falcon was an invitation to new experiences. Yet the beggar was acting strangely, tense and introverted. He apparently wanted to keep his distance. Reliving his past the previous day had disheartened him.

Marco Polo tried to distract him, but his gaze was hazy, without its usual sparkle. He was discreet. Realizing that their conversation would be a monologue, Marco Polo decided to leave and respect Falcon's moment. He felt that it was not worth pressuring those who were unwilling to talk. As he moved away, Falcon said:

"I don't recommend normal people to approach me."

Intrigued, Marco Polo knew that he would not be able to get Falcon to open up unless he provoked his intelligence. He could not afford to be stupid, so he took a chance and said:

"No one's normal without being abnormal and an abnormal person is still capable of being a master."

Falcon looked admiringly at his friend, but struck him back with an unexpected answer:

"I've been told that I'm a danger for your society. What do you expect of me? I am mentally ill. You better disappear."

Marco Polo was silent. He had always been impulsive, but he was learning the difficult art of thinking before reacting. After an introspective moment he said:

"Those who are apparently healthy have always committed more insanity against Mankind than those who are considered to be insane. You are not dangerous except to those who are afraid of thinking."

Falcon rubbed his forehead with his right hand, got up, walked over to a flower and started talking to it.

"You are so beautiful and I am so rough, but thank you for invading my eyes and enchanting me without asking for anything in return."

Marco Polo also got up, walked over to a nearby tree, hugged and kissed it and said out loud:

"You are so strong. You've been through so much. Yet you were strengthened by time and now you provide me, who am so fragile, with your free shade. Thank you for your perseverance."

Falcon subtly looked at the young man and smiled.

The passersby tripped over each other, laughing at the scene and gesturing that both were crazy. Turning towards them Falcon declared:

"Those who have never hugged a tree or talked to a flower have never been worthy of nature's gifts. Don't be insensitive! Learn how to love those who give you so much!"

Ashamed because of the beggar's ideas, everyone walked away reflecting. Thirty yards ahead, a teenager with a punk hairstyle hugged an immense tree trunk and kissed it. An elderly man next to him knelt before a small flower to revere it. A man in a suit and tie also hugged a tree for a moment. Other people repeated the scene. The sensitivity was contagious.

The two friends then sat on a bench and began a long conversation. Marco Polo was the first person, after the Poet, to whom Falcon told his surprising story. Not even his street companions knew certain alleys of his life.

"Why are you called Falcon?"

"The Poet called me that. He said that my intelligence was as keen as the eyesight of a falcon and that my creativity soared high like its wings. But, to tell you the truth, I was born from the ashes."

"What do you mean?"

"I've got a PhD in philosophy."

Marco Polo nearly fell off of the bench. His clouded mind was suddenly cleared. Now he understood the genius that taught him.

"I used to be a philosophy professor at a big university. I used to shine in the small world of a classroom, despite always being a critic of the academic system. I've written papers, oriented theses and shaped a few thinkers."

Then Falcon talked spontaneously about himself. He said that his family had come from a humble background and had been full with problems. His father was an explosive and materialistic man and was also an alcoholic. His mother was a shy and affectionate woman who was the victim of her husband's aggressiveness. He had grown up surrounded by physical and emotional misery. Since they were poor, his parents could not afford to send him to college.

"I had to study and work hard, in order to make my dreams come true. However, I had never worked on my own conflicts."

"Did you ever have your own family?"

One more pause, now it was longer and more painful.

"I was regarded as the best student and the best speaker in college. I enchanted a beautiful young woman who attended the same school. I loved and was intensely loved by her. Her father was a famous and wealthy lawyer – Mr. Peter was fascinated by money and social status."

He continued by telling Marco Polo how he was unable to give his wife the same comfort she had had at her parents' home and how her father had always encouraged her to leave him. His father-in-law had been frustrated with the fact that his only daughter had not married a judge or a prosecutor. Having a philosopher and poor college teacher in the family had always been a frustrating nightmare to him.

"Teachers are anonymous heroes, my friend. They work a lot and make very little money. They sow dreams in a society that has lost its ability to dream."

Marco Polo felt embarrassed when he heard this account. He watched while Falcon talked about himself and could not understand how someone so intellectually brilliant could be completely excluded from society. He wondered if Falcon had suffered losses similar to the Poet's. He drew an imaginary picture of deaths, depression and loneliness.

Suddenly he blinked his eyes, shook his head quickly and came back to reality. He felt that Falcon was dispirited and realized that he no longer wanted to talk about his family. Marco Polo tried to change the direction of the conversation.

"When did you become ill?"

"Six years after I got married, I began to have insomnia. My thoughts were agitated and accelerated. I was anxious and couldn't organize my ideas. Thousands of images rushed through my mind in a continuous process. Little by little, I started to lose the parameters of logic. I could no longer distinguish reality from fantasy."

Falcon dissected his burdens with the precision of a surgeon in the anatomy room. He was able to make such a description because he was a brilliant thinker who had penetrated his own story many times, trying to understand it. Marco Polo felt a weight on his chest and a lump in his throat as he listened to his friend's story.

"I became paranoid. I thought that certain people could read my thoughts and that they wanted to control my mind. The ideas of being persecuted tormented me. Having external enemies is disturbing, but having enemies within your own mind is terrifying. The feeling of being invaded in the only place where we should be free haunted me."

"Didn't you control your own reasoning?"

"At the beginning I doubted the characters in my mind, I was quite aware they were unreal, but they grew stronger and, little by little, I began to fight them as though they were real. They became the predators and I became the prey."

Marco Polo was perplexed with this living story of the destruction of a complex personality.

"In this delirious combat I lost the greatest gift a human being can have: my own critical conscience and my identity. I no longer knew who I was. My mind became a dark theater. Prior to the psychosis, I was the leading actor in this theater; weeks later I was a supporting actor, and months later I became part of the audience of my psychological misery. It was horrible – I was confused, disoriented and frightened. My intellectual structure simply crumbled."

Marco Polo did not know what to say. He had trouble formulating his next question.

Falcon seemed like such a lucid person. He just could not imagine that Falcon had been through such suffering. A few moments after receiving that shocking information, he asked:

"When did you stop teaching?"

"My students admired my eloquence. I was the professor they sought out the most to be the guest of honor. I struggled to make those kids think, not to become formatted, repeaters of ideas, but engineers of new thoughts. However, a disaster struck after my first crises."

Falcon said that those who had known him still respected him, but the others mocked his bizarre gestures. He would go for days without teaching. Falcon paused again and then told Marco Polo how he had been excluded from the university.

Once he was teaching about the ethics of Greek philosophers. The classroom was full. He was speaking enthusiastically when suddenly he interrupted what he was saying and began to argue with his imaginary characters. The frightened students looked at each other.

"I was hallucinating in my delirium and felt that I was in ancient Greece, sitting at a cenacle full of thinkers, including Plato. I raised my voice and proclaimed: Plato, ethics is dying! Violence is part of the social web. People don't know how to examine the hidden needs of others."

While describing the facts that had happened in the classroom, Falcon took a deep breath and exhaled as if to expel the demons of his past. Marco Polo was anxious to hear what had happened.

"After the students heard my speech they applauded and cheered in class, because of the brilliance of my ideas, as well as the madness of the spectacle. They had not understood that it had been a psychotic crisis."

Falcon said that the students' applause had excited him. He had gotten up on a chair and continued his speech with even more vehemence. Some of them cried out, "Madman! Madman!" So he turned to them and provoked them.

- I shouted out at my students: "Here's an audience of Greek servants. They smile at the misery of others because they hide their own misery under their garments. You don't know how to philosophize; all you know is how to be commanded. Servants!" "But your ideas were coherent", exclaimed Marco Polo.

"There's no insane person who isn't lucid, nor lucid person who isn't insane. The problem is that those who are psychotic mix coherent ideas with delirium in the same scene. The thoughts are split between the two worlds. I would stop talking to my students and begin to talk to my characters. I'd rebut one, agree with another one and argue with others."

Joking about his past, Falcon told Marco Polo: "I was so brilliant that Plato was astonished with my thoughts."

But then, looking vacantly into space, he recalled the outcome of that painful moment. After he provoked his students, he went from applause to booing. Some of the students quickly called the dean, who called for three security guards to escort him from the premises. He refused to leave. Other professors gathered to see what the confusion was about. He was grabbed like an animal.

"I felt like Socrates who had been sentenced to death, carried out by consuming poisonous hemlock, destined to eternal silence. And I shouted again: Hypocrites! Drop your weapons! Fight me with ideas!"

With Falcon's brief silence, Marco Polo anxiously asked:

"Did they take you to a psychiatric hospital?"

"While they tried to hold me down, I summoned the strength of a gladiator fighting against ferocious beasts. I was able to escape. I climbed onto a table and recited the hymn to freedom, a philosophical poem I had written during the moments of lucidity."

"Do you still remember it?"

"Just a few phrases."

Falcon stood on the park bench and recited it. A crowd gathered to listen to it.

You can silence my voice, but not my thoughts.
You can shackle my body, but not my mind.
I will not be an audience in this unhealthy society;
I will be the author of my own story.
The weak wish to control the world;
The strong wish to control their own being.
The weak use weapons; the strong use ideas.

After Falcon finished, the crowd applauded him. He sat down, relaxed and went back to talking to Marco Polo. He said that the dean had called the police who had called for an ambulance, in order to take him to a psychiatric hospital. They restrained him in a straitjacket and injected him with a potent tranquilizer.

Falcon watched the paramedics. He felt that he was the victim of the greatest injustice in the world. The spectacle continued while the drug did not induce sleep. He continued to talk to his fictional characters. Due to his resistance, he was considered by the hospital to be highly aggressive. He was kept in isolation in a poorly lit room for a week. The drugs did what no one else had been able to do: silence the philosopher's ideas. Massive doses of medication invaded his brain, acted on the process of memory reading, blocked the windows of his story, obstructed the construction of thoughts and contained his reasoning. He looked like a zombie. His deliria and hallucinations were silenced, and so was the thinker.

He was held in the hospital for two months. It was the first of a series of hospitalizations. After he left the hospital, he went back to the university. His muscles were stiff, his voice was thick and quivering and his reasoning was sluggish. He had lost his eloquence. The medication that had helped him was the same that had imprisoned him. He was in a chemical straitjacket.

A few students made fun of him behind his back in the hallways, but he was aware of it. Others, who had been familiar with his intelligence, approached him and hugged him thanking him for his wisdom, but they were astonished to see him drooling with an unexpressive face. Some of them would leave with tears in their eyes.

"I just wanted to go back to teaching, which is what I love the most. But how could a madman teach? The dean told me that I could no longer teach. He felt that my illness was incurable and contagious, like in the days of smallpox."

They believed that Falcon might disturb the environment with his psychosis. They did not realize that psychotic patients need inclusion and not exclusion. They did not understand that many of such patients were given the gift of a refined intelligence and sensitivity. As if the burden of carrying the weight of their illness was not enough; they also had to carry the burden of rejection.

"You can forget thousands of life's hardships, but the feeling of being rejected is an unforgettable pain."

They demanded that Falcon step down and retire. Feeling useless, his condition worsened. His self-esteem and self-confidence were shattered. He no longer had dignity in the presence of his family or in society.

Thus, he was excluded. He said that he had always felt left out of the intellectuals' niche, but now he had been banished without mercy.

CHAPTER 7

Old Philosophy and Teen Psychiatry

The fear of going insane has always disturbed human beings. Losing one's mind, not being able to discern reality, the disorganization of one's thoughts, breaking the boundary between consciousness of oneself and the world is anguishing for millions of people of all eras and societies.

Many people mistakenly believe that they will go insane because they afflict themselves with absurd ideas, suffer because of fixed thoughts and anguish themselves because of mental images that they never wanted to produce. However, because their reasoning is coherent and they know how to distinguish imagination from reality, they do not develop mental confusion.

Madness is a common name, which is full of discrimination and false fears. The scientific name is psychosis. There are several types of psychoses that appear in various degrees of intensity and, consequently, with several levels of recovery.

The worst form of psychosis had penetrated in the fabric of Falcon's personality, compromising his rationality. Even though he went through periods of serenity, during his crises or psychotic episodes, he lost the awareness of who he was, of what he used to do and, sometimes, of where he was. He was unable to manage his own acts.

Since he was a thinker with refined culture, during his periods of lucidity he tried hard to find the causes of his psychological chaos, a bloodcurdling effort for someone with such a fragmented 'self'. However, the psychiatric treatment did not evolve.

Very few ideas were exchanged between him and his psychiatrists. They did not discuss about "how" or "why" he constructed tormenting characters in his delirium. Psychiatrist and patient lived in distinct worlds and used distinct languages.

Falcon continued to tell his story to his young friend the next day. He felt the need to talk and Marco Polo felt the need to listen, so he asked:

"Were you disappointed with the psychiatrists?"

With a paused voice he replied:

"Not with all of them. I found a few psychiatrists to be humane, helpful and cultured, yet contact was rare. I was disappointed with most of them. Due to paranoid ideas and the fatal belief that I was being controlled, I was diagnosed as being a paranoid schizophrenic. Do you have any idea what it's like to carry the weight of being psychotic?

"I can't even begin to imagine."

"It's really unimaginable! The diagnoses might be useful for the psychiatrists, but they can become a prison for the patients. I was no longer a human being. I was just a schizophrenic one."

Falcon had tears in his eyes. Marco Polo would never forget his words.

"Did you try to help yourself?"

"The only healthy thing I had left when I recovered from my crises was to think about my world, try to understand myself and reorganize my fragmented personality, but they treated me like a mental patient incapable of constructing brilliant ideas and improving internally. I felt as if I were a dammed river. I produced many disturbing thoughts but there was nowhere for them to flow."

"Why are mental patients so discriminated in society?"

"Haven't you ever read Foucault?"

"No."

"You should. Foucault wrote *Madness and Civilization*. This book shows the anthropological roots of how an insane individual is classified. Psychiatry has formatted this classification and has marginalized all behavior that deviated from the behavioral standards universally accepted in a society. Many mistakes were made; many people were labeled as insane, merely because their behavior was unusual."

"What is your definition of insanity?"

"Who can ever define it? Classically, insanity is every long-lasting disaggregation of the personality that differs from the parameters of reality. But what are these parameters? Those who feel they are harassed by imaginary characters are considered to be psychotic. But what about those who harass real characters, such as generals who start wars, soldiers who torture others, police officers who kill, and politicians who control? What are they? Those who have deliria of grandeur, who think they are Jesus Christ, Napoleon or Buddha, are psychotic. But what about those mortals who feel they are gods because of the money and power they possess, who do not care about the pain of others, what are they? In my opinion, there is a rational insanity that is accepted by society and an irrational insanity that is condemned by it."

These words came out of the basement of Falcon's mind, from the most secret place of his being. He revealed that he was a cultured thinker with a shattered past and a profoundly wounded emotion. They would forever be stored in Marco Polo's memory. "A few psychiatrists said that my psychosis was chronic and incurable because it has an organic basis. I was condemned", Falcon added.

"What do you mean?"

"They said that certain substances were altered in my brain and only medication could correct them. To them, the psychological instrument is only a cauldron of chemical reactions."

"Don't you agree with this theory?"

"How can a philosopher believe in such a rigid, limited and foolish theory? Philosophy has been around for thousands of years. Psychiatry has been around for a little more than a century. Its advances have been impressive, but it is still in its teens and, like most teenagers, psychiatry is arrogant. It is an important science, but it isn't yet a mature science. It lacks humility to understand the incomprehensible world of the human psyche."

Falcon had studied the history of psychiatry, its advances, hypotheses and limitations. He had a vast knowledge in this area, surpassing the knowledge of most psychiatrists. Next, he gave a complex explanation on the relationship between the psyche, or soul, and the brain.

He said that many philosophers had talked about metaphysics, such as Aristotle, Augustine, Descartes and Spinoza. He revealed that metaphysics is the branch of philosophy that deals with the human soul, affirming that it surpasses the physical limits of the brain. Descartes, seduced by metaphysics, considered it to be the first object of the world of ideas. Kant submitted it to the limits of reason. However, metaphysics was heatedly debated and criticized following Nietzsche's materialism, Hegel's historical determinism, Marxism, Sartre's existentialism and logical positivism. Therefore, it was no longer debated. "In a materialistic, logical and pragmatic society incarcerated by mathematics and fascinated by the computer age, metaphysics has practically been retired as an object of scientific discussion."

Falcon defended metaphysics as an explanation for the indecipherable psychological phenomena that weave us as thinking beings. He looked at his young disciple and asked: "Are we only a sophisticated brain that is laid in a grave to be nothing else? Does our story end in this brief existence? Are the billions of human beings, who are linked to thousands of religions that believe in a life that transcends death, being foolish? Is the human intellect nothing more than a cerebral computer? I don't believe so. I believe that the brain's biochemical world cannot completely explain the contradiction of thoughts, the territory of emotions and the valleys of fear."

Patting Marco Polo's head, Falcon went even further in his reasoning:

"Remember this phrase, son. Life is a question mark. Each human being, intellectual or illiterate, is a huge question in search of a huge answer..."

He commented that the size of the question determines the size of the answer. Philosophy had asked many questions throughout the millennia and psychiatry, still being young, asked very little and offered quick answers. Those who answer hastily, take enormous risks.

Marco Polo received a jolt of lucidity. He was trying to keep up with Falcon's thinking, but it was not an easy task. His old friend's philosophical ideas and understanding of life would change his views as a future psychiatrist. Wishing to explore the outcome of Falcon's illness, he asked: "What was your relationship with the psychiatrists like?"

"Psychiatrists hold a power that no other human being in history has ever had. Kings and dictators had weapons to wound bodies and imprison them. The psychiatrists have medication that invades the unconscious mind, the place where ideas and emotions are born. A space never penetrated, that not even psychiatrists themselves know."

"Did you need these drugs to combat your deliria?"

With a sad demeanor, the thinker said:

"My brain needed the medication, but my soul needed dialogue. However, when we are labeled as psychotic, it is rare to have someone recognize that we have a complex world with intricate needs. We create monsters during our crises, and we are the ones who have to live with them. It is rare to have someone willing to share them with us."

Marco Polo internalized, looked back at his own story and realized that he had also created monsters and did not share them.

"I believe that all of us create our monsters, our fears, insecurities and mutilating thoughts, but we rarely find people who are willing to share them. When we can't share them, we must face them, otherwise, we don't survive. But most people try to escape their monsters."

Marco Polo began to appreciate philosophy, which would lead him to become a stranger in the cradle of the medical school. As he interpreted Falcon's story, he understood that geniuses and psychotics have always been close; they have always been misunderstood. They were frequently surrounded by loneliness.

He also realized that, deep down, a few tentacles of loneliness embrace each one of us. Some people are able to speak freely, but they are silent about the most intimate aspects of their life. He concluded that a dose of loneliness stimulates reflection, but radical loneliness stimulates depression.

He understood that when the world abandons us, loneliness is tolerable; but when we abandon ourselves, it is unbearable. Falcon broke free of his loneliness, became his own companion and found a great friend, the Poet.

CHAPTER 8

The Worst Part

The following day, Falcon would reveal the most painful part of his story. He wanted to take a walk, move around so he could talk about his emotional ulcer. Marco Polo joined him. In a leisurely manner, he went straight to the point:

"My wife Deborah was a beautiful, affectionate and brave woman. She stood up to her father and society to side with a poor philosopher. She appreciated my simple lifestyle. She took risks to love me and she fought for me. In the beginning she even believed in my deliria. But she couldn't take it anymore. I hurt her unintentionally."

While they walked, his tears came out of hiding and began to run down the wrinkles of his face.

"Have you got any children?"

Falcon looked at the sky. A breeze caressed his face. His long white hair blew in his face. He breathed heavily and, as if he were traveling in time, he nodded.

"A son."

For the first time he showed himself completely unprotected to Marco Polo. The central point of his life was being unveiled. Marco Polo thought that perhaps Falcon's son had died. He did not want to pry but he was unable to stand his friend's prolonged silence.

"Is your son alive?"

Falcon's imagination was filled with mental images as if they were cinematographic representations. He saw himself with open arms and his four-year-old son running towards him for a loving embrace. They boy said "I love you Daddy." The father jokingly replied, "I don't love you, I super love you! I am so passionate about you, my pupil." Pupil was an endearing nickname his father had given him. He used to put his boy on his lap, messed up his hair and tickled him.

When he came back to reality he said:

"Luke is probably alive. I've received bits of information about him over the years."

Marco Polo asked an obvious question, the question that anyone would have asked and that Falcon least needed to hear.

"Why don't you receive news from him?"

His reply was categorical:

"Because any news crushes me with feelings of guilt."

Marco Polo felt a lump in his throat.

"How long has it been since you've last seen him?"

"More than twenty years."

"Twenty years is a too long time", Marco Polo thought. He felt that, if he were in Falcon's shoes, he would never abandon his son, no matter what the circumstances might be. He was fast to criticize Falcon, without knowing the true story.

Falcon continued and told him that when he recovered from his crises, he felt ashamed, judged and watched by everyone, not because he had been delirious, but because he felt he was the most unworthy of human beings. He understood the pain of rejection that the lepers in the days of Christ felt, when they were excluded from society.

After Luke turned five years old, Falcon began to have his crises. However, he loved his son so much that during his periods of lucidity he would make an extra effort to play with him and teach him. His son was his reason to live, but his crises increased.

His last psychiatrist seduced his wife. Deborah was feeling fragile and unprotected and became involved with him. Falcon had found the secret letters that the psychiatrist had written her. Despite the high doses of medication, he was able to cry, his lips trembled, yet he did not react. He knew that he had lost her.

The unethical psychiatrist told her that Falcon would always be a mental patient. He encouraged her to separate from him for their son's sake. Confused, Deborah asked her father for advice. Mr. Peter, who never had liked the poor philosopher, practically celebrated that. He truly despised the psychotic philosopher.

While listening to his friend's story, Marco Polo began to understand him and judge less. Once again he recognized how hasty and shallow his judgment had been. Due to the hospitalizations, Falcon would go for weeks without seeing Luke. The pain caused by the distance of his wife was bearable, but the pain of not being allowed to see his son was indecipherable. Sometimes he missed Luke so much that he'd pick him up at school, despite the gesturing towards his fictional characters. The other children mocked him and the boy, trying to defend his father, got into fights.

"How could a small son defend his father, a grown man? Luke would hug and protect me", he said prideful of his son. But then, he became aware and anxious because he no longer had him.

He had accepted the separation from Deborah although he hadn't had much of a choice. He made it easy on her because he had wanted what was best for her and their son. He had already caused too much trouble. A judge who was familiar with the case had established a one hour visitation period, twice a week. It wasn't enough for one who loved so much.

Falcon was unable to keep the visitation order. The judge, after reading a letter from the psychiatrist, Deborah's boyfriend, considered the father to be dangerous to his son's development. He restricted visitation to an hour a week accompanied by a social worker. He was no longer allowed to be alone with Luke. A judicial wall had separated two great friends.

"Is that why you wandered into the world?"

Falcon shook his head. He would have to touch the epicenter of his emotional misery. Not even the Poet had gone so far in trying to explore the story of the genius of the streets. Thus, he described the most dramatic chapter of his life. His son was about to turn ten. To celebrate his grandson's birthday and his daughter's divorce, as well as to reveal his social status and his mansion's gardens, Mr. Peter had a memorable party planned. Hundreds of people were invited, not only Luke's friends, but also a large number of lawyers, prosecutors, judges and city officials.

On their next to last supervised visit, Luke told his father about the party and naively insisted that he went. The social worker, who was paid by Mr. Peter to control the relationship, was annoyed. She said that it would not be a good idea. Falcon reluctantly said that he would think about it.

The social worker told Mr. Peter that the boy had invited Falcon. Luke was severely reprehended by his grandfather. "Your father will ruin the party. Don't you know he is insane?" Luke started crying and shouted, "He's my father!" Mr. Peter lowered his voice and tried to explain his violence to the fragile child. During their last visit, the boy told Falcon what his grandfather had said. Falcon tried to hide his tears. "I'm ill, but I will get better. Don't be afraid, pupil. I better not go to your party", he confessed to his son.

Falcon had told Luke many times not to mind if he talked or gesticulated to himself. He asked his son to look at his heart. He was concerned about the development of his son's personality and therefore, within limits, he tried to vaccinate him against his disturbances. Luke was rarely ashamed or embarrassed by Falcon.

The social worker supported Falcon's decision about not going to the party. She later gave Mr. Peter the good news. Although he was relieved, he hired security to avoid any trouble. Falcon was very anguished, anxious and lonely on the day of the party. He missed his son tremendously. It was his tenth birthday and he wanted to at least give him a kiss on such an important day. He decided to surprise him so his showed up at his former father-inlaw's mansion.

He wore a tuxedo and pretended to be a waiter, easily dodging security. He walked through the immense garden. He had never seen it so decorated. He spotted Deborah embracing her boyfriend. It was difficult to see such a scene. She saw him and became apprehensive. Her boyfriend whispered, "This guy must be hospitalized immediately" and left to warn the host.

Many of those who knew him looked at each other as if he were a terrorist. Tense and grim faces, whispering, Falcon became the center of attention. Being observed disturbed him, so he quickly left to find his son.

Luke ran into his arms and kissed him. He was ecstatic. He led Falcon inside to see the immense ten-tier cake. On the side of the cake, in large blue frosting letters, he read, "Happy Birthday, Luke. You are a winner!"

"You really are a winner, my son."

"Thank you, daddy, so are you."

They hugged once again. Falcon's emotions experienced a surreal aura. So, to the amazement of the guests he shouted: "This is the best son in the world!"

People gathered around to see what the excitement was about, so Falcon decided to praise Luke with a few phrases by philosophers and thinkers who exalted the fight for life. He looked at Luke and said: "Epicurus stated that if we wish to win, we must engrave our objective onto our soul. Einstein said that there is a force greater than atomic energy: will! Confucius commented that to succeed in life you must demand a lot of yourself and little of others. Pascal said that there will always be light for those who wish to see and there will always be obscurity for those who reject seeing. Sophocles said: 'seek and ye shall find, for unsought things remain forever lost'. Luke, don't be afraid of the light. Search for the treasure that lies within you.'"

Some of the guests panicked, others were ecstatic with Falcon's ideas. Mr. Peter became aware of the situation and, concerned with the disturbance, called security to remove Falcon from the party. The guards circled around the table while everyone began to disperse in fear.

"I suddenly saw a dramatic scene. A man in a black suit pulled out a gun, pointed it at me but didn't shoot. Then, he pointed the gun towards my son and cocked it. When he was about to fire, I threw myself in front of Luke. I fell over the cake and the table tipped over knocking everything onto the floor. People screamed as if they were witnessing a terrorist attack. Confusion took place and the party was over.

"What about the killer?"

"There was no killer. There was no gun. I was hallucinating. It had been a lawyer who had pulled a handkerchief from his pocket and had pointed his finger to Luke and me. Once again, I had deeply hurt my son.

Marco Polo had trouble swallowing. He was shaken and paralyzed. He didn't know what to say or how to react.

"Aren't you going to ask me why I never saw my son again?"

Embarrassed, Marco Polo shook his head. Too much pain was buried under the soil of this man's life. Falcon continued his narrative.

Mr. Peter led Falcon into his posh office. Five lawyers who worked for him joined them there. He said he was speaking on behalf of Deborah, although he was lying. He said that he had an evaluation from a renowned psychiatrist that said Luke could become mentally ill, like his father, if the latter continued to visit him and make him go through such scandals and stressful situations. He said that if Falcon truly loved him, he should disappear from his life. "It's Luke's only chance to be mentally healthy", he completed cunningly.

Falcon picked up the report and read it carefully. He was perplexed and kept pacing back and forth across the room. The idea that his son could be psychotic had tortured him for years. He cried like a child in front of the lawyers.

He anxiously asked out loud, "Where will I go? My parents are dead, my relatives don't tolerate me and my friends have abandoned me. Where will I go?" He then cried out, "Luke! Dear Luke! I love you! Forgive me!" Some of the lawyers were touched. Mr. Peter was as hard and cold as stone.

"So, because I loved my son so much, I decided to disappear from his life and allow him to build a story different from my own. Abandoning one's own child is the highest price one ever has to pay. Perhaps it is more disturbing than seeing one's child passing away."

Marco Polo became immersed within himself. His soul cried profusely. He was ashamed of how he had prejudged Falcon.

"I used the clouds as sheets, the night was my blanket and alcohol was my medicine. I had crises in the streets. I wandered aimlessly. Fortunately, after a few years, I met the Poet. With his help I was able to face my monsters; I fought my deliria, destroyed my ghosts and defeated the shackles of my alcoholism. I rebuilt myself and rewrote my story.

"How did he do that?"

"The Poet advised me to use my own tools to overcome my crises. I meditated, penetrated philosophical texts and then discovered the pearl of wisdom. The Poet had already found it because, despite being a doctor, he had always loved the world of ideas and had always studied philosophy.

"Which tool?" Marco Polo asked admiringly.

"The art of doubting."

"Doubting...? What do you mean?"

"Everything we believe in controls us. If you believe that you are healthy, such a belief will help you. But if you believe in something destructive, that belief will imprison you. So, I used the art of doubting to question everything that controlled me in an unhealthy way, such as anguishing thoughts, unreal images and illusions of being persecuted."

He said that all great thinkers, such as Isaac Newton, Freud and Thomas Edison, had used, intuitively, the art of doubting, in order to refute current ideas and generate new ones. Falcon had used it to combat disturbing ideas and create tranquilizing thoughts. Then he added:

"Those who despise doubt, paralyze their intelligence."

"I'm sorry, but I don't understand how you did that."

He said that while he roamed the streets, he would shout at the characters that haunted him, "I doubt that you exist! Why can't I be free? No one persecutes me; I persecute myself! I have created you and I will destroy you! You are fake!" The Poet would say nothing; he'd follow in silence and in solidarity. When they were in the parks, Falcon would shout within himself. No one heard him, but he was at war against the torturers in his unconscious mind. He practiced this exercise day and night, week after week and month after month. So, little by little, he built a platform within his intellect to distinguish the parameters of reality. The art of doubting stimulated the construction of the art of criticism. Therefore, he began to criticize each instant of any delirious idea. It was a hard, arduous and prolonged task. However, a year later, Falcon had organized his mind.

"There was no need for medication?"

"If the Poet had been my therapist during the period I was on medication, I might not have lost my wife and my son", he said feeling disheartened.

He said that if he had taken medication in doses that had not blocked his thoughts, the application of the art of doubting and criticizing would have been easier and would have structured his 'self' – that represents his decision ability – accelerating his treatment.

"Who's worried about structuring their Self through the art of doubting in this superficial society? Even universities block the Self and obstruct the ability to decide. Millions of students prepare themselves to perform on the outer world, but remain as children in their inner world", the outraged genius said.

"Did you find peace after organizing your mind?"

"No! The same light that illuminates also exposes our sufferings. Lucidity revealed my loss, my mistakes and the scandals. I had nothing. No wife, no son and no classes to teach. Then, the terrifying monster of guilt appeared.

There were times when Falcon had thought of giving up on life. Fortunately, he and the Poet gathered their ruin and helped each other to survive the demon of guilt. They traveled the roads; slept under the stars and journeyed together into the epicenter of their emotional earthquakes. They looked at their losses from different angles, accepted their limitations, sang, smiled, and played with life instead of fighting it.

Marco Polo wished he had taken part in these travels. He felt that they had been more exciting than Hollywood movies. He then asked: "If you recovered your conscience years ago, why didn't you try to find your son?"

Falcon had been afraid that this question would pop up. It had tormented him many times. He looked his friend in the eyes and humbly said:

"I defeated many enemies within me. But I was unable to defeat the fear of not being accepted. I'd rather have the image of my son's love in my dreams than to face the harsh reality that perhaps he doesn't love me anymore. Having a psychotic father had made him suffer; what would he feel if he knew his father was a beggar?"

"I don't know how to answer that", replied the young Marco Polo.

"Perhaps thinking that his father was dead was less painful. But I don't know. We must make choices in life. Every choice implies loss. I made a choice and lost immensely. The capability to choose that keeps me conscious is the same that sometimes wounds my own conscience.

Falcon leaned back on the bench. He was tired because of the weight of his memories. He wanted to rest. The sun was retiring and darkness slowly appeared. The agitated birds found places among the leaves in the trees to rest. Fascinated with everything he had heard, Marco Polo said goodbye to his friend and added something that touched him deeply:

"I wouldn't have made a better choice. If I were your son, I'd be extremely proud of you." Falcon gave a sigh of relief. He stood and embraced him affectionately. He felt as if he were hugging Luke. He kissed his cheek.

"Thank you for listening to an old man."

"No. Thank you for allowing me to listen."

It was truly a privilege to listen to Falcon. Marco Polo had learned more from him than he had in decades of schooling. The thinker then lied down on the bench. He had never felt it so soft. The night was calm. He felt a comfort within.

CHAPTER 9

An Illustrious Visitor

As he walked toward the anatomy lab, Marco Polo was not sure which body belonged to the Poet, but he had guessed correctly. His docile demeanor was immediately recognizable but he told no one about his story. They would not believe him.

Most of his classmates respected him and admired his critical capability. But some of them had a tireless energy to mock – such common thing among youth. They would point at a cadaver and say, "This guy used to be a great artist!" They laughed out loud. When they heard that Marco Polo had a beggar as a friend, the mockery increased, "Where's the genius?" Dr. George neither encouraged nor stopped them.

Tired of the prejudice about those anonymous bodies, Marco Polo once dared to invite Falcon to come to the anatomy lab. He wanted his classmates to dissect the bodies respecting their stories. He had not predicted the consequences of his invitation; he only had the vague impression that the beggar's presence in the lab might embarrass him. He would have to come spontaneously.

"The Poet is being dissected by hands that despise his biography. If you told them his story, my friends and professors might broaden their views on life."

Although he resisted at first, Falcon said he would think about it. And he did. A week later he told Marco Polo that he would go. He felt that he might pay a final tribute to the Poet. On a sunny Monday morning, Marco Polo silently prepared the surprise.

He asked the psychologist and social worker, who had been closed-minded about the excluded, to come. He told them that Dr. George had invited them for a special class. Entering an anatomy room was not a pleasurable invitation, but they could not refuse the request of a respected professor. When he saw them, the professor said that there had been some kind of mistake and became angry with the rebellious student.

When the women attempted to leave, the young man and the beggar entered the room. Silence was broken. Dr. George and his assistants were shockingly amazed with Marco Polo's audacity. Marco Polo excused himself and asked to speak.

"Illustrious Dr. George, you have asked me to bring a beggar who had a good story to tell us. I humbly present my friend Falcon." Everyone smiled excitedly. Dr. George, observing the indigent's profile, felt that Marco Polo would make a fool of himself. However, Marco Polo continued:

"He doesn't look like an intellectual but he's a wise man."

He waited for Falcon to say something. He was finally going to get back at them. Falcon remained silent. Embarrassed, Marco Polo nudged him with his eyes but he remained mute. Each passing second seemed like a day. The beggar's silence encouraged people to make fun of them. Marco Polo was shaken.

Falcon just stood in the doorway. He kept looking around at the crowd seeming to be blocked and inhibited. Realizing the fiasco, Marco Polo began to think that he might be expelled from school because of his intrepid attitude. He also felt that he had put his friend in a delicate situation by bringing him to this place. "I was unfair. I used someone to solve my trauma of rejection", he considered.

The impatient students began to ridicule the beggar. "Speak! Speak!" they chanted. One of the most outgoing students said: "Look at the thinker! He's the man!" Another on replied, "No he's not. It looks like he's had a few." Dr. George and his assistant's egos were inflated. They enjoyed the circus. Only the social worker and psychologist maintained some sign of respect. Marco Polo took his friend's arm and said: "I'm sorry" and then began to take him out of the room.

"Don't worry", said Falcon.

He was not disturbed. Mockery was part of a drifter's menu. What bothered him was everyone's arrogance. To him, pride was one of the most foolish ways of manifesting intelligence. He let go of Marco Polo, turned towards the class and began to speak eloquently about pure philosophy. Their minds were in knots. Everyone was paralyzed. He mentioned the thoughts of several philosophers. He commented on the relationship between the world of thoughts and the physical world. He said that everything we think about the physical world is not real. It is a system of intentions that defines and conceptualizes phenomena but does not incorporate its reality.

Then, he talked about the relation between thoughts and the interpretations we have about our personality. The crowd was even more perplexed.

"Conscious thought is virtual. Everything you think about yourselves is not real. It is merely an interpretation of who you are and not the essential reality of who you are. Your thoughts can bring you closer to your inner reality or take you farther away from it. Therefore, when you think about yourselves, you can be stupid and place yourselves above others trying to control them or you can become your own executioners, diminishing yourselves and allowing yourselves to be controlled by them.

You must learn how to think with a critical conscience. Otherwise, you will treat diseases but you will also be ill…"

The students looked at one another in amazement. Although they understood very little of what he had said, they could see the profoundness of his words. The beggar was far more cultured than the students and intellectuals in the room. There was a mix of reactions.

Those who had always made fun of Marco Polo wished there was a hole they could hide in. Dr. George and his assistants were confronted with how little they actually were. The social worker and the psychologist felt the need to review their paradigms. In five minutes, the genius of the streets had astonished his audience. Next, he changed the focus of his attention and looked at the cadavers.

The audience followed him as he walked around the lab. Falcon approached one of the cadavers and broke the silence:

"General! Here you are! This used to be the great Napoleon of the streets. He fought imaginary armies. He won battles. He wanted to change the world, but death has no respect for heroes. Alcohol defeated him." The audience hesitated.

Falcon took a few more steps. He looked carefully at a fifty-year-old black woman; her face was expressionless due to long exposure to the sun during her life and the formalin after her death.

"Juliet! You too! How many times did you give the little you had, in order to quench the hunger of those who had nothing. You understood that sharing is happiness. At last you have rested. Juliet! Look at all these people who care about you! Everyone wants to study you. It's too bad that they only see the surface of your skin."

Dr. George, absorbed by the indigent's ideas, was paralyzed. Falcon was touched by the sight of his friends. His eyes suddenly broadened their field of view. He acted like the camera of a skillful director searching for a unique image.

Towards the back side of the lab, on the left, he saw the body of a large middle-aged white man, whose body had been punished by time. He slowly came closer and saw the wrinkles on his kind, soft and calm face. Falcon's heart was beating fast.

With every step he took a movie was being played in his mind, rescuing the spectacular experiences he had lived with his friend. They had walked, sang and struggled together. He recalled the Poet lecturing in the parks and praising the humble. Falcon's tears were no longer anonymous and they ran down his face scarred by time.

He stared as his friend's face, bent over and embraced his inert and cold body. Lying on that table was his whole family – his friend who had loved him, understood him and helped him recover his human condition. He felt that the loss of a friend could be as hard as losing the ground to walk on. He cried not caring about what the audience would think.

"What have they done to you, Poet!" he said, observing the shredded body. "Without you, the breeze isn't as gentle. The butterflies' dance is not as graceful as it used to be. Those in misery have lost their inner map. We all long for your sensitivity."

Marco Polo was in tears. The eyes of some of the students were also full of tears. Reflecting on his loss, Falcon added: "We didn't want you to die, but the Gardener of Life knows when to pick his most beautiful flowers…"

He looked at the students and bombarded them with his words.

"There are mysteries in the world, the body holds enigmas, but within the human spirit and mind are hidden the greatest secrets of the universe. You are penetrating this man's body, but you will never penetrate his being. You will dissect his muscles and nerves, you will open his chest and cranium, but you will never dissect his beautiful personality. He was a poet of life, a star on the stage of existence."

Then, he sighed and revealed some of his secrets to them, secrets that Marco Polo was already familiar with: "The man that you are studying used to be a renowned doctor. But since there are unpredictable turns in life, a dramatic surprise was reserved for him. He was driving with his family on vacation when he tried to pass another car and had an accident. He lost everything he loved the most: his wife and his two sons."

He also commented that one of his sons had not immediately died in the accident. The boy had been in ICU for a long time, but had later died. His pain had been indecipherable. He had suffered with serious depressive crises. He felt as if he were the most miserable of men. When Dr. George heard these words, he became pale and rubbed his hands over the back of his neck. It looked like he was suffering a panic attack with tachycardia, lack of breath, excessive perspiration and vertigo. His assistants showed concern for his reactions. Falcon continued to describe the Poet. He revealed that he had been a brilliant therapist of the streets, that he had helped the miserable, the homeless and the excluded ones. While Falcon described the Poet, Dr. George walked towards the body. He looked closely to the cadaver's face and to the wall. Suddenly, with a quivering voice, he began to mumble words that gradually became audible.

"No! This is impossible! It's not possible! It can't be!"

Everyone became even more disturbed. The scene was incomprehensible.

"Look at the picture on the wall", he said.

Those closer to him noticed the resemblance. The man in the picture had the same face as the cadaver. They were the same person. Dr. George anticipated their expectations by saying:

"This man is called Dr. Ulysses Burt. He was one of the greatest scientists in this country and one of the most notable of surgeons. This is the illustrious former director of this institution and also a skillful professor, my most brilliant master. He inspired my entire academic career. But I think that I absorbed very little of his sensitivity."

He delicately held the dead man's hands.

Falcon was surprised. The Poet, always humble, had never spoken about his fame. Dr. George continued explaining that Dr. Ulysses' accident, which had happened over ten years ago, and his disappearance were all over the news at the time. The university had been shocked. Many professors and students tried to find him at police stations, hospitals and hospices, but there was no sign of him.

Before he became a drifter, he had donated everything he had to the medical school. The donation, which was considerable, was used to help build the teaching hospital. Something that no one knew, not even Falcon, and that was only understood after his will had been read again, was that he had authorized the donation of all his organs for transplants. As a surgeon, Dr. Ulysses had performed many transplants. In order to encourage the donation of organs and show the grandeur of such a gesture, he liked to use a phrase:

No one dies when one lives in someone. Donate your organs. Live within someone.

In his will, he said that if it were not possible to use his organs for transplants, he wished that, at least, his body would be used in the anatomy lab.

Falcon finally understood why the Poet had insisted on returning to his hometown. He knew that he was near the end. He had been feeling chest pains. He wished to die near the medical school where he had always taught. He wanted to be found, to be useful to mankind, even after his eyes closed for good.

Professors and students were fascinated with his courage, strength, and love for life. Since there were several photos of Dr. Ulysses on the walls of the different departments, they affixed a plaque under each image containing Falcon's words:

He was a poet. He was star on the stage of life.

Dr. George was extremely moved. He was unable to continue his class. He looked at Marco Polo and Falcon and in his eyes he was saying all the things that words just could not express. He recognized his mistake and demonstrated his gratitude. His friends finally took him from the classroom.

A flower wreath was placed beside the body with the same phrase that had been affixed on the walls. The Poet remained in the anatomy room, in the same room where he had always dissected anatomic parts in his research. His old friends, respected professors, came to see him as if in a procession of a king, a life hero. Gray-haired surgeons who had lost their sensitivity cried when they saw their old friend's open chest and dissected members.

Students who took this class changed their understanding of existence forever. Never again did they have a superficial attitude towards the cadavers. It was a rare moment in the history of medicine, where the sharp blades of the scalpels found poetry while dissecting nerves, arteries and muscles.

Their professional formation also changed forever. Their patients were privileged because the future doctors realized that beneath each pain, each symptom, there were dreams, adventures, fears, joy, courage, setbacks – in other words, a marvelous story that needs to be discovered. Thus, they learned how to treat human beings and not just organs.

The arid soil of the end of the Poet's existence produced an oasis of wisdom within a small group. In life he was brilliant; in death, he shone!

CHAPTER 10

A Spectacular Performance

Time passed and Marco Polo continued to meet with Falcon. Their bond strengthened. Aware of the discomfort his friend suffered, he wanted to get him out of the streets. Falcon resisted.

"You've got to get out of the streets."

"Don't put me in a cubicle. The world is my home."

"But it's unhealthy and risky", Marco Polo insisted.

"No one is at risk when they have so little. This is one of the advantages of being poor." "But you don't get enough sleep; you eat little and dress poorly. Your health is failing." "I don't pay taxes or rent", joked the old friend. His relationship with Falcon made Marco Polo learn one of life's most difficult lessons: being transparent, not being enslaved by what others think and feel about us. Falcon was just what he was; he had no need to prove anything to anyone. Without such an emotional burden, his emotion was peaceful.

They met at least three times a week. The beggar and the young man became so close that they had fun together. They would perform in the parks not worrying if there was an audience or not. To them, life was a game, an adventure to be fully enjoyed.

Sometimes, they were like two clowns; other times, they behaved like children. Boredom did not exist in their dictionary. People who watched them play, and whose lives were a boring routine, reviewed their own lives. They would turn the simplest of things into a spectacle. When they had ice cream, they would say to each other:

"What a flavor! What a wonderful texture!"

Those who were nearby would be surprised. Because they were always in a hurry, they never tasted things the way they both did. When Falcon ate fruit, he would say:

"What a wonderful fruit! Such beautiful colors! How did it come to be? Who planted it? What were the dreams of the farmers who cultivated it?"

Marco Polo had similar gestures. Sometimes, they would contemplate the branches of a palm tree for a long time, observing the symphony of the wind. They looked like two lunatics. The curious passersby would stop and also look up, trying to see what both men were looking at, but they could not see anything. They thought that perhaps they were looking at some supernatural thing or a flying saucer.

When he needed money, Falcon would invite his friend to team up with him. They'd create and dramatize a text on the spot. They did not need to rehearse because they lived existence as a living theater. Falcon would shout out a phrase and Marco Polo would proclaim another one. It was a sure way of making some money.

"*I have no home*", Falcon would say.

"*But I dwell within*", Marco Polo completed.

"*No one can steal my sleep.*"

"*I depend on no one to dream.*"

"*Many people live in palaces.*"

"*But they are miserable beggars.*"

"*What's the use of accumulating treasures…?*"

"*…If they cannot buy happiness!*"

People of all races would stop and sit on benches to listen to the poetic duo. Several of Marco Polo's classmates would show up to see them. They had learned how to appreciate the thinking beggar. Fame knocked on their door, but they ignored it. All they wanted was to live intensely. Falcon taught his friend how to sing Louis Armstrong's "What a Wonderful World". Every now and then they would sing it together, exalting life and nature. They preserved the melody, yet changed the lyrics according to the moment. It was as if there was a symphonic orchestra accompanying them.

"I see trees of green, red roses too", Falcon sang the first line with his deep voice.

"I see them bloom for me and you", the intrepid Marco Polo sang the next line.

"And I think to myself, what a wonderful world", both sang in unison.

"I see skies of blue and clouds of white."

"The bright blessed day, the dark sacred night."

"And I think to myself, what a wonderful world."

"The colors of the rainbow, so pretty in the sky."

"Are also on the faces of the people walking by", they sang together gesticulating to the audience.

"I see friends shaking hands, saying: how do you do?"

"They're really saying: I love you."

When they finished singing, Americans, Chinese, Arabs, Jews, Indians, Brazilians and Europeans would embrace each other in the immense park. Some of them actually had the courage to say, "I love you" to others. Two lunatics – a beggar and a young man, a thinker and an academic, inebriated with joy, attracted everyone.

During one of these encounters, an unusual fact rattled the duo. Falcon was feeling tired, not really up to talking. He only wanted to contemplate beauty. He had walked a lot the previous day. He sat comfortably on the right side of a bench with his head turned towards the sky. The pedestrian traffic was huge, because of the amount of shops and banks around the park.

Falcon observed the clouds. He was fascinated with their floating anatomy. The ecstasy was so great that he just had to say something:

"Such beautiful paintings! Clouds are like wanderers; they drift to faraway places searching for a place to rest. When they do, they distill tears."

Marco Polo also observed them attentively and joined the game:

"When the sky cries, nature blooms in a smile."

Unexpectedly, Falcon looked into the infinite and started interrogating the Creator. He talked to God as if He were his friend.

"Hey, who are you behind the curtain of clouds? Why do you hide behind the veil of existence? Why do you silence your voice and shout through natural phenomena? Why do you like to hide from human eyes? I'm a tiny part of the universe, but I beg for an answer. Please, allow me to discover you."

Marco Polo was amazed with this unique dialogue. However, with airs of an intellectual, he turned proudly to his friend and said:

"Falcon, God does not exist. He is a spectacular invention of the human mind to bear life's limitations. I'm sorry but, in my opinion, science is the god of Mankind."

In a surprising reaction Falcon rose, stood on the bench and began to call everyone who was walking by to gather around him. With overly dramatic gestures he shouted:

"Come! Come closer! I will show you God!"

A group gathered in an instant.

Marco Polo was frightened. He had never seen Falcon reacting this way. He tried to calm him down, unsuccessfully. Falcon continued to shout:

"God is here! Believe me! You will be perplexed when you see him."

Marco Polo thought that Falcon was having a psychotic episode, a hallucination. He anxiously tried to hold him by the arm so that he would sit again. Falcon was suddenly silent. He pointed both hands to Marco Polo and said out loud:

"Here is God in flesh and bone!"

Marco Polo was startled. A mumble could be heard among the crowd.

"Believe me! This young man is God! Why do I say this? Because he has just told me that God does not exist, that he is merely the product of our brain! If this young man has never known the innumerable phenomena of times past, if he's never traveled the billions of galaxies with their trillions of secrets, if he hasn't discovered how he himself can enter his own brain and construct his complex thoughts and, despite all these limitations, he affirms that God does not exist, the conclusion I have come to, my friends, is that this young man must be God. For only God can have such conviction!"

The crowd was aghast. The indigent's speech had been so intelligent that it not only crushed Marco Polo's pride, but also the pride of those who heard him. His young friend was left blushed and astonished.

Falcon got off the bench and sat down. He unwrapped a sandwich and began to eat it. With his mouth full he said to Marco Polo:

"Do you know what this sandwich tastes like?"

Embarrassed, Marco Polo shook his head.

Falcon continued:

"If you are unsure about commenting on something that is so close and visible, don't speak with such conviction about something so distant and intangible. It's not wise."

The young man's intelligence was blocked. For the first time he did not have a rebuttal. He only said: "You didn't need to exaggerate." Falcon replied:

"If you affirm that you're an atheist, you don't believe in God, your attitude is respectable, because it reflects your opinion and personal conviction. But saying that God does not exist is an offense to intelligence, because it is the reflection of an irrational affirmation. Don't be like some of the evolutionist boys."

"What do you mean?" Marco Polo asked intrigued.

"Some philosophers feel that certain theories of evolution are insanely arrogant. I'm not criticizing the hypotheses of biologic evolution, but the unfounded scientific arrogance. Many of these scientists vehemently deny the idea of God because they rely on a few phenomena of their theory. They forget, as you have done, that there are billions of other phenomena that weave the incomprehensible secrets of the theater of existence, which are unknown to them. They are boys playing with science; their pride is built on sand." Marco Polo was shaken with Falcon's boldness, his schematic reasoning and creativity. Darwinists were revered intellectuals. He had never heard anyone, except for the church, criticize the evolutionists so incisively. Falcon had shone a light in this discussion that was not based on religion, but on the limitations of science itself.

Marco Polo tried to gather his thoughts and asked:

"But aren't evolutionists respected by the scientific community?"

"They are respected, but to me they are incarcerated in biology's prison. Unless they break free of this prison and embrace the ideas of philosophy, they will be reducers and not expanders of knowledge. They must follow Einstein's footsteps."

"What do you mean?"

"Einstein said that imagination is more important than knowledge. He shone because he loved philosophy. Unlike many naïve scientists might have thought, he didn't have a privileged brain. He had a privileged imagination. He was only 27 years old when he developed the basics of his theory. He had less academic culture than many college students have nowadays. Yet, why did he shine while college students are opaque? He shone because he used the art of doubting; he set his creativity free and learned to think with images."

Marco Polo was interested about Einstein's story and began to study it.

"Einstein was daring, he wanted to understand God's mind." he said.

Falcon, who was just as daring, had always tried to understand Him in his own way. He loved God, but he was not religious and did not defend a religion. He felt that only an amazing Artist, capable of surpassing the limits of our imagination, could be the Author of human imagination and all of existence.

Falcon said that he and the Poet had learned to relate to God in their psychological miseries and this relationship was one of the secrets that helped them bear their loss and oxygenated their meaning of life. Thus, they survived chaos. To them, each human being, especially scientists, should be an eternal apprentice.

"The wisdom of a human being is not in how much they know, but in how aware they are of what they don't know. Are you aware of this?"

After a pause, Marco Polo said: "I don't think so."

"What defines the nobility of a human being is their ability of seeing how small they really are. Can you see yours?"

"I'm trying", said Marco Polo, feeling cornered by the philosopher's intelligence.

"Never stop trying."

Then, Falcon was silent for a moment. He pondered his attitudes and had the courage to apologize to Marco Polo for embarrassing him.

"I'm sorry. Sometimes I feel that some of my reactions are side effects of my past; of my illness."

"Please, don't apologize. I'm the one who was stupid and arrogant."

Seeing that young Marco Polo was reflecting on the mysteries of existence, Falcon added:

"You can doubt the existence of God, but God does not doubt that you exist. That is what I believe in."

Marco Polo was restless. He rubbed his hands over his face, sighed, held his chin and supported his elbow on his knee, like a thinker, and asked:

"What did the philosophers think about God?"

"Remember what I've told you: many philosophers believed in metaphysics. They weren't afraid of arguing and having discussions about God. Science is afraid of debating about Him out of fear of pending towards a religion and losing their individuality. We know almost nothing about existence's box of secrets. Millions of books are but a drop in the ocean. Remember that we are a huge question searching for an answer in the few years of this life."

"Yet philosophers such as Marx, Nietzsche and Sartre were atheists."

Falcon gazed slowly at his friend and, as if he were enlightened, said:

"There are two types of God: a God that has created men, and another that was created by men. I feel that these philosophers didn't believe in a God created by men. They were against the religiosity of their time, that dilacerated human rights, but they weren't complete atheists. Though, I cannot speak for them."

The young man thought about that and asked:

"Who are we? What are we? Where are we going?"

"I frequently ask myself the same questions. The more I inquire, the more I get lost; and the more I get lost, the more I try to find myself." Falcon then added:

"Look at the people around us. What do you see?"

"Men in suits, well-dressed women, young people showing off their sneakers, teenagers worried about their hair, in other words, people walking about."

"Most of these people live just because they breathe. They no longer wonder who or what they are. They are numbed by the system. Modern human beings don't hear the cry of their greatest crisis. They silence their anguish because they're afraid of becoming lost in the tangle of doubts that is their own being. In the beginning of the 20th century, science promised that it would be the god of *Homo sapiens* and that it would answer these questions. But it has betrayed us."

"Why has it betrayed us?"

"First of all, because it hasn't discovered who we are; we continue to be an enigma, a drop that appears for an instant and soon dissipates from the stage of existence. Second, because despite the advances of technology, science hasn't solved the fundamental problems of Mankind. Violence, hunger, discrimination, intolerance and psychological misery haven't been extinguished. Science is a product and not a god of human beings. You should use it, but not be used by it."

As he traced his intelligence, Marco Polo confessed candidly:

"Pride is a virus that infects my mind."

"It infects us all. Even a psychotic has ideas of grandeur."

"Is it possible to destroy pride?"

"I don't think so. Our greatest task is to control it."

To end the complex class, the philosopher turned to his friend and added:

"Remember: the wisdom of a man is not defined by how much he knows, but by his awareness of what he doesn't know…"

This phrase impacted Marco Polo. He needed to discern it as well as all the knowledge they had covered. His mind had become a cauldron of ideas.

He decided that it was time to leave. A little dazed, he said goodbye to Falcon and left. The setting sun glistened on him and projected his shadow on the ground. His shadow was long. The distortion of the image invited him to a self-analysis.

He always wanted to be great; like a star revolved by all the other celestial bodies. He realized that his search for fame was foolish and that he needed to lessen his social shadow. He needed to find greatness within his smallness.

CHAPTER 11

The Principle of Co-Responsibility

Every time he would lie down on his warm and comfortable bed, Marco Polo thought of Falcon sleeping outdoors. It bothered him and, sometimes, he would wake up in the middle of a rainy night worried that Falcon had not found shelter. The vagabonds lived in precarious conditions and died young. The lack of hygiene, malnutrition, the lack of shelter from the elements and alcoholism shortened their lives in the first years of their journey.

Falcon's survival was an exception. The Poet helped him to get rid of alcoholism and take care of his health. However, the Poet had died and Marco Polo felt that, at least in part, he had occupied his place. Taking care of Falcon's quality of life and helping him to rescue his past motivated the young medical student. But he was afraid to take his friend off the streets and encourage him to find his son. The social system that excluded him was cruel in certain areas. Perhaps Falcon could not endure this stress. The external comfort can generate internal discomfort.

Six months passed and Falcon's health was frail. He was out of breath and refused to go to the university hospital. Marco Polo felt it was time to step in and help him, but how could he do that?

"Falcon can preserve his ideas and way of life when he returns to society. He could be like a virus that feeds on the system to fight the weaknesses of the system itself, as great journalists and other noble thinkers do", thought the young man.

These ideas filled his mind and he gradually lost his fear and increased his determination. He had received a lot from Falcon and wanted to give back at least a little. On the other hand, even though he did not want to leave the streets, Falcon felt that he needed to build a bridge to his past, little by little. His relationship with Marco Polo was different from the one he had with the Poet. Marco Polo was a reflection of his own son. Flashes of Luke sparkled in his imagination as they sang and recited poems. He was plagued by the radical denial of his past.

Marco Polo once addressed the problem directly. "You took great risks to rescue your identity and rebuild your sanity. You taught me to take risks to explore the human mind and fight for my own dreams. How about taking the risk of entering the social system and reevaluating your past? "

Falcon got the message and was dead silent. Marco Polo was incisive and insisted:

"Your son has a right to know that you are alive. The risk of being rejected is the price you have to pay."

These words sent a chill down his master's spine. His security has never been so undermined. He plunged into himself: "I am dead to him. The dead do not disturb the living."

"You said that God hides behind the curtain of existence and screams through the phenomena that He created, but you are not God. So, why do you hide behind the curtain of your arguments? Why do you yell at the phenomena you envisioned? What basis do you have for claiming that you are dead for your son? How many times do you think he searched for you in the crowd?"

Falcon had taught Marco Polo that doubting was the best tool for opening the windows of intelligence and that ready-made responses were the best way to close it.

"Do you love him?" Marco Polo asked the silent Falcon.

"Love is immortal! You can deny, suffocate and bury love, but it never dies. I already told you that my son never died inside me. He still lives in my dreams."

"There are no risks rescuing someone who is dead, but if he is alive, take chances for him!"

When Marco Polo thought Falcon had given in, he built a huge wall. "Our language, interests, views on life and expectations are very different. It would be almost impossible to reconstruct our story. If even family members who have lived together for years do not respect each other, how can harmony be expected between two instruments that have not played together for two decades? "

It was almost impossible to defeat the genius' intelligence. "The shock could really be unbearable," said Marco Polo. "But we fail 100% of the times we don't try."

He had the feeling that no one could overcome the strength of the philosopher's thinking, which was shaped by the psychological crisis and sculpted by life. But he had one last bullet in his intellectual weapon, a strong argument. He had constructed this argument during the period of his relationship with Falcon.

He had polished it patiently as Michelangelo had done it with rough marble in search of his masterpiece. He had smoothed it out, assimilated it and written it down. The time had come to talk to him about "The Principle of Inevitable Co-responsibility". This principle combined certain psychological and philosophical foundations.

"Falcon, you never lived outside of my system. Whether you like it or not, you are part of it."

"This is absurd! Don't confuse my world with yours. In my world, people are transparent; in yours they disguise themselves behind their smiles, behind the aesthetics. In my world, people have time to invest in what they love; in yours, they become working and consuming machines." Marco Polo was confused, but he was not intimidated. "I agree that organized society is sick in many ways, but the principle of inevitable co-responsibility shows that it is impossible to have two different systems. What exists are two ways of looking and acting within the same system. People are never completely separated from each other."

Falcon had never heard of this principle. For the first time, he scratched his head, confused before his disciple. This idea disturbed him. If he convinced himself that there were not two systems, what would his argument be for hiding in his cocoon?

"What principle is that? What thinker elaborated this? He asked suspiciously.

"I did" replied Marco Polo.

Falcon despised it and, infected with pride, looked at the young man with contempt. Aware of this contagion, he composed himself: "I'm sorry. Let's discuss this. Present your ideas." Those words reminded him of when he had a crisis in the classroom during law school. He wanted to be confronted in field of ideas and Marco Polo had challenged him right at that point – and the hardest part was, that it was about the most delicate period in his story.

Marco Polo vehemently defended his thesis. He commented that the principle of inevitable co-responsibility demonstrates that human relationships are a huge multifocal web. It reveals that no one is a physical, psychological and social island within mankind. We are all influenced by others. All of our actions, whether conscious or unconscious, constructive or destructive, alter the events and development of mankind itself.

Any human being, intellectual or illiterate, rich or poor, doctor or patient, activist or alienated, is affected by society and, therefore, interferes in the victories and defeats of society through their behavior. Marco Polo wanted to say that everyone is co-responsible for the future of society and, therefore, for the future of mankind and the planet as a whole. "Our behavior affects people in three ways: it changes their time, changes their memory by recording these behaviors and changes the quality and frequency of their reactions. By changing people's time, memory and reactions, we change their future and story. "Falcon went from indifference to astonishment," Where is this kid trying to get with this?"

Marco Polo went on to say that even little behaviors can interfere with great reactions in history. The sneeze of an American can affect the reactions of people in the Middle East. The attitude of a European, even though little, can interfere with time and actions in China.

Falcon started to see where his friend was going, even though it still was not completely clear. He mindfully observed each of his phrases. Marco Polo went from theory to examples. "A baker who made bread in Paris in the 15th century affected the time and memory of the housewife who bought it, which affected the reactions of her children, which altered the behavior of their friends, neighbors and co-workers. In a way, the chain reaction influenced French society at the time and other generations. Thus, in an uninterrupted sequence of events, the 15th century baker influenced his parents and friends centuries later and, consequently, the formation of Napoleon's personality, which affected the world.

"In 1908, Hitler moved to Vienna to become a painter. The professor at the arts academy who rejected him affected his time, his memory and his unconscious mind. This influenced his affectivity, his understanding of the world, his reactions, his struggle within the Nazi party, his imprisonment and his book. This whole process interfered with the outbreak of World War II, which affected Europe, Japan, Russia and the United States, which changed the direction of mankind. If Hitler had been admitted to the arts academy, perhaps he would have become an artist, even if a mediocre one, and not one of the greatest psychopaths in history. I am not saying that Hitler's psychopathy would be resolved with his admission to the Vienna art school, but it could have been diminished or perhaps it might not have been manifested."

Falcon was surprised. The roles were switched. Marco Polo said that a native of an Amazonian tribe can also affect history. When killing a bird, it will stop laying eggs and having hatchlings, which will affect the consumption of seeds, predators and the entire food chain, the ecosystem and the terrestrial biosphere. Furthermore, the absence of the dead bird's descendents will affect the biologists' observation process, interfering with their reactions, their researches, their publications, their university and their society.

"Those who commit suicide do not stop working in the social world. Suicide alters the time of friends and relatives and, mainly, shatters their emotions and memory, generating an existential vacuum and disturbing thoughts, and memories that will affect their stories and the future of society", said Marco Polo.

"Nobody disappears when they die. Living and dying with dignity must be coveted treasures. Therefore, the principle of inevitable co-responsibility shows that we must not become islands within mankind. There should never be any islands of Americans, Arabs, Jews or Europeans. Mankind is a family that lives in a complex web. We are a unique species and we must love and care for it, otherwise we will not survive."

According to the young thinker, we are all inevitably responsible, to a greater or lesser extent, for preventing terrorism, social violence and hunger in the world. Falcon agreed with Marco Polo's ingenuity of reasoning. Although he was an expert in the art of thinking, he had not realized that he was being captured in his disciple's web. The young man then commented that other people's reactions can affect us in a mild or intense way. Watching a movie, talking to a friend or praising someone can change our lives a little or a lot.

He remembered a friend who was humiliated by a teacher because he was unable to read a paragraph correctly. The teacher made him repeat the text several times while the other students scoffed at him. That experience was registered in his mind and had blocked the student's intelligence, generating stuttering and insecurity, which drastically affected his future as a father and as a professional. He was never able to speak in public again.

After giving this general explanation and example, Marco Polo adjusted his intelligence weapon and hit Falcon with a fatal blow. He had prepared, though without high expectations, a basis for Falcon to question his own behavior over the past two decades and forever change the course of his history. It took twenty minutes to change a life. Marco Polo had cut his friend's resistance like the blade of a scalpel. "You are the master and I am a mere apprentice, but please, after that explanation, tell me: Is it possible to have socially isolated systems?"

Falcon smiled and admitted frankly, "No. There are systems that communicate very little with each other, but not isolated."

"Staying on a park bench and reciting poetry or asking for money to buy bread are reactions that interfere in the behavioral dynamics of those who have been listening, therefore interfering in the lives of their co-workers, their companies, society and international trade. Therefore, enclosing yourself in your own world can be seen as a selfish act! Do you agree or disagree? "

"From this perspective, isolation can be a selfish act," said Falcon, beginning to sweat.

"You were isolated within yourself because society excluded and discriminated you, but you overcame it all and became a wise man. The same society that hurt you needs your ideas and your courage to be transformed because your system has never been separated from mine."

The world weighed on Falcon's shoulders. He was surprised and reflected: "Why didn't I think of that? Marco Polo is right. We interfere with the memory and time of others all the time. Memory and time join us in an inevitable network."

"Your ideas are hard to swallow, but I cannot escape them. I influence your world and I am influenced by it," he said to Marco Polo. The young man looked at the genius and gave him a final blow: "Answer me one more question, you thinker: Why is it impossible to become socially alienated or isolated in a pure, complete and absolute way?"

With a broken voice and already knowing where Marco Polo was going to, the philosopher said sincerely: "Because the absence of reaction is an action in itself, it is the action of non-reaction. The non-reaction contributes to the action of others. Just as a person who commits suicide continues to interfere in the history of loved ones; a father who becomes a vagabond continues to interfere in the life of his own son". Falcon now had tears in his eyes. "Very good, master! I know this is a painful subject, but its absence triggered a series of events that influenced Luke's personality. Every time he looked for you and did not find you or had to explain your absence to someone, you intensely altered his emotions, thoughts and self-esteem. Therefore, you have never ceased to be co-responsible for it."

Falcon got up and started to walk in circles. Never have so few words generated so many consequences on his intellect. He concluded that even his speeches in the park and getting people to travel inside were facts that influenced society and indirectly affected his son.

The question was not whether his absence had been better or worse for Luke. The point is that he never managed to be isolated from him. The thinker was defeated in the only place where his life path could be changed: in the field of the ideas. Fearful, he said sincerely: "We cannot escape from others because we cannot escape from ourselves. I will take risks to find my son again!"

He decided to break out of his cocoon. He would have to pay a high price to reconstruct his story. The problems he would face would be enormous. He would have to face his internal and external predators. He could be rejected for being a beggar. He would have to face his ex-father-in-law, his ex-wife and his former co-workers. Worst of all, Luke could blame him, be indifferent to him and be ashamed of his father. He might not even be alive. The price was incalculable and the risks were unimaginable. "I am scared!" he said.

Marco Polo had never heard Falcon say those words. He always considered him unbeatable. "Afraid?! But you have always been fearless!"

"I am afraid of myself. I'm afraid to face myself. I am afraid of walking the paths I have not traveled in a long time and I thought I would never travel again."

As he was learning the art of producing witty phrases, Marco Polo surprised Falcon once again: "Fear can be an excellent teacher. It removes kings from their thrones and teaches them to be what they have always been: mere fragile human beings."

Falcon laughed despite his pain. Trying to console himself, he looked again at his invisible audience and said: "We all have a child that we must find – some within and others on the outside. I must find the child outside without losing the one inside."

He asked to stay on the streets for one more day. He would have to say goodbye, at least temporarily, to his lifestyle and the outdoor home where he had lived for so many years. He wanted to hug more trees, talk to more flowers, play with butterflies and watch the stars before closing his eyes for another night's sleep.

Marco Polo agreed to pick him up the next morning. His roommates who shared a house with him would be leaving to go home and the house would be empty. Falcon was going to spend the weekend with him. Together, they would plan the long trip to his hometown.

Falcon was slow to say goodbye. He hugged a dozen trees. He felt the breeze and heard the serene sound of the wind. He knelt in gardens, kissed the roses and talked to God. He concluded by saying, "God, you have been my friend throughout my madness, my misery and the homeless nights. I am afraid that you will not be my friend in times of abundance and comfortable nights. It is so easy to forget you. Walk with me."

While he lay down, the stars did not induce sleep as usual. The old blanket didn't warm him up as usual. The park bench was uncomfortably pressed against his ribs. He had nightmares. He saw people laughing at him and despising him. His mind had become a whirlwind of menacing images.

The next day, Marco Polo took him home. Falcon showered, trimmed his beard and long hair. Marco Polo lent him some clothes, but since he was four inches shorter than his friend, his pants and shirt looked funny.

The old man that looked to be between seventy and eighty suddenly looked younger. He now looked to be his true age of 55 again. Marco Polo laughed at his friend's new look. Falcon looked like a big kid wearing short clothes. "I still look good!" he teased doing an awkward pose.

"Good enough not to scare me." They went out to buy him decent clothes. For Falcon, any outfit would do. They entered a store and Marco Polo chose a green long-sleeved shirt and red pants. Falcon tried them on and found the clothes beautiful; they reminded him of red roses with green stems in the gardens. Fortunately the saleswoman intervened and they bought two white shirts and beige pants.

Upon leaving the store, Falcon felt artificial as if he were wearing a costume. He walked upright, serious and without spontaneity. For years he did not care about other people's eyes. He felt he was being watched. It was not a feeling caused by his old paranoia, but having to represent what he did not feel, having to smile when he was feeling miserable.

Marco Polo saw his friend's face gradually sadden. Nothing cheered him up. He turned on the TV so that Falcon could watch a news channel, but that only made things worse. Since he left for the world, Falcon had never watched TV again.

He saw a reporter denouncing the famine in Ethiopia, showing images of extremely thin and hungry children, only skin and bones, without any facial expression and in a deep state of melancholy. The children had almost no muscle strength to move. They were supposed to be playing, but instead, they were starving. Falcon tilted his head forward as his eyes widened.

The reporter said that, according to FAO (United Nations Food and Agriculture Organization), a child dies of hunger every five seconds. Shocked, Falcon shook his head and started shouting: "This is not possible! They are letting the children die! "

He then saw another ghostly image. A father ran desperately and screamed as he carried his bloody son. He had been a victim of a terrorist attack. The images that jumped from the screen seemed more insane than the hallucinations that disturbed him during his most drastic psychotic phase. And that was real. Falcon started to feel bad. He was having palpitations and excessive sweating.

Then he watched the reporter's facial expression. To his surprise, his face did not translate the drama of the news; it just showed an air of dismay. Later, the same reporter quickly changed his behavior, smiled and talked about an eccentric millionaire who appeared on the screen petting his horses in luxurious stables. This new one struck Falcon's intellect like an earthquake. He was incredulous.

He realized that the process of transmitting information destroyed viewers' affectivity. He looked at his young friend and pointedly commented, "Doesn't this society disgust you?"

"These are bad things that are happening," agreed Marco Polo.

"Bad? They're horrible! All of you have adapted to social rubbish. You are no longer affected by them!"

"No! We hate those images!"

"Your eyes hate them, but your emotions don't react to them."

Marco Polo was shaken. He felt that Falcon was right. Even though he wandered the streets and saw certain types of suffering, he had no contact with some of the most disgusting miseries created by the system. His sensitivity was not sick or exaggerated; he was numb.

Marco Polo suddenly had an insight. In a quick moment of lucidity, he analyzed psychoadaptation in the anatomy room. The first images of the corpses, as well as the smell of formalin, provoked strong reactions in the students, but little by little these reactions were diluted in their unconscious mind. The smell of formalin became bearable. Some of the students who had cried because of the tension on the first day, now played with the corpses, moving their limbs as if they were alive.

Marco Polo drew a parallel between the anatomy room and the social environment. The impact caused by the grotesque images on the nightly news lost its effect as viewers watched them day after day. He realized that human sensitivity was dying. It became a horror show. Thus, he humbly admitted: "We are sick".

Still completely indignant, Falcon used Marco Polo's own speech on the principle of coresponsibility to ask: "Are society's leaders adults?"

"Of course they are."

"Then answer me: are the rulers of the rich countries and the entrepreneurs who dominated the world co-responsible for all this misery?"

"Yea."

"Do they suffer from insomnia because of all this suffering?"

Feeling trapped, the young man did not know how to respond, so Falcon answered for him. "If they can sleep and feel at peace, they are children. Only a child is unaware of the misery of others and is not responsible for them. Only a child can eat and sleep in peace while other children are starving."

Falcon and the Poet often entertained children in the parks and skillfully taught them to think with their ideas and gestures. According to the two excluded thinkers, children were the only pure thing in society and its greatest treasure. Seeing them being mistreated overwhelmed his feelings.

Suddenly, Falcon opened the windows of his unconscious mind and rescued his emotions from the days after abandoning his son. He relived his first nights as a wanderer and recalled his screams for Luke. He would look at random students' faces on the streets and see his son's face. He wanted to hug them, but their parents wouldn't allow it.

These images in his mind were mixed with the TV scenes increasing his anguish. The images of the horses in luxurious stables with the images of starving children were confusing in his mind. Restlessly, he walked around the room. It was as if the children were experiencing pain.

He felt like throwing up. He wanted to vomit his outrage. He looked at his invisible audience and started teaching a class as if he were in crisis. Nearby neighbors could hear him shouting. Marco Polo watched, motionless.

"Insane! Stupid! A species that destroys their little ones is committing suicide! What society is this that allows children to be treated like animals and animals like children? Don't mistreat them! Let them play! Let them live!" Internally asphyxiated, Falcon left the house suddenly. He needed to breathe.

CHAPTER 12

The Reencounter

Walking on the streets, Falcon was apprehensively accompanied by Marco Polo from a distance. On the street, however, little by little, Falcon started letting go. He started dancing and making faces for the children and encouraging them to smile. He greeted everyone, even those he did not know. He hugged a tree. He went back being the usual Falcon. He had recovered, yet he had not forgotten the images.

He returned home and, together with Marco Polo, began to organize things for the trip. They left before dawn from Sunday to Monday in the young man's old car. The trip lasted more than six hours. When the day broke, they were still on the road. The first rays of sunlight penetrated his eyes. Falcon was convinced that he needed to rediscover the basements of his past, open some wounds that were never healed and face the ghosts that never died.

Falcon's real name was Socrates. His mother had chosen the name of the Greek philosopher without great intellectual pretensions, just because she thought it was pretty, sonorous. But this name had influenced him to take an interest, during his high school days, in the extraordinary thinker.

He discovered that Socrates had been a questioner of the world, but had left nothing written. His disciples wrote about him, just as Marco

Polo would one day write about Falcon. Fascinated by the philosopher's intellectual stance, the young Socrates decided to pursue a career in philosophy.

To me, you will always be Falcon - commented Marco Polo.

'I'm not Socrates anymore."

Finally they arrived at the city. It was difficult for Falcon to recognize the streets, squares and bars. The city had had changed, but not substantially. He managed to get around. His heart was racing, his hands were sweating, his muscles tightened. He found the old Italian canteen, next to his house. He asked to stop.

It was a simple but pleasant place. In that canteen, around a table and holding a glass of good wine, he had had great debates about topics such as politics, social crises and human relations. Customers listened to him in awe. They learned to philosophize as in Ancient Greece. Falcon remembered some sweet passages. However, it was also from this canteen that his friends had to drag him out when he had his psychotic outbreaks.

The walls were faded, the checkered floor was the same, but dull, the flowered tiles with a white background remained untouched. Tony, the owner, a little older than Falcon, was fascinated by his intelligence, and they became great friends.

He got out of the car slowly. He looked down the street, gazed at the buildings. He breathed in the morning breeze, it was still ten o'clock. Marco Polo, taking him by the right arm, gently pushed him into the establishment.

Falcon asked about Tony. The young man at the counter said that the owner had suffered cerebral ischemia and was walking with difficulty, but he had not lost his lucidity.

He said he would call him, but first asked who was looking for him.

"Say it is Falcon, or rather, Socrates, an old friend."

The clerk opened the back door, where there was an old residence. A gray-haired man, upon hearing the news, was astonished. With a shaky walk, he anxiously struggled to walk faster. As he approached, an incredulous smile appeared on his face. It looked like he was seeing something out of this world. After all, a dead man had just reemerged.

"Socrates! Socrates! It can't be you! - He said, trying to run.'

The scene was almost indescribable. The eyes read the 'letters of the time'. The two friends hugged each other for a long time without saying a word. It was not necessary. The silence was more eloquent.

Tony always thought Socrates was a genius. He had suffered intensely from his friend's psychotic crises. He said that the fact of being a genius had driven him crazy. His disappearance had made him a taboo in those areas. Even recently they commented on his case. After the affectionate hug, Tony asked where he came from.

"I come from everywhere and nowhere. I belong to the world, my friend."

Tony was delighted with his answer. He realized that Socrates was still sharp in the short, but far-reaching phrases. Marco Polo watched everything as an attentive spectator.

After a few minutes of conversation, Falcon entered the arid terrain of his past and asked his friend, "What about Luke?"

Falcon had brought his son to the restaurant many times. Tony knew the story well. He knew about the long and painful separation. He paused. The pause froze Falcon's feelings. Then, he heard the great news. "Luke has become a great man."

"What do you mean?" asked Falcon, feeling ecstatic and relieved. "The seeds you planted have spawned a thinker."

"I didn't plant any seeds. My son had a psychotic father!" he said humbly. Disagreeing with him, Tony repeated a phrase coined by Falcon himself. "Do you remember saying that the greatest favor you can do for a seed is to bury it? You buried a seed in your son's heart. It seemed to have died, but it flourished. Go to Central University and see for yourself."

Tears streamed down Falcon's face as his old friend continued: "Your son has come here many times to hear me talk about you. He knew your intellectual talents."

The street thinker was no longer able to get up. He had been through long years of suffering. Seeing Tony again was surreal. He sat down and said: "That's impossible! My son looked for me!" Marco Polo took a deep breath. At that moment, he was sure that he had taken the right path. Tony offered them something to eat and drink.

"I'm sorry, my friend," said Falcon. "My soul's hunger and thirst are more urgent."

They went to the university, the same one where Falcon had taught and been expelled. The long corridors and the dark granite floor opened his memory windows. Once again, pleasant and frustrating memories filled his mind. He was apprehensive.

They went to the Secretary and asked for Luke. They found that he had gone far. He was a doctor of sociology and dean of the university. He was 32 years old. Falcon was surprised by the news. How could the son of a mental patient, who was distressed by his father's crises, have reached the height of the academic hierarchy at such a young age?

Falcon knew that psychological illnesses were neither contagious nor genetically determinant. Most of them generate influences that can be dissipated by the educational environment. He was aware that the psychological universe was so complex that the children of psychotic and depressed parents were able to overcome the stressful environment of their homes and be happy, safe and become leaders.

He lived with Luke for ten years. The foundation of his son's personality had already been formed. The fear that his absence might have damaged the boy's personality had always haunted him. The current news about Luke refreshed his emotions.

The secretary said that Dr. Luke was in the department of judicial sciences giving a lecture on the "Crisis in the formation of thinkers". Feeling unsure, Falcon said he would be back another time. Marco Polo took him by the arm and asked to be pointed in the direction of the amphitheater. The room was almost full when they arrived.

There were a few seats in the front row. With no alternative, they sat down very close to the speaker. Dr. Luke quickly interrupted his speech, waited for the newcomers to calm down and then continued.

Falcon was completely unrecognizable with his relatively long, shaggy gray hair, his skin dry and wrinkled from the adversities of the streets. Some of his former colleagues were also in the audience.

Hearing his son speak confidently set off innumerous triggers in his memory. A hurricane of images passed through his mind. He remembered countless moments in little Luke's life. It seemed unbelievable, even surreal, that after so many years he was in front of him again. His eyes were fixed on his face. He had a desire to interrupt the conference, run to him and hug him. But he controlled himself because he did not know how Luke would react.

Luke ended his talk by saying that universities had multiplied, but the shaping of thinkers had not. He said that one of the causes for this was that knowledge was separated, divided, forming professionals with a unifocal view, instead of a multifocal view of reality. He said that mathematics, physics and chemistry must unite with sociology, psychology and philosophy, in order to build a humanistic science capable of producing tools that change the world. "Humanistic knowledge produces ideas. Ideas produce dreams. Dreams transform society...", he concluded under the loud applause of the audience.

After finishing, he encouraged the participants to discuss their ideas and experiences. The audience was hesitant, as if the speaker had left no room for questioning.

Marco Polo boldly signaled Falcon to speak, but he remained silent. Once again, he encouraged his friend by whispering, "This is your big chance to help people and impress your son. You are a master of this theme. Let's go!" "I can't," Falcon murmured.

Marco Polo then remembered a lesson that Falcon had taught him when he foolishly said that science was the god of mankind. He felt that now it was time to return the lesson. He suddenly got up, walked to the front of the audience, took the microphone and went up to the stage where Dr. Luke was standing.

When he saw Marco Polo's attitude, Falcon realized that he had gotten himself into one of the biggest problems of his life. His disciple learned fast.

From the stage, Marco Polo said boldly: "Dear audience! I am going to introduce you to one of the greatest contemporary thinkers. He has toured several universities in the world. He is under so much demand that he has no address. He is so eloquent that he is able to give a lecture from a park bench. He understands the crises of the thinker like no one else." Everyone laughed with admiration. Then Marco Polo pointed both hands at his friend. "I give it to you, Dr. Falcon!"

There were more than three hundred participants in the auditorium. They found the debater's name strange. Dr. Luke, as a sign of respect, stood up and applauded. The crowd joined him. Falcon had no other choice. He went up on stage and looked at the audience for a long time. He managed to recognize some of his colleagues, despite their white hair. He remembered how they mocked him and turned their backs on him. His penetrating gaze invaded and breached their intelligence.

He started to speak in a slow, yet vibrant voice. It was as if he had never left the classroom microcosm. He said that great men produce their brightest ideas in their youth while they are still immature. "Why were they so productive in their youth, ladies and gentlemen? They were so productive because they were not afraid to think. And why weren't they afraid to think? Because they were not servants of the old paradigms and concepts or their truths. They were not trapped by preconceived knowledge."

"What is more important in the formation of a thinker: doubt or a preconceived answer?" Falcon asked the audience.

"The doubt!" they responded in unison.

"What do you teach?"

Taken by surprise, most professors of law, psychology, sociology, engineering and pedagogy responded honestly: "We teach preconceived knowledge".

"Ladies and gentlemen, excuse me, but even if you are not aware of it, by transmitting pre-conceived knowledge, you are forming repeaters of ideas and not thinkers. The academic system has imprisoned human beings and has not released their intelligence".

While Falcon was speaking, some people in the audience had the feeling that they knew him. His audacity and sharp thinking took them back to the past. Falcon, focusing on former professors and researchers, hit them head on: "Perhaps many of you have been handcuffed by this system without knowing it. At the beginning of your careers you may have doubted, ventured and produced more knowledge than you do now. A successful career and titles that value scientists can work as a poison that kills your boldness and creativity. In reality, we should not be doctors, ladies and gentlemen, but eternal apprentices."

Luke listened attentively to the cultured and provocative man. As director of the university, he knew that many distinguished professors hid behind their titles and did not produce any science. Luke became a fearless thinker; his success had come from his chaos. He had grown up in one of the worst environments, but his father, before his psychosis and in the moments of lucidity between crises, led him to be unafraid of new things, to explore the unknown, to get wet in the rain, to build his own toys and to face his insecurity and feelings of humiliation.

Falcon looked at Luke, Marco Polo and then at the audience and concluded: "Our students consume knowledge as if it were a fast food sandwich. They do not digest or assimilate it and do not know how it is produced. They receive degrees and prepare for success, but not to deal with frustrations, losses, challenges and failures. Universities, with some exceptions, have generated servants and not authors of their own stories."

The public was shaken by this critical and incisive explanation. There was an explosion of applause. Everyone asked Marco Polo where the professor had come from. Marco Polo told them that he had come from everywhere and from nowhere.

In an embarrassed voice, Falcon thanked him and said: "I would like to direct the applause to someone here who is more important than me. During his childhood, I played with him, kissed him and loved him more than anything in this life. But also someone who I hurt and disturbed with my crises. To spare him, I set out on a long journey where I overcame my crises. But I didn't have the courage to return. I was afraid of myself."

The confused audience could not understand the change in the lecture and neither could Luke. Falcon was crying. He stopped once more to contain his tears. "My son suffered a lot, he lost a lot, but he used pain to succeed. He became a brilliant thinker and a generous human being."

Falcon looked at Luke as he spoke. He was in shock. In a trembling voice, he lowered the microphone and wiped the tears away with his hands and said: "I love you, my son. Forgive me, my little pupil."

Luke had never forgotten the affectionate nickname his father had given him. Like lightning, Socrates' last words opened the craters within him and lit up the dark alleys of his story. He recognized his father. He was transported to the past. Countless images immediately emerged from the patchwork of his memory and became visible in the conscious stage. He started to see and hear his father calling him with open arms. He was ten again and saw his own frightened face looking for his daddy in the crowd.

Luke wept many times during his adolescence, crying out for his father in silence. He did not care that people made fun of him. He loved his father the way he was, his dear father. Now, Socrates was on stage with his fiery intelligence as if he had never left the stage of his life. He looked unreal. Luke started to cry. He could not react.

It was not the meeting of two intellectuals, but of two broken souls. A father and his son, whose stories had been mutilated by the misfortunes of existence, but were now gathered together.

Luke stood up sobbing and murmured, "Dad! Dad! Is that you...?!"

They embraced for a long time. They comforted each other's pain. They kissed each other with affection. Time stopped. The audience was in awe.

Moments later, Luke looked at Falcon and said: "Dad, you have no idea of how long I've been looking for you! I lived through sleepless nights and nightmares."

"My son, my son! Forgive me! I wanted to be a hero, but I was a coward!"

"No, daddy, you were the most courageous of men. My grandfather, on his deathbed, confessed to me and my mother what he did to you. He said he paid for a medical report from a psychiatrist to keep you away from me. But I never stopped loving you."

They embraced again. The audience stood up and applauded without really understanding all the facts. They were just aware that they were witnessing a scene showing one of the most beautiful demonstrations of love...

Marco Polo could not stand the excitement. He walked to a window, opened it and felt the breeze caress his face. He observed the smooth swaying of the leaves and flowers. In a moment of introspection, for the first time he whispered a few words that were more like a prayer: "God, I don't know who you are. I also don't know who I am. But I thank you for life and for all the joys and sufferings that turn it into a unique wonder!"

Falcon turned to Marco Polo, hugged him and thanked him. He introduced the student as an adopted son and, following his sense of humor, he joked: "Crazy people live more adventures than normal ones. Never be too normal, Marco Polo..."

Hearing this phrase, the young man rescued the phrase from his father, which was immersed in his unconscious mind: "Never be ordinary, my son!"

Marco Polo shook his head and got the message. He decided to release his creativity and walk fearlessly through the twists and turns of existence. He wanted to honor his name and turn his life into a fascinating adventure.

CHAPTER 13

The Student's Boldness

Luke took Falcon and Marco Polo to his house. He was already married and had a twoyear-old daughter. They talked for a long time. The next day, Falcon's ex-wife Deborah appeared. Luke gave her the surprising news. She was shaken and skeptical. Socrates' return was like a dream and, especially, the fact that he had rescued his lucidity.

Deborah's relationship with Falcon's former psychiatrist did not last long – nearly a year. They lived together for six months. Like any relationship without roots, which often happens between therapists and patients, they were not able to overcome their difficulties. The psychiatrist, who was so kind and friendly during the first few months, became intolerant and did not like to talk. They broke up and never spoke again.

Deborah had had other boyfriends. For four years she lived with a judge who was friends with her father. But this relationship had no emotional ties. It lacked intimacy and affection. The judge tended to isolate himself; he lived to work, instead of working to live. He was an excellent professional, but he did not know how to invest in what he loved most. He could not understand Deborah's hurt feelings or Luke's lonely world. As a fact, since Socrates departure, she never found love again. She had been alone for the last two years.

Deborah arrived at Luke's house by surprise. When she entered the room, her eyes and Falcon's met. The moment was filled with tenderness. Kindness and pain were intertwined. His eyes were teary; hers were full of tears too. Only silence could decipher the magic of this moment.

Lucas was silent. Marco Polo, who was ready to go home, remained quiet. He knew Deborah by Falcon's words. The look on his friend's face let him know who was in front of him. After a quick introduction, Marco Polo and Luke left, in order to give them some privacy, but Falcon and Deborah decided to take a walk. They needed to walk the avenues of their past.

Deborah remembered the time when she could not stand his crises and left him for his psychiatrist. She slowly lowered her head and said softly, "I don't know if it's possible for you to forgive me, but please forgive me for leaving you when you needed me the most…"

Shaking his head, Falcon quickly tried to ease the weight of her guilt. "I understand you. I understand you."

These words have rarely been so eloquent. He then reflected on his jealousy and added: "I also need you to forgive me. Forgive me for my paranoid jealousy. Forgive me for all the times when, in my delusions, I accused you of cheating."

"You weren't aware of that."

"Aware or not, I hurt you. I can't even imagine what you went through. I know it must not have been easy to live with my madness."

"Underneath your madness, there was a wonderful human being."

She then hugged him tenderly. He kissed her gently on the cheek. She was still beautiful in his eyes. Hand in hand, they continued talking. From that moment on, they became great friends.

Falcon was readmitted to the university. Some of his former colleagues acknowledged their mistake with gestures, but not with words. They had discriminated him for being a psychiatric patient and were wrong to label his mental illness as a completely disabling illness. There were other victims at many other universities.

Falcon's return to his professional activities was more than an act of compassion by society with the aim of social inclusion. It was one of the rare occasions when society recognized the wisdom of an ex-psychotic patient and gave him the opportunity to prove that many of those maimed by life have a lot to teach for those who have a lot to learn.

Falcon kept his nickname. Still provocative, he urged his students to open the windows of their own intellect, to dare to build critical ideas against everything that held their minds. With a penetrating look and sharp words, the street master was back, igniting the small world of the classroom.

Marco Polo went home. While driving on the highway, he watched the sunset. The sun's rays surpassed the spaces between the clouds, leaving golden bands. It was an enchanting heavenly anatomy. While observing the nature around him, he immersed himself. After a moment of silence, he thought out loud: "I will spend my life exploring the human mind, the most complex and dazzling of the worlds. I will be a gold digger who finds treasures in the rubble of those who suffer".

That thought would change his life forever; it would guide his conduct and gradually make him view psychological disorders from other angles. Over the years, his thinking would be different from the current thinking of science. He would not see psychoses, depression and other psychological disorders as an attribute of the weak, but as the complexity of the human personality.

His close contact with Falcon made Marco Polo a medical student who questioned and criticized more than ever. He was a type of student that was rare in the academic world. Most of his colleagues were afraid to voice their doubts and criticisms. He, on the other hand, although trying to be kind, could not bear to be silent. He caused turmoil in the classroom with his audacity to question his teachers who were prepared to teach a passive audience.

Some students, very well behaved, would get better grades than Marco Polo, but they did not get better grades in the most important functions of intelligence. They did not exercise their ability to think before reacting, their safety, sensitivity and boldness. They were serious candidates for becoming professionally and emotionally frustrated.

Not being afraid to be different was not always the most comfortable path for young Marco Polo. There is a price for those who want to shine on their own and not be in the shadow of others, but he was willing to pay for it. He felt that a diploma was just an appendix. As Marco Polo used to think a lot and analyze the internal and external facts of his life, he was a distracted person. He always forgot where he had left the keys of his battered car and sometimes forgot where he had parked it.

Once, during his first year as an intern, he was supposed to take a patient whose leg was immobilized with a cast and who needed to use crutches to the orthopedics department. But he forgot that the patient was following him. He went up several floors, went down, walked down long corridors and entered the refectory of the great hospital. When he got there, he realized that someone was following him. It was the patient using crutches. He apologized and said humorously: "You are doing better than me". The patient smiled. Some of his patients said: "Doctor, I have a bad memory." "Don't worry, mine is terrible," he replied playfully.

He was getting almost as distracted as Hegel in his old age (the illustrious philosopher once entered a classroom wearing only one shoe. Without realizing it, he left the other one stuck in the mud). Despite his distraction, Marco Polo was extremely generous and kind to his patients.

During their practical classes, their teachers gathered groups of eight students around the patients' beds and began to describe their illness, its causes, treatments and life expectancy. They referred to certain diseases using codes, like "C.A." for cancer, so as not to embarrass patients. However, the patients would always get anxious.

After the group left, Marco Polo would stay behind with these patients. He wanted to know their stories, relieve their anguish caused by being in a hospital and the anxiety of death. He became friends with them. Fascinated by medicine, he thought: "One day, sooner or later, every human being will become sick and need a doctor. Rich or poor, famous or anonymous are all the same in the face of pain and death. They are the most democratic phenomena in existence."

Over time, despite his appreciation for medicine, Marco Polo was disappointed with what he saw. Modern medicine had specialized in eliminating physical and emotional pain, but had not learned to use it minimally. The urgency of trying to eliminate the pain, delayed the relief and blocked the patients, preventing them from using it as a tool to correct their ways and polish their maturity. By detesting pain, medicine, as well as modern society, specializes in treating the suffering of human beings and not of human beings who suffer.

Medicine became logical and objective, a slave to technology. Nowadays there are many devices, many tests and many procedures, yet very little sensitivity to discover the emotional and social causes. Anxiety was not taken into account as the genesis of heart attacks.

The stress hidden behind the scenes of cancer had scarcely been analyzed. Anticipatory thoughts behind gastritis, hypertension, headaches and muscle pain had rarely been investigated.

Marco Polo was already an intern in the emergency room. The atmosphere there was bleak, overly technical and not very affectionate. He was unable to accept the attitudes of certain medical professors towards the symptoms that some women had. They had severe headaches, abdominal pain and chest pain, but they did not have any physical illness to justify the symptoms.

Doctors prescribed painkillers, sometimes tranquilizers, and sent them away, discourteously, saying that there was nothing wrong with them organically. At best, some would suggest that they seek help from a psychotherapist.

After the patients left, some teachers complained about them to their students. They said they hindered their work, simulated symptoms and invented diseases because they had nothing better to do. They denied that they had an internal conflict that massacred them.

Marco Polo once argued with a professor, Dr. Flavius, who had been rude to a woman. She came every week to be examined for chest tightness, tachycardia and difficulty breathing. When Dr. Flavius saw her again with the same complaint, he asked rudely, "Don't you have anything better to do? How many times have I said that there is nothing wrong with you physically? Get a life! Go see a psychiatrist." The woman started to cry.

Marco Polo took her gently by the arm and asked her to wait outside. He turned to the teacher and said: "Instead of criticizing her, why don't you talk to her about the psychological causes of these symptoms? Why don't you investigate her story? "

One of the most difficult tasks in the world is teaching a teacher who has lost the ability to be a student. Feeling offended, the teacher raised his voice and authoritatively, in front of three other Marco Polo's classmates in the room, said: "Listen here, boy, don't lecture to me. I am a medical emergency doctor and you're a mere student. We don't have time to take care of nonsense."

Marco Polo boldly replied: "If you, cultured and healthy, were offended by my simple words, imagine how offended this patient was by your words."

The professor swallowed dry and Marco Polo added: "Going to an emergency room is not the most pleasant thing to do. If this patient had the courage to come to this tense and unhappy environment, it is because she must be suffering a lot. Don't you think that her symptoms, although imaginary, are a cry for you to talk to her?" The other students were shaking because of Marco Polo's boldness.

"I am not a psychiatrist." replied Dr. Flavius.

"I'm sorry, professor, please forgive my ignorance in the face of your competence, but don't you think that maybe we divide patients between biological and psychiatric medicine? Maybe she doesn't need a psychiatrist now, but a specialist like you to listen to her, support her, understand her and make sure that there's nothing really wrong with her."

The students looked at each other apprehensively. The professor was disturbed and did not know what to do, but after a moment of silence, he showed a gesture of rare humility, "Bring her back in."

Dr. Flavius asked her full name and whether she could tell her story in front of all the students or if she preferred to speak with him in private. Catherine said she did not mind talking to everyone. She was a woman of beautiful features, but marked by chronic anguish. She was thirty, married and had an eighteen-month-old son.

To the professor and his students' surprise, she spontaneously said that she had lost her father in the previous year, one of the people she loved most, victim of a heart attack. He had always been a friend of hers and had always been by her side in the most difficult moments of her story. Now, she was going through a serious problem, but she no longer had his shoulder, his comfort and his advice.

Four months ago, her husband was in a serious car accident, he had a spinal cord trauma and was in a wheelchair. He cried every day wishing he could walk, play sports and see his friends. His house, which used to be a garden of joy, was now arid land. The doctors said he still had a chance of walking again, but she feared it would never happen.

The fear of life, the fear of tomorrow and the fear of having a paraplegic husband dominated her. Insecure, she began to fear other things: fear of not being able to support her home, fear of dying of a heart attack, just as her father, and fear of leaving her son alone in the world.

She no longer had her father to share her pain and could not tell her husband how she felt. In addition, her husband did not have health insurance or unemployment insurance. She had to work to support her home, but her salary was barely enough for her family to survive. And while she worked, she kept thinking about her husband sitting in a wheelchair and her helpless son. As she told all of this, she started to cry. She was not sleeping; she was depressed and completely lonely. She felt unprotected.

While looking at Catherine's distress, Dr. Flavius kept thinking about everything he had and took for granted. He felt completely selfish. His wife was healthy, his children were wonderful and he had a housekeeper to take care of the house and had no financial problems. He had everything that Catherine didn't have, but he was dissatisfied and always complained about life and work.

Marco Polo told her: "You have reasons to display these symptoms, Catherine. They are the tip of the iceberg of your suffering."

To the patient's surprise, the teacher who had offended her kindly added: "I'm sorry for my initial attitude. I agree with Marco Polo. Your symptoms are light despite so much tribulation. You are a hero Catherine. I believe you are stronger than all of us. You can be assured you have no major physical problems. Your tests have shown that your heart is fine. Come here as often as you like. You will always have a few friends to listen to you." Marco Polo added: "You are channeling the anxiety caused by your loss to your body. Fight your fear, fight for those you love, fight for your child and your husband."

Dr. Flavius was impressed with his patient's conflicts and his student's altruism and strength. Deeply moved, Catherine thanked him and left, feeling happy and willing to face life for the first time. She now knew that she had a safe haven, with friends to count on. She understood and became convinced that her symptoms had an emotional origin. When they appeared, she no longer revolved around them. She rescued her self-esteem and her security.

Unfortunately, the condition of her husband was irreversible and he would remain paraplegic forever. Catherine encouraged him to never give up, to find joy and freedom within his limits. Supported by his wife, he was no longer miserable or felt self-pity.

Instead of being depressed, he found happiness in his son. Despite being in a wheelchair, he took care of the child while Catherine worked. Rarely did a father enjoy so much time with his son. He later got a job. The boy went to nursery school. They became a wealthy family, even though lacking large financial resources.

Catherine never returned to the emergency room as a patient. She returned only to introduce her husband and son to her new friends. She had overcome the dungeon of fear.

CHAPTER 14

Turning Things Upside Down

Marco Polo frequently wrote Falcon and they would visit each other at least once every six months. They still had adventures together. Their unusual attitudes of hugging trees, contemplating nature for long periods of time, improvising poems and reciting them continued to draw people around them.

Graduation day had arrived. Marco Polo's classmates, who now admired him, chose him to be the valedictorian. His speech rescued his experience from the days in the anatomy lab and blended philosophy with a critical view of medicine and psychiatry. He ended his daring speech by saying:

"Some day we will all end in the solitude of a grave. A day-old child is old enough to die. Death is the defeat of medicine. However, despite the limitations of science, we must use all of our ability not only to prolong life but also to make this brief existence an unforgettable experience. Doctors should be people who have a rare sensitivity, who are artisans of emotions; they should be professionals who are capable of seeing the anguish, anxiety and the tears behind the symptoms. Otherwise, they will treat organs and not human beings. Above all, doctors, as well as every practitioner who takes care of human

health, should be salespeople of dreams. For if we are able to make our patients dream of just one more day of life, or a new way of looking at their loss, we will have found a treasure that not even kings have acquired..."

Marco Polo was applauded with enthusiasm. His speech had made everyone reflect. But he had no idea that one day he would go through difficulties and that he would have to use this audacious speech as the central pillar of his life, otherwise he would not survive. He would have to sell and build dreams.

Just after graduation, Marco Polo began his residency in psychiatry in a large psychiatric hospital called Atlantic. The hospital treated over eight hundred patients. His professors frequently held meetings to discuss the most complex cases.

The Atlantic Hospital was comprised of three buildings with beautiful facades and richly crafted lathed window frames. The buildings resembled one of the buildings on the old side of Paris. However, on the inside it was a far cry from being enchanting. The walls were white and faded. The leisure areas between the buildings were enormous yet underused, and the extensive yard was poorly kept.

Hospitalization was already discouraged in Marco Polo's day. In theory, patients should be hospitalized the least time possible but there were still countless hospitals and many patients who were hospitalized and abandoned by their families. The young thinker would become saddened when he realized that society insisted on separating the normal from the abnormal. The problem consisted in knowing who was less ill, those on the outside or those on the inside.

Certain psychiatric hospitals were more humane than the Atlantic Hospital was. In these more humane hospitals, patients who were not severely ill, would spend the day at these hospitals and would go home in the evening. But the old hospital, despite being a national reference, was more like a deposit for the mentally ill.

The nurses were impatient and anxious. The psychiatrists rarely smiled and were always in a bad mood. The sadness was contagious. There was a lack of joy and sympathy in the famous hospital. Marco Polo was shocked with what he saw. In the beginning of his residency he frequently asked himself, "What am I doing here?" This world was completely different from the society he had grown up in.

Although he had had brief contacts with a few psychiatric patients while he was in medical school, he was now in their city. All around him he could see people with an unstructured and broken self, lacking identity and parameters of reality. The patients were expressionless and their muscles were contracted. Their treatment was based only on medication. Such a procedure went against everything he had learned from Falcon's story. Marco Polo was indignant.

Some patients thought, in their deliria, that they were great historic characters. Others felt that they were being controlled, persecuted and felt that their minds were being invaded by voices, such as Falcon, during his episodes. There were others who saw images of threatening animals or objects. There were also patients who were victims of alcoholism, drugs and depression.

Psychological illnesses do not pick color, race, nationality or social status. Those admitted in the hospital came from all social backgrounds, from simple employees to executives. Lawyers, engineers and even some doctors were part of the Atlantic Hospital population.

According to the unconscious ingenuity, each patient built their deliria and hallucinations with their own frequency and characteristics. Each mind was a world, a world that enchanted Marco Polo.

As soon as he began treating patients, the young thinker realized that psychiatric treatment created an industry of prejudice. People in society were afraid of seeing a psychiatrist because they felt that these were doctors for insane people and those who had been committed were so depressed that they would sentence themselves as ill, spontaneously proclaiming their diagnosis, "I'm schizophrenic", "I'm a manic-depressive psychotic."

There was no sparkle in their eyes; there was no hope. To Marco Polo's distress, he concluded that if there was one place where dreams died, that place was inside psychiatric hospitals. Penitentiaries were less caustic. It was as if psychiatry sold nightmares instead of dreams.

Some discriminating people used to consider committed patients as society's sewage, not realizing that they deserved solemn respect. The patients could not be blamed for their psychological disorders just as AIDS, cancer and heart attack patients could not be blamed for theirs. However, the society of the "normal people" loves to find superficial explanations and find people to blame for the problems they do not understand.

Marco Polo also discovered that those who suffer mild emotional disorders would easily lose their self-esteem. They labeled themselves as depressive, phobic and stressed. "What are the roots of this prejudice since no one is psychologically healthy in society?" he thought indignantly.

He suspected that the patients "wore" the label of psychiatric diagnosis and felt condemned to live with them throughout their life. They lost the greatest gift of their intelligence: recognizing that, despite our psychological maladies, we are human beings and, therefore, we have a fascinating personality. Shaken, Marco Polo better understood the rejection that Falcon had suffered because of his crises before he went out into the world. It did not take long for Marco Polo to shake things up. He gathered the patients in the hallways, lounges and examining rooms, looked at them and told them with confidence, "You are not mentally ill ones. You are human beings who have a mental illness. Believe in your intellectual potential. Don't give up on yourselves. You are strong and capable."

Some patients would cry, touched by the comfort they had never received before. Others did not understand what he meant. Others would become euphoric with enthusiasm. Others felt that he was just another patient posing as a doctor. They would say, "What a cool lunatic!"

Marco Polo would smile. His fame gradually spread. A fox had appeared in the Atlantic Hospital's henhouse to awaken closed minds and disturb the dogmas.

He felt that there should be more romanticism and pleasure in such a horrible place. He criticized the bad mood of the hospital's practitioners. Thus, he began to revolutionize the relationship with the patients. The formalities were dispensed. The distance between doctors and patients was narrowed. Marco Polo began to cheerfully and enthusiastically call each one by their name. He hugged them and praised them whenever he met them, "Joanna, you look marvelous! Edward, you look cheerful today! James, it's great to see you again!" The psychiatrists and nurses were surprised with the young psychiatrist's attitudes. Certain petty people said that he was running for office.

One fine day, Marco Polo examined a 75-year-old woman who felt depressed, was pessimistic and excessively critical. Her name was Naomi. She had innumerous *killer* windows in her unconscious mind. These windows are conflict zones that generate a large volume of tension, which is capable of "killing" or blocking one's ability to think in certain moments, making one react instinctively with aggressiveness.

Any annoyance, even a stare, detonated an unconscious trigger that made Naomi open the *killer* windows, which made her react without thinking and impulsively offend and criticize those around her. She was as angry and anxious as always, when she entered Marco Polo's office, but he disarmed her. He stood up, walked to the door, greeted her with a smile, called her by her name and praised her, "Naomi, you look beautiful!"

She hadn't visited a hair dresser in ten years. She cut her own hair and rarely styled it.

Embarrassed and admired by the psychiatrist's gesture, she felt happy and tried to straighten her hair. "Thank you for your kindness doctor. You are very nice", she said, repaying the compliment quite unconsciously.

"I would like to hear your story."

Naomi was an introverted woman who was incapable of paying compliments to others, not even her three children. She opened a few chapters of her life during the first examination. On her next session she opened up even more and this time she was wearing more presentable clothes and her hair was done. She had gone to the hairdresser to get her hair dyed and styled.

She used to treat people aggressively and they would treat her in the same manner, completing the cycle of anxiety. Marco Polo's small gesture began to break the vicious circle of her pessimism. Little by little, he encouraged her to criticize the way she faced life, to rethink her past, to work on her pessimism, to extract pleasure from the little things and especially to learn how to place herself in the others' shoes.

Naomi did not only need a psychiatric treatment but she also needed to learn how to live again. And she did. At the age of 75, she reedited her *killer* windows, developed her solidarity, kindness and altruism.

Marco Polo became bolder in breaking the paradigms in his sessions. He left his office to greet his patients in the waiting room. He always praised them with a smile on his face, which was a characteristic of his personality. Feeling flattered, the patients felt valued instead of ill. They'd enter his office with an elevated self-esteem, breaking the conscious and unconscious barriers that caused a blockage, which would prevent them from getting in touch with their own reality. The sessions, despite tense moments, full of tears and stories of loss and anxiety crises, were generally pleasant.

Marco Polo felt that modern society was impoverished, had lost its amicability and affability. People were educated like no other generation before, but they had lost the power of kindness and praise. Medicine had been contaminated by this insensitivity.

He was gentle not only with the patients but also with the lowest employees of the hospital. He bantered with the doormen and the nurses. He hugged the janitors. He brought joy to the somber atmosphere of the Atlantic Hospital.

He also tried to conduct group therapy not only with intelligence but also with humor. An unusual event happened once. One of the patients in the group was called Ali Ramadan, a Palestine who had lived in Iraq for many years. He had been tortured by Saddam Hussein's police force. He had been able to escape but had lost the majority of his family. His father had never gotten out of Abu Ghraib, the most notorious prison complex of the regime.

Ali Ramadan had developed his psychosis at the age of 25. He had been tormented for years with the image of extraterrestrials. As his illness evolved, the degree of his torment increased. He began to talk to aliens and would obsessively talk to people about them, especially with the other patients at the Atlantic Hospital. During one of the group sessions he asked Marco Polo, "Dr. did you know that there are beings from other planets?"

"I don't know whether there are beings from other planets, but I do know that there are many monsters within us that disturb us."

Caught by surprise with the answer, Ali Ramadan smiled for the first time as he spoke about the aliens. Realizing that his relaxed state was a precious opportunity to help him have a critical conscience, Marco Polo took advantage of the moment and added, "Dear Ali, don't worry about beings from other planets. The monsters we create everyday in our mind are enough. Fight them and criticize fearlessly. Be free!"

"My head is full of little monsters. Do you want some Ali?" said Sarah spontaneously. "No. My aliens are enough," he answered contemplatively.

Everyone laughed. Marco Polo did not waste time saying that the patient had hallucinations. It was not the moment for that; instead, he used Ali's intellectual potential so that he himself could see the incoherence of his ideas and understand the real source of his distress.

The patient became pensive, which was not one of his characteristics. He opened the windows of his intelligence and gradually began to make progress in group therapy. He began to criticize his fantasies and to boost the effect of his medication. The young doctor and Ali constructed a long friendship.

Marco Polo gradually became the subject of conversations of the hospital administration. The hospital had lost its routine with the irreverent young man. Once, he could not resist when he contemplated a tree in bloom with yellow flowers in the middle of the immense hospital yard. He embraced its trunk, kissed it and said a few words. It was a scandal to those who witnessed his display.

Many patients began to imitate him. A long line was formed in front of the tree. Each patient would hug the tree for a few minutes and then kiss it. They would leave feeling relieved.

James, a biology teacher, who after many crises had been abandoned by his family, enjoyed the experience. He had not hugged anyone for years, not even those responsible for his health. When he hugged the tree he felt its vigor and ran around the yard. He hugged and kissed all the trees in front of him and shouted, "You are marvelous!"

The case had come to the attention of the arrogant and authoritarian Dr. Mario Gutenberg, the director of the Atlantic Hospital. Dr. Gutenberg was an intelligent, perspicacious and radical European. He was a respected doctor but he was very inflexible. Marco Polo was summoned to explain himself.

"What are you teaching your patients?" "I don't understand Dr. Gutenberg."

"You don't understand? Dozens of patients are out there kissing trees."

With a lump in his throat, Marco Polo said: "I didn't ask them to do this. Every now and then I like to hug a tree and kiss it. It's the way I found to thank nature for the gift of life."

"Gift of life? Are you treating patients or do you need treatment yourself?"

"We all need treatment."

"Where did you learn how to be so insolent? Your behavior can precipitate patients' crises."

"Hugging trees can trigger crises?"

"I don't know but they are euphoric, different."

"If psychiatrists, psychologists and nurses embraced patients and were more affectionate with them, perhaps they wouldn't need to hug trees."

"What an insolence...! You're not even a specialist in psychiatry and you want to turn our system upside down? This institution is almost a century old. Don't disturb it. I'll have my eye on you."

Chapter 15

Marco Polo got involved in another argument with the doctors – now, much more serious than before. There were more than forty psychiatrists and ten resident doctors working at the hospital. He was participating in a meeting to discuss cases. The meeting consisted of ten psychiatrists, which included a few professors and five students. Dr. Alexander, a psychiatrist of great reputation and a renowned professor, conducted the discussion. He concluded the meeting by saying "Those who do not learn how to diagnose will be terrible psychiatrists."

After the applause died down, Marco Polo replied, "Diagnoses might be useful for me, but is it ethical to categorically tell our patients?"

"Yes, our patients have the right to know the truth."

"I agree that patients should know the truth, but what is this truth that we construct in psychiatry? Isn't it true that our theories are subjected to change over the years?" "Are you questioning psychiatry?" the professor asked impatiently.

"Certain areas must be questioned. I'd like you to answer me this: should we place our patients within a theory or a theory should be placed within our patients?"

The professor thought about that but had no answer. He had written many scientific articles but had never thought about that. Marco Polo tried to simplify his question:

"If the theories are above human beings, if they are irrefutable, then we should place our patients within them and label them according to what is presumed. However, if human beings are above the theories and their personalities are so distinct from one another, we should be careful with our diagnoses. The same diagnosis that might serve to direct my conduct might also serve to control a patient's life and to commit atrocities."

His other colleagues felt powerless. Dr. Alexander was shaken with Marco Polo's argument and boldness. He had never faced a situation like that. But he tried to avoid the issue, "The fact that patients might suffer because of their diagnosis is a myth." "There are millions of people who live under the dictatorship of labels and who affirm that they are depressive, schizophrenic or bipolar." "Don't you think that you are awfully young to be criticizing psychiatry?" said Dr. Alexander feeling annoyed.

"Professor Alexander, if I lose my capacity to criticize I'll become a servant of the theories and not a servant of mankind."

Marco Polo saw differences between communicating a diagnosis to a patient with a physical illness and to a patient with a psychological illness. When a patient knows he had suffered a heart attack or that he has cancer, he can collaborate with the treatment to overcome the disease and as a result, improve and expand his quality of life. Therefore, Marco Polo added:

"Cancer or heart attack patients are rarely discriminated because they suffer such illnesses. Instead, they frequently receive affection, support and are visited by friends and family. On the other hand, patients who suffer from manic-depressive psychosis or schizophrenia are rejected by family members, socially excluded and are rarely visited by friends. Labels in psychiatry generate a cruel and unjust isolation."

"I don't label my patients", said another professor.

"I'm sorry but sometimes we label them without wanting to. The manner we use to give them our diagnoses can generate an emotional disaster. They lose their identity as human beings and introject the fact that they are ill." He took a breath and added, "And what about the power of labels? Einstein once said that it is easier to disintegrate an atom than to overturn a prejudice."

The professors were intrigued by the young doctor's culture and intrepidness. Philip, who was also a resident said: "Einstein was a genius. If he said that, we must be careful. We might cause more damage than good to the patients."

Marco Polo completed: "Einstein himself suffered from prejudice on two occasions."

"When was that?" another psychiatrist asked.

"The first time he was a victim of prejudice, and the second time he was the agent himself. Einstein demonstrated that time and space are interchangeable and they belong to the same structure. However, the space-time structure, as a whole, does not vary, it isn't relative. Therefore, Einstein himself wanted to change the name from theory of relativity to theory of invariance but he was unable to." "Why so?" he asked looking at Dr. Alexander.

"Because the word "relativity" had already become popular", he answered.

"Correct! The greatest theory in physics was perpetuated with the wrong name. Prejudice had won."

Marco Polo became silent. He did not tell them what the second prejudice Einstein had suffered from was. He had something very important to reveal, perhaps never revealed before about the worshiped scientist. He waited until their curiosity produced a healthy level of stress in those present, capable of opening the possibilities of thought.

Anxiously, one of the psychiatrists couldn't wait any longer and asked, "What was the second situation?"

"One of the greatest geniuses of Mankind also generated a mentally ill son. His son was schizophrenic. Everyone looked at one another. They hadn't known that. Marco Polo completed: "There's a great lesson here. Except for genetic causes, a question comes to mind: if one of mankind's greatest geniuses generated a mentally ill child, who is spared from generating them? This question leads us to an anguishing answer: no one is immune to this drama. However, it needs to be rebutted with another question: Einstein was the exponent of logical science, of the physical world and of mathematics, but to generate psychologically healthy children we must be exponents in another world, the illogical world of emotions, of sensitivity, of flexibility, of dialogue and of forgiveness."

They were intrigued by Marco Polo's reasoning. They looked at their own story. It would be expected that psychiatrists or psychologists rarely generated unhealthy children. But they also knew that several mental health professionals, including some of the psychiatrists in the audience, had stressed, depressed, phobic, timid children who also had other conflicts.

All the logical knowledge about the human mind they possessed had not been enough to guarantee the success in forming their children's personality. They understood that to educate was to toil illogical soil. Every human being has difficulties walking this sinuous terrain, including psychiatrists and psychologists. Another psychiatrist asked, "What was Einstein's reaction to having a psychotic son?"

"It couldn't have been worse! That time Einstein wasn't the victim, as a matter of fact he was the agent of prejudice."

"What do you mean?"

"Einstein visited his son at the psychiatric hospital only once. He abandoned him and allowed loneliness to be his companion. And rejection and loneliness, my dear friends, are not as fast as the light studied by physics but they are more penetrating than light."

The audience was silent. After a few moments of deep reflection, Dr. Alexander himself asked humbly, "Within the limitations of interpretation, what were the causes that you detected that made Einstein abandon his son if we exhaustively recommend that families do not abandon their patients here in this hospital? Why was one of the most brilliant minds of mankind so opaque in this situation?"

Marco Polo took a deep breath and said: "In my humble opinion, there were four causes for Einstein's prejudiced attitude, which was incompatible with his intelligence. First, the emotional blow he received when he saw the inhumane conditions of the hospital where his son had been staying. Notice that, to this day, our hospitals are depressive. Second, the lack of hope that his son could overcome his psychosis. Third, the dramatic anguish that his son's hallucinations and deliria caused him. Fourth, the fear of having to face his own impotence in an unknown world.

"Einstein's mind was avid for answers but he must've been disturbed by the lack of answers to explain the fragmentation of his son's intelligence", Dr. Alexander concluded.

After a brief pause to catch his breath, Marco Polo continued, "These four causes reveal that the man who best understood the forces of the physical universe hadn't understood the psychological forces, which are the most complex in the universe. Einstein was a gentle man who loved peace, but prejudice had incarcerated him. His 'self', in this area, was imprisoned by the *killer* windows or zones of conflict recorded in his unconscious mind. His fascinating story reveals that it is easier to deal with the atom and with the immense space than with psychological afflictions and tribulations."

He then concluded by saying: "Gentlemen, each mind is a universe to be explored. Welcome to the most complex area of science!"

Dr. Alexander was inspired by this last phrase. He had always been a mature person. Like everyone else, he would become defensive when questioned or contradicted but after being convinced about his mistake; he had the courage to shake hands with his student:

"Marco Polo is right. I recognize my mistake. Psychiatry and psychology, as well as medicine in general, cannot look at a disease as if it were a product, like in the capitalistic world. Over time we have become disease technicians and we have lost our sensitivity for the ill. Let us become vaccinated against the industry of prejudice. Use diagnoses but don't be used by them.

Thus, the meeting ended. The small audience's understanding of the fantastic world of the human psyche was expanded.

Chapter 16

Over two hundred practitioners worked at the Atlantic Hospital, among them were: doctors, psychologists, nurses, social workers, attendants, security guards and others. Most of them did not know Marco Polo well and were suspicious of him. A few psychiatrists and the hospital director saw him more as an insubordinate than as a competent professional. Less than a tenth of the patients knew him, but those who did, loved him. They'd greet him from afar.

Philip had straightened his ties with Marco Polo. They had become close friends. But, even though Philip criticized the hospital's system of treatment, he was quiet, discrete. He disliked scandals and was concerned with his future and social image.

On a Monday afternoon, Marco Polo and Philip were walking around the grounds where the patients sunbathed and tried to have fun. Looking at the saddened, hopeless faces, like prisoners in the worst of prisons, the psychological prison; Marco Polo went over to a small gazebo. Worried, Philip asked him, "What are you doing?"

"I'm going to prospect for gold."

"For gold?!"

Marco Polo recalled the speeches he and Falcon used to give in the parks to guide people to take an inner journey. Then, he recalled what he had promised himself after he had left Falcon at Luke's house, "I will turn my life into a great adventure, I'll find a treasure hidden within the rubble of psychological illness."

As these images came to mind, he looked at the patients of the Atlantic Hospital and was frustrated. He saw a few patients a day; therefore, he knew that he would never have the opportunity of talking and getting to know most of them. Driven by a strong impulse, he solemnly exclaimed, "Dear friends, gather round! We can show you the way, but only you can open the doors of your mind and walk towards freedom. We can give you a pen and paper, but only you can write your story. You are temporarily ill! This is not your home! Your home is the free world! Dream of being happy!"

The patients had never seen a performance such as this one. Several of them did not understand what Marco Polo was saying but they clapped enthusiastically. Those who did understand his message had tears in their eyes. Among them was Dr. Vidigal, a general practitioner who had bipolar disorder. Dr. Romero, a psychiatrist who for over 15 years had been the victim of psychotic schizophrenia, had his lips quivered as he approached the young psychiatrist and kissed his hands.

Hundreds of people gathered around the gazebo. Innumerous security guards and nurses began to check out what was happening. At first, they thought that it was just the deliria of one of the psychotics but then the nurses realized that it was the future psychiatrist creating turmoil once again.

Mr. Bonny, an eighty-year-old man who had been admitted to the hospital twenty times and who knew a few of the psychiatrists well, smiled and shouted, "I vote for this man! Out with Dr. Mario!"

James, who had become a tree kisser, was extremely excited with the speech. He accepted Mr. Bonny's suggestion and began to chant, "Marco Polo! Marco Polo!" The other patients joined in. The audience was full of enthusiasm. It was the first time, in the institutions one hundred years, that the patients experienced a collective euphoria. Everyone unanimously applauded and shouted, "He's our man! He's our man!"

This was an election that Marco Polo would never want to win. Dora, the head nurse, grinded her teeth in anger as she witnessed the disturbance he had caused. He saw her conspiring with other psychiatrists and security guards to try to contain him but he wasn't intimidated. He looked at the audience for a long time, he observed the patients' quirks and once again exclaimed, "I don't deserve this applause. You do. Who's more important: we the psychiatrists or you the patients?"

"The psychiatrists are!" they all shouted without hesitating.

"No! The psychiatrists only exist because you do. You are more important than we are." And he added, "Look at the nurses. Are you inferior to them?"

Some of the patients closer to the nurses, kissed their hands as if they were divas, goddesses of survival. The attention they gave the patients was fundamental so that they had the minimum comfort but many nurses had very little patience with them.

One of the patients walked over to nurse Dora and tried to kiss her hands, but she didn't allow it. Fifteen years earlier, Dora had been an affectionate and sympathetic professional, but working years at the Atlantic Hospital had made her affection as arid as the Sahara. The atmosphere made her nauseous.

Dr. Vidigal, with a trembling voice because of the medication he took and forgetting that he had once been a respected doctor, exclaimed to Marco Polo, "Doctor...We aren't...aren't...anything. Nothing at all."

Forgetting that he had once been a psychiatrist, Dr. Romero, with tears in his eyes, said: "We are trash doctor! We have no value to society."

Marco Polo knew them both and was deeply touched. He had intensely criticized prejudice but he now realized that its effects were more serious than he had imagined; it was an emotional cancer. "If both doctors, who are patients in the hospital, feel like trash, imagine what the self-esteem of the other patients who don't have their culture, is like", he thought.

With teary eyes, Marco Polo called a few patients he knew by name and encouraged them, "Dr. Romero, you are a person of great value, the world might despise you but never diminish yourself. Sara, look at the treasure hidden within you! Ali Ramadan, my friend, you are intelligent and capable of overcoming your inner ghosts. Your wife awaits you!

James, you are a poet of nature. Fight for your dreams, your children need you."

Then, he took a deep breath and shouted in a very loud voice so that the entire audience could hear him, "You are stronger than many generals. You have faced your crises, borne the pain of discrimination, the rejection of friends and the distancing of family members but you still managed to survive. Great men in history wouldn't be standing if they had suffered such loss, but you still stand. You haven't given up on life. You are heroes! At least, my heroes!"

These words moved Philip. On an impulse he got up on the gazebo and shouted, "You are my heroes too!"

Encouraged by his friend's attitude, Marco Polo gazed at each one of the patients' faces, pointed to them with his hands and proclaimed several times along with Philip, "You are heroes! You are heroes!"

The patients, who had no social value at all, were astonished by this clamor. They had never felt so important. While the two friends proclaimed these words, something poetic and very beautiful happened. The crowd of patients began to collectively cry. It was the first time that there had been a collective cry of triumphant joy in such a depressive place.

Those who had always been anonymous now gained visibility. The weak ones felt big, the low-spirited gained strength and the rejected felt loved. The two irreverent doctors had excavated the patients' psychological ruins and unveiled precious relics hidden there. They had exercised the beautiful art of anthropologic psychology.

The scene, which evoked an indescribable emotion, touched the patients' collective unconscious. They began to hug one another like soldiers in a war who bear the weight of fallen friends. They felt understood and loved. They felt like actual human beings.

Suddenly, a few patients began to gather their things to leave. The nurses, security guards and other psychiatrists were apprehensive. "Where are you going?" they asked harshly.

Some said: "I'm going home. I need to kiss my children." Others commented, "I need to hug my wife." And others affirmed, "I don't belong here. I want to be free."

"You're crazy!" Dora said, trying to stop them with the help of the guards. Dr. Vidigal replied, "A little less crazy now. I'm a hero for having stayed here."

As they tried to leave, they were barred by the hospital security. Some of the patients were pushed and fell. They were weak due to the effects of the powerful sedatives.

Sarah, who was very sensitive, panicked and began to cry inconsolably. The atmosphere became tense. Marco Polo incisively told the nurses and security, "Don't touch these patients! There is no greater madness than exerting aggressiveness to convince people. Talk to them with respect and they will listen to you."

Marco Polo, fearing for the patients' safety, begged them, "Dear friends, do not leave yet.

With this ardent desire for freedom you will speed up your treatment and will soon be discharged. Then you will be free."

The patients listened to him and backed down. Dr Mario told the guards to grab Marco Polo and take him to his office where he, the clinical director, Dora the head nurse, the head of security and a few of the institution's senior psychologists gathered. Dr. Alexander wasn't present. Marco Polo's days at Atlantic Hospital seemed to have come to an end.

Dr. Mario was infuriated. According to the distorted report given by Dora and some of the other psychiatrists, Marco Polo had not only put the lives of the patients in risk but also the institution itself. No one had ever brought such a threat to the renowned hospital. Dr. Mario feared a scandal in the press, which could represent the end of his career.

Before he passed judgment on Marco Polo, Dr. Mario sent a team of nurses with injections and straitjackets to repress the euphoria and possible excesses committed by some of the patients. Dr. Romero, Ali Ramadan and several other patients were chemically contained. James resisted. He shouted, refusing an additional dose of sedatives, but to no avail, he received the injection by force. Thus, they silenced the so-called rebellion.

Philip was present at the meeting. Marco Polo came forward and said: "Philip is not to be blamed for anything. I take full responsibility for what happened."

"You take full responsibility for your irresponsible actions?" the director asked angrily. "I'll take the blame but not for being irresponsible," replied Marco Polo who might lose the war but not his courage for combat.

"I've investigated your life doctor. I've learned about your medical school days: rebellious, irreverent, class disrupter and world questioner. You file is a bomb!"

Those in the room became apprehensive with those words. They considered Marco Polo as a threat. The director continued, "You chose the wrong place to be insolent you...you rebel."

"My actions might have been wrong, but my intentions were good. I wanted to..."

Before he could finish his phrase the director interrupted him, "Don't be cynical. You disrupted the hospital routine, the patients' tranquility and put the hospital in danger."

Marco Polo knew that he would be expelled from the institution. He then remembered one of Falcon's memorable phrases, "You might imprison my body but not my ideas." Thus, he was convinced that they might exclude him but he wouldn't be unfaithful to his conscience. He looked Dr. Mario in the eye and then looked at those present and with assuredness said:

"I wanted to show the patients that they are human beings who should fight for their own freedom. I told them that they are "presently ill" and not "permanently ill". You can expel me but I will never be silent about what I think."

Marco Polo's intrepidness shook the group. Cornered and feeling both angry and fascinated with his courage, Dr. Mario decided to give the young adventurer one last chalice of mercy. "You are here to learn and not to teach. Don't forget your place. Your attitude is punishable with expulsion but we'll give you only one more opportunity. Don't forget that you will not get a second chance." And thus, the meeting was drastically ended.

Chapter 17

Ever since Marco Polo began to disrupt the environment at the Atlantic Hospital, the place became more cheerful. People talked to each other more, some nurses became more affectionate and some psychiatrists were in a better mood.

After the meeting, Marco Polo was more contained but not less bold. He continued to perform small transformations, this time with the acquiescence of his superiors. He painted the patients' rooms with colorful paint. He organized competitions and a theatrical performance among the patients. He thought about creating a support group where the least serious patients would help the ones with the most serious cases. He wanted them to feel useful. Dr. Mario felt impelled to approve some of Marco Polo's suggestions as long as they were under his control. He was afraid of his creative freedom. To avoid more serious problems, Dr. Mario made sure that Marco Polo was constantly watched. Security guards kept an eye on him at all times. Some had the nerve to knock on his door and ask if everything was fine.

Marco Polo was showing signs of distress. He continued to admire the universe of his patients but he was saddened by the fact that he was being watched. In this state of mind, he wrote a heartfelt letter to his old friend. His soul exhaled his views on life and human suffering.

My Dear Friend Falcon,

You once told me that you and the Poet could see God's signature in the flowers, clouds and also in the crises of those who have psychological disorders. At the time, I honestly thought that this was a delirium; that it would be impossible to find beauty within chaos. Well, you were right. I have found indescribable wealth in those who suffer. They are neither miserable nor susceptible to misery. What they do need is to be understood, supported and encouraged. I have found a psychological wealth of inestimable value within tears and despair.

I have discovered an amazing creativity in those who suffer from psychosis. Although they are disturbed by deliria and hallucinations, they reveal an exceptional creativity and an unprecedented intellectual ingenuity. Not even the best screenwriters in Hollywood have such imagination. It's too bad that classical psychiatry despises their immense intellectual potential.

The intelligence of those who suffer from manic-depressive psychosis astonishes me. They are true geniuses. During their manic phase, the excitement, fast thinking and the sheer volume of thoughts they produce transport them to the clouds in a state of grace, far away from reality. In this phase, their self-esteem is intensified. They feel that they are invincible, vested by a supernatural power. On the other hand, during their depressive phase, their euphoria collapses, their thoughts become pessimistic leading them to get stuck in the quagmire of feelings of guilt and experience the lowest levels of self-esteem. If they learned how to steer their thoughts and to manage their intelligence so as to not abandon the parameters of reality, they would shine more than any "normal" person. Unfortunately, they misunderstand themselves and are misunderstood by the society they're in.

I have found a rare sensitivity among those who are depressed. They are so sensitive that they have no emotional protection. When someone offends them, it ruins their day, week, month and sometimes their life. They are so enchanting that, without being aware of it, they live the principle of inevitable *co-responsibility in an exaggerated manner. Thus, they become disturbed by the future and suffer intensely because of problems that haven't happened yet. They are so concerned with others that they live the pain of others! They are great to society but are terrible to themselves. Falcon, I have no doubt that if political leaders had but a small dose of the sensitivity that depressed people have, societies would be more sympathetic and less unjust. I feel that my own emotions are cold and dry when compared to theirs.*

Among those who have the panic syndrome, I have found an enviable desire to live. When they are struck by a panic attack, their brain goes into a state of attention trying to protect them from a serious situation of risk, a non-existent risk. They suffer tachycardia, breath shortness and perspire intensely trying to escape losing consciousness or death, an imaginary death that only exists within the theater of their own minds. If only they could learn how to rescue the leadership of the 'self' during their crises, they would become free of the prison of fear. I wish the drug users, those who live dangerously, terrorists and those who promote wars would have awareness of the finiteness of life and the grandeur of existence that those who suffer from the panic syndrome have. Despite the suffering imposed by panic, they are passionate about life. I wish I could love life as they do and live each minute as if it were an eternal moment.

Falcon, you are right when you say that society is stupid. It really only values aesthetics and not content. I am disappointed even with those who are apparently cultured. They don't realize that each human being, especially those who suffer psychological disorders, is a unique gem in the amphitheater of existence.

My challenge as a psychiatrist is not only to medicate them and conduct psychotherapy sessions, but also to show them that the most exuberant flower can bloom in the most rigorous emotional winter. Those who have crossed their psychological deserts and have overcome them have become more beautiful, lucid and richer than they were.

Isn't that what has happened to you, my dearest friend? Through the drama of your psychosis, you expanded your noble intelligence and became a master, my master. Now, my patients have taught me. Sometimes I learn more from them than from my professors. I hope that my capacity to learn never dies.

I decided to specialize in psychiatry to get to know the fascinating human personality and treat its illnesses. However, just as you questioned what madness was, I have been questioning "what is psychological health? Who is healthy? Are my psychiatric colleagues, who are incapable of greeting their patients with a smile and a hug, healthy? Are the parents, who listen to the characters on TV but are unaware of their children's fears and frustrations and are impatient with them, healthy? Are the teachers, who hide themselves behind their desk or a computer and are unable to talk about their own story with their students, healthy? Are youth, whose emotions are incapable of extracting plenty from little and whose pleasures are fleeting, healthy? And what about those who focus on making money but are unable to fight for what they love; are they rich or poor?"

I have also been questioning my own quality of life. I thought I was healthy because I say what I feel, I fight for what I love and I try to protect my emotions, but I have discovered that I only know the living room of my own being. I lack tolerance, affectivity, wisdom and tranquility. The day that I no longer admit the things I'm lacking, I will be sicker than my patients. Thank you for teaching me that I am merely a traveler and there's still a long road to travel...

From your friend and admirer,
Marco Polo

Falcon was touched as he read the letter. He recalled the difficult moments of his story and the wonderful times he had with Marco Polo. He was pleased with the humanist psychiatry that he and a few of his colleagues were practicing. He believed that Marco Polo could do a lot for mankind but very little for his own pocket.

A few days later, Marco Polo went through an experience where the Atlantic Hospital almost came tumbling down on him. A patient who was suffering from severe depression associated with a psychosis characterized by mental confusion, loss of identity and difficulty of finding himself within the space-time boundary, was the cause of this turmoil. His name was Isaac.

Isaac belonged to a Jewish family that was very rich and politically powerful in the region. Due to his depression, his feelings were dull. He avoided any form of social interaction and refused to leave his room, to talk, to bathe and to eat. Thus, he had developed anorexia nervosa.

He would frequently just lie in his bed. He had a strange and unusual behavior, a psychotic projection; he would affirm he was something he was not. He continuously repeated he was a frog. He would frequently open and close his mouth imitating the behavior of this amphibian.

When someone approached him to ask him something, Isaac would simply say that he was a frog. He eliminated any possibility of interpersonal interaction. He wanted to live and die within his cocoon. This bizarre behavior had lasted for weeks. The patient was gradually losing weight. He simply refused to live.

His treatment was ineffective. He was given various medications in several dosages. Psychologists also tried to help him but he wouldn't come out of his cocoon. Some of the psychiatrists then decided to try a few sessions of the traditional and questionable electroshock therapy, once again with no results. Isaac was in a life threatening situation.

They presented the case to Dr. Mario. He was concerned with the patient's drama and the institution's image of not being able to produce results. Dr. Mario had already treated Isaac other times. Even though he knew him, Dr. Mario ignored the seriousness of his current crisis. "I can't believe that after two months with the arsenal of medications we have, you haven't been able to relieve the patient's depression, get him out of his psychotic episode and bring him back to lucidity! I have brought this patient out of his crises many times. We need more efficient professionals in this hospital," he arrogantly told his team.

Some mental health professionals are capable of helping others, but incapable of helping themselves. That was Dr. Mario's case. He was recognized as an excellent professional, he had a doctorate in psychiatry, he was an eloquent professor and he had published countless scientific papers, but he did not know how to deal with his own emotional conflicts. Under stressful situations, he was unable to think before reacting or empathizing with others. The world had to revolve around his truths. Like many well-meaning but authoritarian leaders, his posture blocked the intelligence of his subordinates.

After questioning the psychiatrists' efficiency, he asked them to give a report on the procedures and anti-psychotic and anti-depressive medication that had been used as well as the respective dosages. After the report was concluded, it was clear to him that Isaac had had an extremely serious crisis, unlike the previous ones.

However, so as not to lose his composure as the boss, he invited some of the psychiatrists and residents, among them Marco Polo and Philip, to evaluate the patient in his room. He wanted to teach them a lesson.

In the room, Isaac demonstrated his usual indifference towards them. The director introduced himself and proceeded to ask him a few questions. "What's your name?" Isaac remained silent but Dr. Mario insisted, "What is your name, please?" "I'm a frog."

"How old are you and where do you live?"

"I'm a frog."

Dr. Mario asked a few more questions about his relatives and where he had worked but the answer was always the same. The conversation would not evolve. He was being embarrassed in front of his students. He gave a few quick explanations about this type of psychosis and the impotence of psychiatry in some cases and ended his visit. But feeling frustrated for not being able to teach a brilliant lesson, just before he left the room, he asked, "Since when have you been a frog?"

The patient looked at him and replied, "Since I was a tadpole."

Although the students respected the patient and the director, they couldn't contain themselves. They put their hands over their mouths to suffocate their laughter. The director shook his head unhappily and insisted, "Mr. Isaac, you are a human being. You have the head, arms and legs of a man. You can't be a frog."

The patient looked at him and once again said: "Frog. I am a frog."

He was enclosed within his world and there was nothing that would make him change his mind. Everyone left his room, except for Marco Polo. Being an observer, he noticed that while people insisted on telling Isaac what he wasn't, he maintained his obsessive conviction. However, when Dr. Mario unknowingly entered into his delirium by asking him since when he had been a frog, he formulated a different phrase, "Since I was a tadpole!"

So, he decided not to question the delirium but enter into it. His case was different than Ali Ramadan's; Isaac's case inspired more care and imposed more risks. Isaac couldn't carry a logical conversation.

Marco Polo had not forgotten that imagination is more important than knowledge. He used his imagination and said: "Look at that beautiful pond over there. Look at how beautiful the stars are. Listen to all the frogs croaking."

Marco Polo gradually stopped being an intruder in Isaac's world. Thus, he began to open up and distinctly formulated other phrases. "Where's the pond?" he asked.

"Look! It's right in front of you. Can you see it?"

"Yes!"

"Where do you live in this pond?"

Isaac began to think spatially, "Over there."

"How big are you?"

"Can't you see me?" he said incisively.

After this brief dialogue, Isaac once again became enclosed and would only repeat that he was a frog. Marco Polo was euphoric with his words. He then remembered that there was a porcelain frog in the hallway next to Dr. Mario's office. He went there to get it.

A security guard immediately told the director. Curious and apprehensive he told the guard to intercept the student; he wanted to check out Marco Polo's intriguing behavior himself. Inquired about his methods, the young man answered him that he was trying to enter the patient's world, the universe of his deliria and gain his trust. After gaining his trust, Marco Polo wanted to stimulate his critical capacity.

"Don't waste your time. Professionals with far more experience than you have tried and failed. Besides, if this case couldn't be solved with antipsychotic medication, it won't be solved with words."

"But why did you take us to Isaac's room and talked to him then?"

"Well, I was teaching you a lesson," he justified while feeling embarrassed.

"Professor, I know your competence, but I believe in the strength of psychology and not the exclusive use of medication. Let's give him conventional medication and, despite my lack of experience, allow me to try to help him."

Reluctant, Dr. Mario decided to allow it. "Go ahead but come to my office after you see him," he said incredulous trying to keep everything under control.

Marco Polo went back to Isaac's room; he took the porcelain frog out of his smock pocket and said: "Isaac, this is a frog. Do you look like this frog?"

The patient was shocked. The porcelain image wasn't the same as the hallucinated image he had created in his mind. Despite his confusion, the impact made him open the doors of his reasoning a little bit more. "Take the frog Isaac."

Isaac took the frog, thought for a minute and said: "I'm not a frog."

Thus, their conversation began to evolve. Later on, Isaac became fixed with another idea that intrigued Marco Polo. Since they had been talking for over half an hour, Marco Polo decided to call it a day. He could see he was worn out. He decided to come back another day.

Marco Polo headed towards Dr. Mario's office. Several psychiatrists were already there. On one of the rare occasions when the director was in a good mood he asked, "Tell me researcher! What were you able to get out of the frog-man?"

"I was able to carry a brief conversation with him."

The psychiatrists were skeptical. They thought he was bluffing. "You were able to get him to speak about other thoughts?" one of them asked.

"How did you do that?" asked another.

"I entered into his delirium and from then on I led him to doubt his own fantasies. Now he says he's something else."

Suspicious, Dr. Mario quickly asked, "What does he say he is now?"

Marco Polo paused and apprehensively answered, "He says that now he is something better."

"Come on, tell us," said those dying with curiosity.

"Isaac said that he's Dr. Mario."

The psychiatrists, who rarely exaggerated their behavior in the presence of the director, were unable to contain themselves. They laughed out loud. They thought it was the funniest joke they had ever heard. Even Dr. Alexander was unable to control himself.

"A little better," someone jibed.

Dr. Mario, feeling humiliated and angry, got up and told the psychiatrists to follow him to the patient's room but before he left he said: "Pack your bags. You're leaving this institution. You have made a serious mistake that will ruin your career forever: an ethical breach with your director and with your patient.

They quickly headed towards to Isaac's room. When they got there Dr. Mario asked him, "Who are you?"

He raised his head, stared at the director and said: "I'm a frog." The psychiatrists froze. They liked Marco Polo. It was the first time a psychiatry student would be expelled from the Atlantic Hospital. Marco Polo was tense. He felt like saying something to try to extract other words from Isaac, but, if he had bombarded him with questions trying to get him to say something he did not want to would be an ethical breach.

Since their discussion on Einstein's personality traits and prejudice, Dr. Alexander had become Marco Polo's friend. Trying to defend him he anxiously insisted, "What is your name? Where do you live?"

Dr. Mario was already walking out of the room when he heard Isaac say, "I'm Dr. Mario." It was Dr. Mario's turn to feel a chill run down his spine, move up to his head and stop at his throat. Besides being deeply embarrassed in front of his colleagues, he was being intensely unfair with Marco Polo.

He knew that Marco Polo, despite being irreverent, was bold, sensitive and intelligent. He was not just "another" professional, he was a builder of knowledge and he loved his job. However, he couldn't stand his audacity. Ever since he came to the institution a year ago, Dr. Mario had been disturbed with his behavior and had been silently questioning his own practice and inflexibility.

He sometimes went through nights of insomnia trying to get Marco Polo out of his dreams. Expelling him from the hospital would be painful for him, therefore, despite his shame, he was happy for his student and for the patient's small evolution.

Marco Polo humbly told Dr. Mario, "Because he's known you for a long time and admires you, Isaac has identified with you."

"Don't try to justify my mistake. I'm sorry. Take over the case."

With these words he quickly left the room. It was the first time that Dr. Mario had recognized a mistake in public and also apologized for it. The unbeatable man began to see what he had always been, a mere human being, and as such, subject to failures and mistakes. From then on, he became more flexible. Abandoning his throne didn't make him less of a leader or less admirable, it was just the opposite.

Taking over Isaac's treatment, one of Atlantic's most difficult cases was a herculean task, but since Marco Polo hated routine, he openly embraced the challenge. Any sign of improvement was met with a huge compliment by the young psychiatrist.

"Who am I? Where am I?" Isaac would say while he walked around in agitation. "Congratulations, Isaac, you're getting better! Don't be afraid of thinking! Don't be afraid of life!"

The patient did not really understand the compliment, but he did understand the warmth and affection. The effects of the medication started taking more effect after he began to cooperate with his treatment.

Over the weeks, Isaac began to eat better and to talk in more complex phrases as his consciousness returned. He slowly faced his harsh story, which had made him abandon reality and lose his identity. One day, as he became fully aware of himself, he broke down and cried. "I didn't have a childhood, doctor…" he then paused.

"Don't be afraid of talking to me, I'm here to listen to you."

"My mother had always had psychological problems. My father, despite his wealth, drank. He had been a practicing Jew but he abandoned his religion."

He paused again. "I was in love with my wife. Elisa was the most beautiful and kindest woman in the world. Then we had a wonderful son. My family was my oasis. Fifteen years later, my marriage became a sterile ground. I caught my wife in bed with my best friend, the manager of my company. I used to be a rich man but I felt miserable."

Isaac sobbed. "My wife begged for my forgiveness. I hesitated and didn't leave her, but I never forgave her."

Marco Polo sympathized with him in silence. Then he asked, "What about your son?" "Later on, my dear son Gideon became a heroin addict. If he'd go for a day without the drug, he'd run a fever; vomit and his body would ache. It was horrible to see my fifteen- year-old son in such despair. He tried to find heroin like a person who is choking desperately tries to find air to breathe. I was afraid he would die. I tried to help him in every way I could, but he became aggressive, closed within himself and alienated; he was impenetrable. He accused me of never having been his friend. He is now nineteen years old, he lives alone, his dependency has worsened and he is HIV positive. He has refused to speak to me for a year now. I have nothing left."

Marco Polo finally understood the causes of Isaac's psychotic depression. His 'self', which represents his conscious will, would rather immerse itself into a state of unconsciousness than bear the weight of his loss and frustrations.

"Do you like ponds?"

"Fishing used to be my favorite pastime. I've always enjoyed the peacefulness of a pond."

Trying to relax him, Marco Polo said: "You're smart Isaac. A pond is one of the best places to escape reality."

Isaac smiled and Marco Polo added, "Do you think that this is a healthy mechanism?" "No!"

"We all face suffering in life, some more, others less. Trying to escape from ourselves produces a false sense of relief and besides, it destroys our psychological health." Isaac looked at the hospital walls, thought about the process of his illness over the last four years and said: "The price was too high." "Facing our ruin is never easy, but it's the only way that we can be the authors of our own story and not the victims of it."

"But what will I do in life? I've lost everything I love the most."

"Everyone loses something in life. Some need to take responsibility for their loss; others need to pick up the pieces of what's left. What are you going to do? No psychiatrist or psychologist can make that choice for you."

Isaac was impressed with the way Marco Polo conducted the psychotherapy sessions. He provoked his intelligence and didn't treat him with pity. He encouraged him each step of the way to make his own decisions.

"All that is left are the pieces. I need to pick them up."

"Pick them up with courage. No matter how much some people disappoint you, you love them and you can't erase them from your life. If you erase them from you consciousness, you won't erase them from your unconscious."

Besides using these techniques, Marco Polo recalled how Falcon had rid himself of his crises. He asked Isaac to do an intellectual exercise everyday within the silence of his mind. "Everything you believe in controls you. If you believe in something that incarcerates you, then you will be a prisoner; if you believe in something that liberates you, then you will be free."

Isaac had become a chronic case. No one expected anything from him, not even himself.

"How do I become free of the shackles that have made me mentally ill?"

"Doubt your disturbing thoughts. Question your feelings of incapacity and why you are programmed to be unhappy. Shout at yourself. Criticize your escape. Criticize your fantasies. Strategically determine to appease those around you. Remove your Self from the audience. Enter the stage of your mind and practice being your own leader. Do this daily and silently."

Isaac learned how to manipulate the art of doubting, criticizing and determining with a substantial improvement despite small lapses. All the professionals were enthusiastic about his recovery. A month later he was doing so well that his medication was decreased. He was soon discharged. He'd continue to receive treatment as an outpatient. Before he was discharged, Marco Polo gave him a few recommendations. "Isaac, the weak condemn, but the strong forgive. You accuse your wife and your son accuses you. We all make mistakes. Forgive her and if you feel the need, apologize to you son, discover him. And especially forgive yourself; don't carry the monster of guilt with you. Surprise them and allow yourself to be surprised by them."

Isaac hugged Marco Polo and simply said: "Thank you for making me believe in myself and in life! Thank you for making me believe that it is possible to survive after one loses everything."

Isaac consciously traced his own paths. He made his own choices. He returned to the arms of his wife. He allowed himself to be loved by her and also to love her. He began to see his son from different perspectives. He discovered that Gideon's greatest problem perhaps had not been the drugs but having felt that he was an orphan with a living father. He began to enchant him, captivate him; talking less about the drugs and more about himself. He became a storyteller. Gideon got to know the story of Moses, Abraham, King David and Solomon. A few weeks later, he felt he was important to his father, despite his dependency. He gained strength to fight against the drugs. Later on, Marco Polo treated him and helped him.

Marco Polo broke barriers and distances and became a close friend of Isaac's family. He also became the friend of Ali Ramadan's family after he was discharged from the hospital a month after Isaac had left.

Although he did not have much time, he visited them at home. He appreciated both Jewish and Arabic cuisine. In fact, he had an enormous appreciation for these fascinating races.

Six months later, Marco Polo introduced Ali Ramadan to Isaac. Ali wanted to live on another planet because the Earth had been the stage of his loss. Isaac, on the other hand, wanted to live in a lake because the Earth had also been the stage for his loss, an arid desert. There had been so much loss and pain that they were able to weave a beautiful relationship. They became great friends.

They frequented each other's homes. They would have wonderful dinner parties and would have long conversations about the Middle East. Both were descendents of Abraham. They had more in common than differences.

They would respectfully comment the beautiful passages of Moses' Pentateuch, the Psalms and the surahs of the Koran. Marco Polo at times was invited and enjoyed listening to them. Besides learning from them, Marco Polo liked to talk about the intelligence of the Master of sensitivity, Jesus, which he had learned from the philosopher beggar. All of them respected one another, all of them learned and all of them ate non-stop. Their meetings were a festivity. The only one missing was Falcon.

Once again, a phenomenon that excited the heart's eyes was born: an exuberant flower bloomed in the chaos of the psychological winter.

Chapter 18

Dr. Mario had followed Marco Polo's brilliant results with Isaac and was astonished. He developed a special fondness for the young professional. The other psychiatrists also began to respect him and became more creative. Each mind is a planet and each planet has its own route and requires a distinct "flight plan" to be reached.

Psychiatrists and psychologists lost their fear of touching, connecting and playing with their patients. The degree of trust and empathy grew between them. They became more cheerful, sociable and sensitive. Psychiatry and psychology took a qualitative leap and broke the superficial and unhealthy model extracted from business relationships where bosses and employees cannot come close to each other, where the hierarchy must be maintained for the good order and progress. Such a model serves to discipline an army, but not to shape thinkers and free creative people.

Even though the environment at the Atlantic Hospital had improved, Marco Polo was still dissatisfied. He felt that the patients spent a long time immersed in their negative ideas and morbid thoughts. Something was missing.

Through his clinical observation, he discovered that hyperactive children with attention deficit disorder, whose mothers had developed the pleasure of listening to classical music in their childhood, decelerated their agitation, expanded their concentration, diminished their anxiety and became more productive.

A month later, he brought a stereo for the hospital and asked that it be installed in the yard. He bought Mozart, Chopin and Bach CDs and asked that they be played during the patients' recreation period. Two weeks later, the patients were more serene, more motivated, happier and less pensive. Even their crises diminished.

Marco Polo and the other psychiatrists suspected that the music generated a sublime abstraction that exalted the universe of affections, broke the cycle of the anxious and intensified the construction of thoughts, which liberated endorphins and increased the effect of the medication in the brain's metabolism. But this was only a hypothesis, which needed to be proven. The background music began to be used in patient rooms and in the infirmaries.

Claudia, a patient who was frequently discouraged and had a curved back, became cheerful with the music. She was sixty years old but she looked like she was eighty. The music invigorated her. No one knew that she had once been a dancer and a dance teacher in her youth. She was a specialist in waltzes. Motivated, Claudia told Marco Polo about her past. "I used to shine on the dance floor, Dr. Marco Polo."

The young psychiatrist was enchanted with her story. "You can still shine, Claudia."

"I don't know. When a storm goes through our mind, art gets blown away."

"Not really. Many artists produced their masterpieces during the worst moments of their pain and frustration. Suffering lapidated their art."

Claudia left deep in thought. One day, while many of the patients were gathered in the yard, Marco Polo showed up with a CD of classical music. Some of the patients mumbled their disapproval. Next, he played a beautiful waltz.

Claudia became excited when she heard it. She was standing at one corner of the yard. Marco Polo walked over to her and in front of everyone, asked her to dance. She was ecstatic and at the same time unsure. He took her by the hands and led her to the center of the yard. She hadn't danced in twenty-five years, at least not in public. Her friends formed a circle around them and cheered her on. "Dance! Dance!"

She could not resist. Marco Polo placed his hands on her back in the wrong way. She delicately corrected him. He was not a good dancer and Claudia's muscles were stiff. During the first thirty seconds, they had trouble getting the steps right.

Then, she loosened up and corrected his moves. The other patients were enchanted. They applauded cheerfully. They had been unaware of the artist in their midst. Claudia felt like a princess. Her mind brought back sweet images from her glorious past.

Little by little, the patients paired up and also began to dance. Some of the patients had to pair up with members of the same sex since there wasn't a pair for everyone. Dora, looking upset, walked over to the yard. "Marco Polo has gone too far this time," she thought.

When Marco Polo saw her irritation, he asked Claudia to pair up with Dr. Vidigal, who was standing alone in a corner. Dr. Vidigal was about to be discharged from the hospital and had never danced a waltz but he was eager to learn.

Marco Polo walked over to Dora and asked her to dance but she refused. Suddenly, everyone stopped to pay attention to the tension between them. "Life is so ephemeral and goes by so fast; allow yourself to relax", he insisted.

She turned her back to him to leave but the crowd shouted again, "Dance! Dance!".

She took a deep breath and suddenly turned to Marco Polo. Everyone was surprised because they thought she might slap him. With incredible assuredness she took his hand, placed it firmly on her back and began to dance with an incredible agility.

Dora had studied classical ballet during her adolescence and knew how to ballroom dance with a unique dexterity, but she had lost her ability to dance the waltz of life.

Astonished, Marco Polo allowed himself to be led by her. After the applause, everyone began to dance again.

Dr. Mario and other psychiatrists heard about the confusion in the yard. He was perplexed when he arrived there. "Even Claudia, who is so reclusive, has been affected", he thought. Although he liked Marco Polo, the scene was unbearable for him. After all, he knew that no psychiatric hospital in the world had background music. Everyone dancing a waltz was too much for him.

He was about to turn the stereo off when he felt a hand touching him on the shoulder. It was Dora. She delicately stopped him. The patients once again became silent. "Dora, you have always been so restrained. What's going on here? Have you all gone crazy?".

Smiling, Dora said: "A little less now."

Claudia then came forward and said: "Dr. Mario, please dance with me?"

He resisted, scratched his head and found the invitation absurd. However, in a flash he became contemplative and anxious. He had treated Claudia once during a psychotic episode and now she wanted to lead him to the center of the stage. She was secure and he wasn't. The roles had been switched. "My God, what's happening here?", he thought.

The craters of his unconscious quickly opened to disturb him even more. He realized that despite being the most respected psychiatrist in this grand institution, he was also ill. He was afraid of going onstage, of being observed, of failing, of being ridiculed, of being mocked, the same symptoms that many of his patients had.

During those few seconds of intense reflection, Dr. Mario glanced towards the crowd of patients and discovered that they possessed something of extreme value, which he had lost: spontaneity. Spontaneity, one of the basic personality characteristics for psychological health, had become scarce in modern societies. Dr. Mario then realized that it was no longer part of his life's vocabulary.

The euphoric audience began chanting again, but now they called out his name, "Dance, Dr. Mario! Dance, Dr. Mario!". Under the watchful eyes of those who had been mutilated by life, he divested himself of his untouchable position. He decided to dance too. He took one of Claudia's hands and placed the other on her back. She didn't have to correct him. His first steps were unsure and he tripped but to everyone's surprise he transformed his stumble into a dance step. The audience liked it. He quickly loosened up and danced magnificently in the circle formed around them. He knew how to dance very well but he had become a working machine. Like Claudia, he hadn't danced in twenty years.

He treated magnates and celebrities in his private clinic, he was a specialist in solving problems but he had unlearned the art of living and didn't follow his own advice. During the first years after he graduated from medical school, he had been relaxed, light and happy. Over time, he had become prudent, introspective and had lost his simplicity. He didn't even care. Observing the director's skill and grace, Marco Polo thought, "If only we wouldn't hide our identities behind our titles. If only psychiatry, without losing its scientific basis, were more romantic and generous."

Dr. Mario and Claudia formed a marvelous pair. They weren't psychiatrist and patient dancing; they were two human beings who needed to rescue the pleasure in the little things. After Claudia got tired, he took

Dora in his arms and they began to dance. Two other psychiatrists left, shaking their heads in indignation and saying to each other, "Dr. Mario had gone mad."

Other psychiatrists, however, including a few security guards, took the opportunity to really show some moves on the improvised dance floor. Dora approached Marco Polo and apologized for the arrogant way she had treated him. Complacent, he simply said: "I understand you." "We work in one of the saddest places in the world. We need to relax a little bit more", Dora added.

"This is a huge challenge. The greatest paradox of modern psychiatry is that it uses antidepressants to treat a sad mood but it doesn't know how to produce joy. But look at what we have accomplished. With so little we have made people very happy."

"I need to change my lifestyle," she said.

"We all do. I believe that the tense and sad atmosphere at the Atlantic Hospital is merely a reflection of the society we're building."

Dr. Mario, without them noticing, had been listening closely to their conversation. He interrupted and said: "Unfortunately, it seems like we unlearned how to live. The society outside isn't less ill than in here."

Relieved, he placed his hands on his young friend's shoulders and said: "Thank you so much, Marco Polo! Thank you for teaching me that it is always possible to start over again."

Smiling, he said something that he had never said before, "We must thank our patients for teaching us the path to simple things."

He said goodbye and left. As he was leaving, he saw the director hugging every patient he met along the way. He gave more hugs in those few minutes than he had in thirty years of practice.

After these events, the Atlantic Hospital was changed forever. There was a sparkle in people's eyes. The abilities of patients were put to use.

Claudia set up a "dance school" at the hospital. She shined like never before. Her gratuitous dance school became her masterpiece. Those who knew how to paint, act, write or even do crafts taught those who wanted to learn. Patients improved at a faster rate and hospitalization time decreased significantly.

Some patients felt so useful that after they were discharged, they came back as volunteers. The art of pleasure filled their lives. It was the first time that anyone had heard of patients who loved a psychiatric hospital.

Chapter 19

Marco Polo ended his residency in psychiatry. Every now and then, he would visit his friends at the Atlantic Hospital. While he became a prominent professionally, he wrote down his ideas on the intangible world of the human mind. His restlessness for new discoveries and his incapacity to passively accept what went against his conscience were not appeased after he graduated; they had intensified.

He agreed with Aristotle, "Man is a political animal". In Marco Polo's point of view, human beings were social actors. Psychiatrists and psychologists should get out of the microcosms of their offices to act socially. They should contribute to the prevention of psychological disorders and not live at the expense of a system that produces ill people.

Marco Polo gradually became an influential psychiatrist in his town and surrounding areas. Due to the boldness of his ideas, he was frequently invited to give lectures at colleges. He was once invited to give a lecture to the senior class of a psychology college. There were over a hundred people in the audience. The theme was "Depression, the ailment of the century." He moved the students with his finishing statements: "Future psychologists; depression is the most dramatic experience of human suffering. Only those who have crossed such valleys know the dimension of this pain. Words are not enough to describe it. We must learn how to respect these patients, listen to them openly and make them stop being passive spectators of their emotional chaos. We must lead our patients to manage their thoughts, protect their emotions and reedit the movie of their stories.

This is psychology's great task. Those who practice psychology should be passionate about life and above all, should develop skills to find the treasures buried under the rubble of those who suffer. The map to this treasure cannot be found in our theories, but within the behavior subtly expressed by the patients themselves. Allow yourselves to be taught by them. Never forget that we don't treat those who are ill because we are healthy, but because we know that we are ill…"

Marco Polo received an enthusiastic round of applause from the students. They became introspective and even positively shocked by his ideas. Because of the audience's enthusiasm, he told them that there would be an international psychiatry conference the following month and the main theme would be on depression. If they'd like to learn more about the subject, they could participate.

Next, he opened a debate. Since the subject was of general interest, several engineering, pedagogy and law students, who were walking through the hallways of the amphitheater, heard Marco Polo's eloquent final words and asked to attend the debate. They sat down on steps of the aisles. Right off the bat, a student boldly approached a sensitive issue. "Professor, certain psychiatrists don't refer their patients to psychologists. They trust the power of medication and give little importance to psychotherapy. Some of them feel that psychotherapy is a waste of time. Why is psychiatry considered to be superior to psychology?"

It was controversial, but a real and serious matter. Although psychiatry and psychology should walk hand in hand, many times they were separated from each other, competing for patients and jeopardizing their evolution. There was a lack of ethics and knowledge in this delicate area. Recalling and agreeing with Falcon's wise words, Marco Polo said:

"Psychiatrists have a power that no dictator or king has ever had. Through antidepressants and tranquilizers, they enter the world where thoughts are born and emotions bloom. This power can be very useful, but if it is used in the wrong way, it is capable of controlling and not freeing the patients. In theory, medication produces immediate effects, while the effects of psychotherapy last longer. However, that doesn't make psychiatry superior to psychology. Both sciences complement each other."

"And why are they separated?" wondered an intrepid student.

This was a short question but its implications were huge. It touched the evolution of science, the formation of dozens of thousands of professionals (psychiatrists and psychologists) and affected the lives of millions of human beings who become psychologically ill every year. Since Marco Polo was not afraid of giving his opinion, he incisively said what he thought: "To me, psychiatry and psychology are separated because science is ill. Psychiatry and psychology developed separately in the 20th century." Psychology became a separate school and psychiatry became a medical specialization.

They should be united, for the human mind isn't divided, the human being is undividable. In my opinion, psychiatry should be a specialty of psychology and not of medicine.

The students were ecstatic and applauded the elevation of the status of psychology in relation to the powerful psychiatry. They had never thought that they would hear such an opinion from a psychiatrist. Marco Polo added:

"Psychiatrists have a deep understanding of the brain's metabolism and the action of medication, but they do not have a good understanding of the personality. Psychologists, on the other hand, have a good understanding of the personality but not of the brain and the action of psychotropic drugs. Psychiatrists can perform as psychotherapists but psychotherapists cannot perform as psychiatrists and prescribe medication. This is a scientific injustice."

"Is the fact that psychiatry is separated from psychology, damaging to patients?", called out a curious Law student who was sitting in the middle of the aisle.

Marco Polo was pleased with his interest. "In certain cases it is very damaging. When a psychologist treats a serious case, which needs immediate drug intervention and refers the patient to a psychiatrist, there might be a dangerous interval of time until the patient is seen by the psychiatrist. For example, during this interval, the patient might commit suicide, have a psychotic episode or panic attacks. If psychologists were given two more years of residency in psychiatry, they'd study the human body, the biology of the brain and the effect of medication better, and thus, would be qualified to prescribe them. But unfortunately there's a competitive market on the backstage of science. Human beings don't always come first."

Then, a student brought up yet another important and usually misunderstood topic, "Sometimes psychologists, because of their lack of knowledge or the fear that they'll lose their patients, also don't refer them to psychiatrists. When should we refer them to be medicated?" "There aren't any set rules but I'll give you a few principles. Every time there's a condition of mental confusion, a risk of suicide, an intensely depressive mood, serious anxiety or insomnia, the patient should be medicated. Please, don't forget that you are dealing with lives. Each patient is more important than all the gold in the world. Always use your common sense."

The students became pensive. They had been studying psychology for years but these parameters had never been clear in their minds. Certain psychologists put their patients' health in jeopardy for not referring them to psychiatrists. They were worried about working together. "Why should insomnia be medicated?"

"Because sleeping is the engine of life. It restores all the energy we have expended. The lack of sleep triggers or intensifies many psychological and psychosomatic disorders. You might try to eliminate or work on the causes of someone's insomnia, but don't insist on it for long. Refer your patient to a psychiatrist or even to a neurologist if it's a simple case. And don't forget that you might fight against the world and survive, but if you fight against your bed, you will lose. Oh, and don't take your enemies to bed with you. Forgive them, it's a lot cheaper." The group smiled. "What percentage of the population is depressed?"

"There are different statistics. In the past, they believed that 10% of the world's population was depressed. Nowadays, we're approaching 20% of the population. This indicates that over a billion people will sooner or later have a depressive episode and unfortunately, because of prejudice or a lack of a public health policy, most of them will not receive treatment, which will cause serious psychological, social and professional consequences."

The audience was in awe. The situation was extremely grave. According to the projection, ten to twenty of the students in the amphitheater would develop depression. Some of them had already developed it. Since 70% of the students were female, a young woman asked, "Who has more emotional disorders: men or women?" "Women tend to have more emotional disorders than men."

The class became agitated. The guys mocked the young women. Marco Polo looked at them and said: "Women don't have more emotional disorders because they are more fragile than men as has always been the belief of male chauvinists for millennia. Except for metabolic causes, women become more ill because they love, worry and give of themselves more to others than men do. Besides, they are frequently more ethical, sensitive and sympathetic than men are. They are at the frontlines of the battle of life and thus, find themselves more unprotected. The soldiers at the front of the battle have a greater chance of being targeted."

Marco Polo sighed and asked, "Please applaud the women in this audience. Without them our mornings would have no dew and swallows wouldn't fly across our skies."

The future male psychologists blushed and the future female psychologists were on cloud nine. Marco Polo then gave them a small but precious piece of therapeutic advice to them, "Dear women, you can live among thousands of animals and not become frustrated, but if you live with one human being, as good as the relationship might be, there will be disappointments. Give a lot of yourselves, but don't expect much in return from others. This is one of the best tools to protect your emotions."

Because of this word of advice, some of the women avoided having psychological disorders in the future. They began to apply this principle with their future patients.

A girl, an engineering student, who was standing against the wall couldn't contain herself, "Professor, I'm only here out of curiosity. I'm an engineering student but I am so impressed with the level of ideas that I think students from all courses should hear these words. We learn how to deal with numbers and data but we leave college completely unprepared for life. Why do universities have this flaw?"

Marco Polo thanked her and answered, "The academic system doesn't need to be fixed; it needs a revolution. It produces giants in logic, but children in emotion. Students don't learn how to free their creativity, to be enterprising and to lead with risks and challenges. College teaches the love for the podium but doesn't teach how to use the defeats." Recalling the stories of the patients at the Atlantic Hospital, he added, "As careful as you might be, you might suffer a few defeats, and sometimes they'll be hard to bear. But remember this phrase: no one is worthy of the stage if they don't use their defeats to achieve it."

The students applauded enthusiastically and another student asked in a quivering voice, "What percentage of people in society is stressed?"

Like many other people, she was a shy person. Every time she spoke in public she'd get cold sweats and tachycardia. In fact, most of the people in the audience were timid to some degree. They weren't used to debating but Marco Polo had created such an instigating atmosphere that they were unable to stay silent.

As a critic of the social system, Marco Polo gazed at the audience and said with conviction, "The system transforms us into consuming machines, a bank account to be explored. We have been slaves living within democratic societies. Are you free to think and feel whatever you want to? How many times have you been tormented by things that haven't happened yet or by pseudo-needs?"

The students felt their throats tighten. Marco Polo then calmed his tone of voice and said: "Even though there is a healthy form of stress that encourages us to dream, to plan and to face challenges; modern societies have become factories of unhealthy stress, which blocks our intelligence, obstructs our pleasure, generates anxiety, muscle pain, headaches and excessive fatigue. According to certain statistics, over two thirds of people are stressed in modern societies."

A student jokingly pointed to his agitated friend and said: "Professor, this one here is overstressed!"

Marco Polo also joked with the audience, "Nowadays, being stressed is considered normal and being healthy is considered abnormal. If you are stressed, then you are normal."

The relieved audience smiled. Another student asked, "But who can be free in this crazy and agitated world?"

Marco Polo took a stroll to his past. "Those who hug trees, talk to flowers and see the world through the eyes of a falcon."

The students whistled and laughed thinking that he had told them a joke. There was one student, sitting in the front row on the left of the class, called Anna. She was the only one who did not demonstrate any reaction while Marco Polo answered the questions. He had noticed her air of sadness. Only when he talked about hugging trees and talking to flowers did she smile. Marco Polo added, "This isn't insanity. I'm not kidding. Hug trees, contemplate the shapes of the clouds, hug your doorman, greet the school's security guard, don't hide your feelings from those you love and talk about your dreams. Allow me to philosophize: existence is a beautiful book. No one can read this book well unless they learn how to read the little words…"

With this, Marco Polo ended the debate. The students were impressed with what they had heard. He had spoken poetically at a debate on depression. They had never seen the human psyche from this perspective. They could see psychology courting philosophy.

Marco Polo left under a round of applause. In the hallway he approached Anna and greeted her. She timidly and coldly shook his hand and excused herself and left with a friend. He thought that her attitude was strange but since the students had gathered around him he couldn't follow her. After they left he went outside to try to find her.

He saw her, approached her and said: "Excuse me, but what's your name?" "Anna, but excuse me, I have to go."

Marco Polo was puzzled. Only Anna had not applauded him. It was not the fact that she had not applauded that bothered him, but her constrained emotion. In a few months she would be a psychologist. "How would she be able to practice psychology?" he thought. Thus, he insisted, "Can I talk to you some other time?"

"No!"

"There isn't a 'no' without an explanation. Do you have a boyfriend?"

"No! I'm sorry but I don't want to talk."

"Then it was my lecture that you found terrible", he argued.

"It isn't you, the problem is me" said Anna with the words barely coming out of her mouth because of her insecurity.

"Are you afraid of talking to me?"

She gazed at him and without hesitation said: "You are the one who will be afraid of talking to me!" And she left without saying goodbye.

Marco Polo was disturbed by her reactions. Once again, he had confirmed that each human being is a box of secrets. He had treated so many people and he had known so many types of personalities but Anna had intrigued him.

Chapter 20

His never ending appetite to explore the soil of the human mind led Marco Polo to want to discover the mysteries that involved Anna's reactions. However, something subtle and unexpected hooked him. Anna was a tall brunette with long curly hair. She attracted him.

He went over to the college to see her again. When the students saw him, they gathered around him again. He thanked them but his eyes were searching for someone else. When Anna saw him from afar, she disappeared into the crowd of students.

Her attitude bothered him. He was trying to distance himself to be able to interpret her reactions, yet her behavior hurt his pride. Not only had the psychiatrist been struck, but also Marco Polo the man. He was embraced by an ambiguous feeling.

He wanted, at least, to find out what was causing the resistance. He would rather have her criticize him and consider him foolish than reject him. He had learned how to protect himself from frustration, but since emotions don't follow mathematical rules, he felt fragile.

The following week he made a last attempt to meet with Anna, but she was not there. When he asked one of her friends she simply said: "Anna is a spectacular person, but her behavior is strange every now and then. She isolates herself from everyone. She cuts classes and seems to be afraid of facing something."

Marco Polo wondered if his insistence had provoked or worsened her isolation. He felt that he might have crossed the line. He criticized his foolish attitude of wanting answers for everything. He was struck by a feeling of guilt. "I should have given her the right of not talking to me, even without an explanation. After all, no one is forced to like me", he reflected.

In reality, Anna had a mutilated past, which she had not revealed even to her friends. Her reactions were disguised. She smiled on the outside but cried on the inside. She had been chronically depressed since childhood. Her friends tried to get close to her, but Anna was impenetrable like granite. Despite her facade, she was affectionate, sensitive and loyal to her friends. She loved reading. Goethe was her favorite author and Faust was her favorite book.

Despite her periods of absence, she was a model student, at least on her exams. She got the best grades in her class. She tried to cover her low self-esteem with her high grades. Like many students, she had consciously chosen psychology to become a psychotherapist, but unconsciously she chose psychology to understand who she was and to overcome her own conflicts. However, she had been frustrated because her emotional illness resisted and had perpetuated itself throughout college. She understood that it would be easier to help others than to help herself.

Anna was a prisoner in the only place where she ought to be free: within herself. Extremely beautiful on the outside, yet sad on the inside, she could not take criticism, offenses and or be confronted. She was tolerant towards others but she was self-punishing and self-demanding. Her perfectionism stole her enchantment for life and imposed a serious anxiety on her.

Her former boyfriends could not understand her crises and periods of isolation. She was never completely open in her relationships because she feared losing those she loved. When a relationship began to get intimate, she'd back off and break it up.

She had seen several psychiatrists and psychologists over the years. The results were not consistent. She alternated periods of improvement with crises. Her emotion was like a ship with no anchor, incapable of navigating safely in the beautiful and tumultuous ocean of emotions.

Certain renowned psychiatrists gave her the incorrect and inadequate diagnosis for her psychological illness. They said that she would have to live with her depression for the rest of her life because she had a deficiency of serotonin in her brain.

For a future psychologist, who had always dreamed of helping people become healthy, it was difficult to accept her depression as an *ad infinitum* guest of her personality. The dream of freedom that had inspired human beings to write poetry, climb mountains and break free from iron bars did not exist within Anna, for it had melted in the heat of her crises.

Marco Polo loved challenges. Anna loved routine. He decided to respect her space and wouldn't try to find her anymore.

The following month he went to the famous International Psychiatry convention. Thousands of psychiatrists from all over the world came to the event. Sparks of hope would be announced for the treatment of psychological disorders, especially depression.

Marco Polo had spoken at the psychology school about the hidden treasures within the rubble of those who suffer. His sensitive manner of speaking about the psyche led dozens of future psychologists to participate in the event. They were enthusiastic. They didn't know that their expectations were about to become a nightmare.

Anna was bold enough to go too. She avoided Marco Polo but his ideas attracted her. The students expected to be intellectually enriched; after all, they would soon receive their diplomas and would have to treat the most complex disorders, those that reach the invisible world of the psyche. They thought, "Soon, the life of a human being will be in our hands." Some of them felt chills imagining this huge responsibility.

Most conferences at the convention were about pharmacology (the study of drugs), the launch of the latest generation of antidepressants and the metabolic causes of psychological disorders. The power of medication would be exalted. The power of social interaction, of techniques to protect emotions and the expansion of wisdom to survive in the stressful modern societies would have little value.

Marco Polo was glad to see the students in the immense lobby of the hotel where the convention was held. He hugged them. He saw Anna and was happy but greeted her discretely.

After the moment of camaraderie, he became apprehensive. He looked around and felt embarrassed looking at the pharmaceutical laboratories installed in luxurious stands, enticing the visitors. He had encouraged the students to come to the temple of psychiatry but was worried about the unpredictable facts that could occur.

The pharmaceutical industries, especially those who were releasing new drugs, sponsored the event, the expenses of some of the lecturers and the cocktails. Besides, they paid for the registration fees, plane tickets and hotel bills of certain renowned psychiatrists so that they would participate in the seminar.

Up to the 1970's in the United States, most clinical research to produce new drugs was financed by public funds. With the decline of the North American economy in the 1980's, resources became scarce and academic researchers began to receive grants from companies.

By the 1990's, the situation was even more serious. About 70% of all research was now financed by pharmaceutical industries, but the situation was still positive, for most of the research was still conducted in universities where the verification of data was more detailed and more committed to the health of human beings and less concerned with the profits.

Marco Polo was aware of these changes in the scientific production, which was rare among psychiatrists and scientists. Analyzing data, he realized that these changes had intensified in the 21st century. Most of the research, besides being financed by the pharmaceutical industry, was now conducted within the industry itself, no longer in universities. The goal was to cut costs, reduce bureaucracy and achieve quicker results.

Such a change was not an unethical process in itself because the industry had contributed a lot with the world health. Marco Polo knew this. However, he felt that the same way that courts and law enforcement are useful for society, they sometimes make serious mistakes. Unfortunately, the pharmaceutical industries were exempt from making mistakes, especially because they dealt in unimaginable sums of money.

The research for new drugs within the laboratories of the pharmaceutical industry was the reason for his concern. He was concerned with three types of controls, which, if done inadequately, could jeopardize the health of a significant part of mankind: the research process, the research results and the manipulation of these results and their release to the medical community.

The third type of control bothered him the most. In the field of psychiatry, as well as in other medical specializations, it was easy to manipulate inadequately the results of research and propagate them in a harmful way.

Every medication has side effects. Omitting such effects was a dangerous way of releasing a new drug. But what concerned Marco Polo the most was the way the pharmaceutical industry produced printed material and distributed them among doctors around the world. They used rich printed material, expensive paper where the positive effects of the drugs were in bold print and the side effects were almost imperceptible footnotes. Since doctors work excessively to survive and are always stressed, they don't have the time to assimilate the universe of information presented to them at conferences and in scientific magazines; they end up trusting the synthetic information in the didactical material produced by the pharmaceutical industry.

Based on that information, some doctors prescribe unnecessary medication that isn't adequately efficient or that has side effects that compromise their patients' health. Data is fundamental in medicine. The manipulation of this data, even if minimal, dilacerates ethics and maximizes the risks.

The powerful pharmaceutical industry has become a business like any other business, where profit is of utmost importance. The life of millions of people is at stake in a game where the referee isn't always impartial.

Marco Polo was especially concerned with the huge laboratories that synthesize the drugs, which act on the delicate and indecipherable human brain; such as tranquilizers, sleep inducers and antidepressants. Ever since his close contact with Falcon, he began to question the pressure and the seduction doctors are submitted to in order prescribe their drugs.

Besides this pressure, there was the permission to advertise medication that required medical prescriptions. Advertisement of such products was only allowed in the United States and in the beautiful country of New Zealand. TV commercials showed professional actors as depressive patients who took the medication and had an emotional qualitative leap and cheered to happiness.

The images of these commercials penetrated the population's collective unconscious, generating the belief in the miraculous power of these drugs and not taking into consideration the need to learn how to navigate the turbulent waters of emotion, to reevaluate their lifestyle, to work through their psychological conflicts and to overcome disappointments.

Many patients would already require from their psychiatrists the medication they would like to take. The patient wanted to control the doctor and the atmosphere between them became terrible. If a doctor refused, the patients simply went to another professional and they could always find a doctor who would prescribe the medication of their preference.

As a result, medicine, especially psychiatry, which should be the exercise of a free spirit and of a conscious intellect, became pressured by the strength of marketing. The laws of the market contaminated medicine.

But another problem appeared on the horizon. The Internet access of information on illnesses and treatments has made many patients self-medicate. The democracy of information has also created side effects.

Certain web surfers made their own diagnosis, they wrote out their own prescriptions and self-medicated. They forgot the singularities of each body, of each illness and of each medication; analyses that only real doctors have been trained to do.

The modern world was in conflict; it was in a true process of transformation. Digital doctors, manipulation of medication data, market pressure, all of this created discomfort in Marco Polo. His only concern should be in making money, securing his future, enjoying his vacations like any other professional. But he could not escape his passion for mankind.

Some of his friends could not understand this feeling for mankind; they wanted to feel a little of what Marco Polo felt, but it was difficult for them. This passion had begun with his father's stories and expanded when he had to face the bodies without a story in the Anatomy room.

Later, it was forged in his friendship with Falcon and sculpted when he discovered the fascinating universe of society's "wretches". Therefore, his passion for mankind was not driven by Messianism. Ever since he developed the *principle of inevitable co-responsibility* he could not be individualistic and live exclusively for himself.

He felt that no mentally ill patient was less in greatness than any political or artistic celebrity. Some people are artists because they act in Hollywood dramas; others are artists because they produce their own dramas on the stage of their mind. He felt that fame was an intellectual stupidity and criticized the propagation of gurus by the media because he believed that each person should build their own story. He truly believed that each human being was worthy of all dignity, including those who were anonymous or special children.

Because he was an excellent observer, he analyzed certain paradoxes of modern societies that disturbed him. He felt that the entertainment industry: TV, video games, Internet, sports, music and movies had never been so big and yet human beings had never been so sad and anxious. People had never been so crowded together in offices, elevators and classrooms, yet so lonely and silent about themselves. Never before had knowledge been multiplied to such a degree but still the forming of thinkers had never been so destroyed. Never before had technology made such gigantic leaps and, contradictorily, never had the *Homo sapiens* developed so many psychological disorders and had so much difficulty in being the author of his own story.

The drama of these paradoxes led Marco Polo to think that if science did not change its focus and the huge amounts of public and private funds were not spent on research to avoid the illnesses of human beings, mankind would implode.

He felt that it was completely unfair and a social crime to wait till people had developed anxiety, psychosomatic illnesses or depression and, only then, treat them. He considered that an insult to his psychosocial principle.

What suffocated his soul the most was this thought: "If the powerful pharmaceutical industries depend on the existence of unhealthy people to be able to sell its products, what is their interest in having disorders disappear?"

A battalion of employees and professionals dressed for the occasion could be seen at the convention. They had been hired by the laboratories to approach psychiatrists and doctors of other specializations. Several psychiatrists followed their conscience and did not let themselves be seduced, but it was hard to escape from any involvement.

To entice them, they gave away trips and gifts and distributed richly informed folders. The future psychologists were not used to so much luxury. They did not know that behind this intense advertising of medication, billions of dollars were at stake. Psychology conventions were less ostentatious and more humble. Ideas overlapped aesthetics.

There were several simultaneous conferences at the event. Feeling uncomfortable with the students' tense looks, Marco Polo recommended that they attend a lecture by a renowned psychiatry professor in the main auditorium; Dr. Paul Mello was a highly regarded researcher in neurosciences. He would be talking about the causes and treatments of the most insidious and anguishing psychological illness.

After his conference there would be a roundtable composed of illustrious psychiatrists and an open debate for the participants. Among the members of the roundtable was Dr. Mario Gutenberg, head director of the Atlantic Hospital.

Anna, eager to discover more about the valleys of her pain, accepted Marco Polo's suggestion. He didn't know it, but he had made a terrible choice for the future psychologists because at the conference, the complex workings of the mind would be treated as if it were the fruit of a cerebral computer. The intangible human being would be confined within the limits of logic. The manner how the theme would be dealt would make the young students, who had nourished beautiful dreams with psychology, nauseous.

However, Marco Polo was there and his presence was an invitation to shatter the paradigms and disrupt the atmosphere. A commotion took place.

Chapter 21

Dr. Paul Mello was not merely an internationally renowned scientist; he was also an eloquent speaker. He was not afraid of exposing his ideas. During his presentation, he commented on the biological foundations of mental disorders. He said that the deficiency of neurotransmitters, especially serotonin, was the basic cause of depression and other psychological disorders.

He explained how neurotransmitters were like mailmen of the brain that convey the messages within nervous synapses; that is, in the small pocket of space between the neurons or brain cells, where they can pass messages to communicate. Its deficiency created a lack of communication within the network of neurons, reducing emotional responses and causing depressive crises. The role of antidepressants, he said, was to preserve these mailmen in acceptable doses in the brain's metabolism.

The audience composed of psychiatrists was paying close attention to his ideas, but the psychology students did not like them. He hadn't talked about the conflicts in parent-children relationships, social stress, family crises and the malformation of the 'self' as causes for psychological illnesses.

They felt as if they were in a different world than the one they had lived in during the arduous years as psychology scholars. It was as if the illustrious professor was talking about another species, another kind of human being that they hadn't studied in college. They realized what they had already suspected: certain areas of psychiatry were so far apart from psychology as the Sun is from the Earth. They became frustrated with Marco Polo's invitation.

Feeling troubled, Marco Polo gestured with both hands as if to say, "Be patient! Calm down, the conference hasn't ended yet". It would have been better if it had ended. Moments later, disappointment had reached new heights. Dr. Paul Mello was even more radical in his speech by affirming:

"The soul or psyche is chemical, fruit of the brain's metabolism. Therefore, every psychological illness is originated by a chemical error and consequently, needs a chemical correction to solve it, in other words, it needs medication."

The future psychologists saw the world come crashing down over their heads. They felt wounded and humiliated. "If the psyche is chemical and psychological disorders are chemical mistakes, what room is left for psychology? What is the role of psychotherapeutic techniques in this situation?", they wondered. Some of them felt like leaving. They could not bear the insult.

Marco Polo had never attended one of Dr. Paul's conferences, he only knew of his fame. He knew that many neuroscientists had a strictly biological and chemical view of the psyche. He was also aware of the prodigious psychotropic pharmaceutical industry being complacent with this view, using it and helping disseminate it in the laymen press: newspapers, magazines and TV.

Several journalists, uninformed about the foundations of science, reported with certainty that the deficit of serotonin and other neurotransmitters were the cause of psychological illnesses and that this deficit needed to be corrected through medication. They didn't know that this information was merely an assumption and not an irrefutable scientific truth. They unknowingly published a serious and restricted theory that the psyche was chemical and, unaware, contributed to the extremely high profits of the pharmaceutical industry.

Marco Polo felt that he had been extremely naïve to invite the psychology students to come to this event. They might feel fragile at the outset of their careers. Unconscious scarring might occur. Visibly concerned, he gestured to them not to leave.

The renowned lecturer concluded by giving a fatal blow to psychology. He did not know that there was a group of psychologists in the audience; he figured that his audience would be composed of doctors, especially psychiatrists.

"We need medication that is more and more efficient, such as the ones I presented in my lecture. Psychologists will be replaced by the latest generation of drugs. Neurosciences will triumph over psychology. No one can oppose its advances. The progresses of neurosciences announce a healthy future for mankind."

The students were incredulous with what they heard. They weren't aware that behind this scene was more than the opinion of a scientist in a psychiatry convention. Dr. Paul's lecture was a reflection of the dangerous path that modern science was trailing.

A serious intellectual dispute was being played out in the backstage of science on the nature of *Homo sapiens*. Many of the actors who took part in this game, including scientists and professionals, for knowing more and more about their areas of expertise and less about everything else; that is, for being specialists in their areas, were not aware of the game itself and even less of its consequences for mankind. Marco Polo had already been thinking and worrying about these consequences for a few years.

The argument was if the human psyche was merely a biologic computer, a chemical device, or not. If thinking, producing ideas, feeling fear, loving, hating, dreaming, daring and retreating were merely fruit of the brain's metabolism. If human beings have a spirit; a psychological world that surpasses the limits of logic and biochemical reactions; the eternal debate about who we are and what we are was at stake. Science's last frontier was in question. Judging by the psychotropic industry's view and the thinking of many neuroscientists, the game was over and they had already won. If the neurosciences actually won this dispute, as was seemingly happening, the consequences for the future of mankind could be devastating. Psychology would disappear, or at least lose its relevance. There would be a massive use of medication. Psychotropic drugs might be diluted in water to collectively treat certain psychological disorders. Lives would be controlled.

Besides, if the human mind were merely a complex biologic computer, it could be fed by electronic computers. Teachers would disappear; they would be replaced by sophisticated, cheaper software and wouldn't complain. The Internet would become an electronic nanny as was already happening during Marco Polo's times.

Electronic games, multimedia software and TV programs could become the most excellent source of pleasure and personality formation. There would be no need to contemplate beauty, hug trees, cultivate flowers or extract joy from the simple things. Marco Polo felt chills just thinking about it.

He sensed that youth was becoming sadder worldwide. Back in his day, youth had already lost its capacity to argue against the madness of adults, as was the case during the counterculture period. They no longer criticized the poisons of capitalism; quite the opposite, they fought to drink from it in ever-greater doses. They exploited their parents. They were avid consumers, victims of a chronic and insatiable dissatisfaction.

Besides, the triumph of the neurosciences might also announce the triumph of transhumanists, the ever-growing number of people who emphasize the improvement of the human species through genetic manipulation and the usage of cloning. Some transhumanists have their bodies frozen after their death to be revived in the future when sciences become more advanced. They dream of accelerating the process of human evolution. In this scientific rush, those who do not support to this evolutionary process or do not fit into its quality control might be excluded. The risks would be very grave.

Religions would also disappear if the notion that the human soul is only a fantastic biological machine prevailed; the existential void, the restlessness of the spirit, the search for the Creator and the transcendence of death would be merely biochemical disorders. Once the disorders were corrected, the existential conflicts would dissipate putting an end to human religiosity.

Religions have tried for millennia to understand the intrinsic nature of human beings and realized that it is indecipherable. Now, the time had come for science to make this fascinating attempt, but there was an obvious risk. Science could become the most closed and dangerous of all religions if it sold its postulates and hypotheses as unquestionable truths.

As he analyzed these factors, Marco Polo sensed that the scientific world was inside an immense coliseum. Although there were several interconnections between both parties, on one hand there were the neurosciences, of which biologic medicine, pharmacology, neurology, a part of classic psychiatry and computer sciences took part. They talked about neurotransmitters, limbic system, amygdala, frontal lobe, in other words, the brain's anatomical and metabolic structures as the grand source of the indecipherable personality. On the other hand, there were the humanistic sciences, which included another part of psychiatry, anthropology, sociology, law, philosophy and especially a significant part of psychology.

Although they did not state a clear thought about human nature, the humanistic sciences saw the phenomena of the psyche in a more complex manner, capable of surpassing the limits of the physics and chemistry laws. To them, solidarity and tolerance could not be achieved with computer software, the human spirit should be educated, wisdom should be lapidated, sensitivity would need existential experiences, the role of the masters would be irreplaceable in the development of the most important functions of intelligence, such as thinking before reacting and placing oneself in other's shoes.

After speaking about the domain of neurosciences, Dr. Paul Mello ended his conference. He received an ovation, some stood while they applauded him. He then sat down; satisfied with the reception he received.

There were more than five hundred participants in the audience. In addition to the 42 psychology students, there were also psychiatry professors from several international universities, clinical psychiatrists, neurologists, pharmacologists and pharmaceutical laboratory directors.

The students noticed that Marco Polo also felt apprehension in the face of the lecturer's radical thinking, but they thought that there was nothing he could do, for he was like a small fish compared to the shark that was on the stage. But they did not know him.

The debate began. Some of the members at the table wove quick considerations and compliments to the lecturer. Next, they opened the debate so that the audience could participate. A dead silence took over the auditorium

Marco Polo suddenly stood, walked to the center of the amphitheater and hurried towards the microphone at the right side of the stage about twenty-five feet from the table. Audacity was his main characteristic. He quickly thanked them for the opportunity to speak and without stalling, confronted the lecturer staring directly at him.

"Dear Dr. Paul. Do you know what the *dictatorship of the hypothesis* is?

No one understood the term. It did not exist in scientific literature. It had been coined by Marco Polo's ability in synthesizing ideas. Trying to show confidence, Dr. Paul answered:

"No young man, I've never heard of this dictatorship. Please explain it."

"I don't need to. You have just committed it during your conference."

The audience of psychiatrists mumbled. "Is this young man questioning the illustrious lecturer? That's impossible!" they muttered. The students also had no idea of where Marco Polo was going with this but they felt encouraged. Dr. Mario, who was sitting at the table, put his hand over his head for he knew that a thunderstorm was ahead. Embarrassed and irritated, Dr Paul asked:

"What do you mean by that?"

Marco Polo taught by inquiring. He did not pass on readymade knowledge. He led his opponents to think and come to their own conclusions even while it seemed like he was combating in a coliseum. He had learned this technique with the street master. Instead of responding, he asked another question:

"What is a hypothesis and what is its distance from a scientific truth?"

Dr. Paul became worried with the young man's daringness and answered:

"A hypothesis is something one believes in, that one supposes, while a scientific truth is a fact that is accepted unanimously by the scientific community. The distance between them might be small or great, depending on the quality of the hypothesis."

Then, Marco Polo gave him the first intellectual blow:

"Is the deficiency of serotonin as the cause of psychological disorders a hypothesis or a scientific truth?"

"It's a hypothesis."

"Congratulations, doctor! You have just confirmed that you have committed the hypothesis' dictatorship, for you have sold this audience your hypothesis as a scientific truth."

The psychology students looked at each other and applauded him. Disturbed by the applause, Dr. Paul replied aggressively:

"This is an outrage! I only exposed my ideas."

"No, doctor! You imposed your ideas. You should have said that the deficiency of serotonin was a hypothesis. Besides, you had the nerve to sentence psychology to extinction. You overvalued the brain's metabolism and the action of pharmaceutics (drugs) and despised the complex emotional and intellectual world that makes us an intelligent species."

"Young man, forget the empty arguments and present your ideas so that we can have a true debate!"

Marco Polo wasn't intimidated. He lived for challenges.

"Tell me, illustrious professor, is it possible to go to New York City wearing a blindfold and finding someone's residence without knowing their neighborhood, their street, their apartment number?"

Feeling that Marco Polo was lost in his ideas, Dr. Paul answered him with disdain:

"No. It would take you decades of trial and error."

"So, how do you find, wearing a blindfold, in a thousandth of a second, the address of the verbs and nouns within your memory, which is thousands of times more complex than New York City, and insert them into the chains of thoughts?"

Embarrassed, he said:

"I don't know. But who knows how this occurs?"

"Two more questions, master. Do you know how our existential consciousness, which makes us realize that we are unique beings on the stage of life, is built? Do you know how this consciousness reconstructs the past or anticipates facts of the future, although the past cannot be brought back and the future is inexistent?"

The audience became uncomfortable. Dr. Paul's mind became confused with all the questions, but he candidly replied:

"The current phase of science is barely scratching the phenomena that construct thought and develop consciousness."

Suddenly, changing the subject, Marco Polo asked:

"Congratulations, master! One more question: Do you believe in God?"

"That is a private issue. We are in a scientific arena. I don't wish to talk about foolishness."

Raising his voice and opening his arms, Marco Polo shouted out to the audience: "God is here, everybody! He is present in flesh and bone. I introduce you to God." And he pointed his hands towards Dr. Paul, like Falcon had done to him.

"You are having a religious delirium, a psychotic episode!" said the lecturer jokingly, trying to relax the audience.

The audience laughed at Marco Polo.

"It's not a delirium! If you are unaware of the incomprehensible secrets that weave human intelligence, if you don't know how the existential consciousness thinks and develops, and yet you are bold enough to affirm that the psyche is the brain, that the soul is chemical, then you are God. For only God is capable of such conviction. Millions of people have tried to discover this secret and took their questions to their graves, yet you have solved it. You must be God."

The audience laughed and even the neuroscientists loosened up. But Dr. Paul tried to dodge by saying:

"You are offending me."

"I apologize. I accept that you have the right to express your opinion, but I can't agree with the fact that you impose your ideas. My criticism is that many professionals, trusting the theories of illustrious scientists such as yourself, accept them as being absolute truths and thus, make serious mistakes. If you and the other neuroscientists exposed your ideas with the status of hypotheses, the democracy of ideas could be exercised. Those who read or heard your ideas would be able to criticize and filter them."

The audience was silent. The future psychologists squeezed each other's hands in a sign of approval. And Marco Polo paraphrased Shakespeare:

"There are more things in the brain and the human soul, than are dreamt of in your science!"

The audience smiled once again.

"I have a postdoctoral degree in psychiatry and psychopharmacology. And what about you, sir? What theses have you defended?" asked Dr. Paul arrogantly. A member at the table, trying to help, added:

"Dr. Paul has over 50 articles published in scientific magazines all over the world.

"No, 150 articles!" the lecturer corrected.

"Yes, 150 articles. How many articles have you published? What are your credentials as a scientist?"

Some of the psychiatrists in the audience whistled. They thought that their young colleague had lost his voice.

"I am Marco Polo, an explorer of worlds," he answered without faltering.

This time the audience laughed out loud. The students applauded.

"Come on, young man, reveal yourself."

With their insistence, Marco Polo added:

"I have explored the canyons where disturbing ideas appear and the archipelagos where emotional defenses are raised, even the defenses present here, but I haven't defended any theories or published any articles. I'm aware that I am a young psychiatrist when compared to your credentials. But I'm also aware that the most lucid science debates the ideas of a thinker based on their content and not on the titles the author presents. I believe that true scientists love the debate and not submission."

The audience became restless and started applauding, sympathizing with Marco Polo. Universities had been seduced by the bearer's titles and fame. They were no longer temples of debate searching for the exemption of prejudice, as in ancient Greece.

Psychiatry and even psychology conventions were usually boring. The participants had not seen such a rich discussion with so many scientific implications in quite a while. Several psychiatry professors were vibrating with this cauldron of ideas. They took notes with gusto.

"Are you telling me that I'm not a real scientist? The atmosphere here is unbearable," said Dr. Paul in a cold sweat and threatening to leave.

Dr. Mario did not allow the lecturer to get offstage. He took the microphone and said: "Your ideas are very interesting, Dr. Marco Polo. If there's anything else that you'd like to add, please do so."

Dr. Paul felt a chill and sat down. He had not known that they knew each other. Marco Polo tried to be gentler and praised the lecturer trying to open the windows of his intelligence. He had to tell him and the audience the things that were caught in his throat.

"I know that you are one of the most renowned psychiatrists in the world. I have much to learn from your spotless knowledge." Dr. Paul was flattered.

"But in my opinion, medication, when necessary, is a supporting actor and psychotherapy is the leading actor of a psychological treatment."

"That is so naïve! You love poetry and I love science. We're in the 21st century and you don't know the spectacular advances of the neurosciences? You've never used tranquilizers and antidepressants in psychological illnesses? You must be a psychologist to be thinking in such a way."

Some of the psychiatrists thought it had been a mean joke.

"I'm a psychiatrist, doctor, and I use medication with a certain frequency. I know, although not completely, what their advantages and limitations are. But my theory is that if we don't nurture the 'self' of our patients, which represents their capacity to decide, to become the leading actors in the theater of their minds, we won't create free people, capable of managing their thoughts, making choices and constructing their own story."

The future psychologists were excited with this approach. Anna, in an uncommon attitude, stood up and applauded. Marco Polo observed her in admiration. Dr. Paul was deeply irritated.

"That is cheap philosophy."

"I respect your position but I insist on defending what I think."

Another member of the table, Dr. Anthony, a 65-year-old serene psychiatrist, who had a calm voice and was an icon in the academic world, was delighted with the heated debate. Showing extreme interest, he asked Marco Polo:

"Do you disagree with the hypothesis of neurotransmitters as the cause of psychological illnesses, doctor?"

"Dr. Anthony, to me, this is a poor theory if taken into consideration solely. There are other hypotheses that are just as or maybe even more important, such as childhood conflicts, social stress, existential loss, interpersonal frustration, the incapacity of freeing creativity and preserving emotions. However, in my opinion, truth is an intangible end. What should happen is a combination of the hypotheses of neurosciences with those of psychology."

"What is the soul to you, my young man?" asked Dr. Anthony.

Marco Polo took a deep breath. He would have to touch a delicate subject, one that science felt was almost forbidden to discuss. However he was not afraid to express his thoughts. He used poetry.

"When I see a mother, who forgives her son even though he doesn't deserve it, when I see someone believe in a friend when no one else does, when I see a cancer patient believe in life despite being near death or when I contemplate a beggar share his bread in spite of not having any value to society, I'm enchanted and ecstatic. I think to myself: What a wonderful world is the human mind."

He became emotional with his memories but continued:

"I realize that loving, singing, tolerating and backing off are reactions that surpass the linear limits of the brain's physical-chemical laws. Computers will never have such reactions, they will never be aware of themselves; they will always be slaves of programmed stimuli." The audience became agitated. "Your ideas shock science. If we are more than an organized brain, then what are we and who are we?" asked Dr. Anthony.

"I don't know who we are, but I can talk a bit about what we are. In my opinion, the psyche is a complex and indecipherable field of energy that co-inhabits, co-exists and cointerferes with the brain, surpassing its limits."

Now the audience was perplexed. They had never heard a postulate of such a dimension. Dr. Anthony introspectively commented:

"Congratulations on your innovative ideas. You have touched the last frontier of science. If our species proves your theory, it will give an unprecedented leap towards the future. However, despite the depth of your theory, there is no way to prove it. The only argument we have is faith. And faith is a scientific uncertainty."

"I have a few arguments that can support this theory, but they are still being elaborated."

"You see? I told you that his ideas were cheap philosophy!" exclaimed Dr. Paul with enthusiasm. Dr. Anthony quickly corrected him:

"The debater's ideas are of great breadth, and it is science's theory of theories. Our neuroscience conventions have been dry, morbid and unifocal. We don't discuss the dictums of the human spirit. We are afraid of entering into unknown terrain, but that is essential in life. We are afraid of penetrating the delicate boundary between psychiatry and philosophy, between science and religion. Sometimes, I think that this boundary doesn't even exist; we have created it. It would be nice if our arid conventions dealt more with emotions, education, spirituality, existential crises, social conflicts, and less with the brain's metabolism."

Several psychiatrists rose and applauded Dr. Anthony, agreeing with him. The discussion would've ended right there if Dr. Paul had not shown disrespect towards the serene Dr. Anthony.

"Excuse me Dr. Anthony, but this is the third millennium and mixing faith with science, psychiatry with philosophy, is scientific naïveté; a cultural retrocession. It's moving backwards a thousand years in time. You no longer produce science. Nowadays you are merely a retired professor and are isolated from the great researches. Neurosciences are closer and closer to proving that the soul is a chemical device."

To Marco Polo there were no winners in this debate, but rather distinct theories, which should be discussed with respect for the good of mankind and not for the benefit of groups. In the face of Dr. Paul's arrogance, he stepped forward and elevated the level of the debate. He raised a few questions that had been elaborated since the days of his friendship with Falcon. Very few understood his initial reasoning.

"Dr. Paul, we know that a group of patients have new depressive crises after the interruption of antidepressants, even if they were used for a long period of time, such as six months to a year. But another group, after the interruption of the drugs, no longer has crises. Is this information correct?"

The professor gestured for him to continue.

"Well, I ask you this. Why is it then that the latter group of patients no longer had crises?"

Without hesitating, the professor immediately responded:

"The patients' surpassed themselves. They defeated their difficulties, reorganized their conflicts and learned how to face their stressful stimuli."

"Did the serotonin deficiency or chemical imbalance remain in this group of patients who had a successful treatment?"

The professor felt his throat tighten. Marco Polo had trapped him by using his own arguments. Some psychiatry professors realized the trap that Dr. Paul had fallen into. They thought, "What a fatal argument". However, other psychiatrists hadn't realized where Marco Polo was headed. Dr. Paul timorously answered:

"Yes, the deficit probably continued." "Congratulations, professor! You have just questioned the future of the neurosciences. After the suspension of antidepressants, the deficit of serotonin continued, for the metabolic disorder that produces the deficit wasn't solved through medication. If the disorder continued and the patient no longer had crises, this indicates that overcoming difficulties, reorganizing oneself and resolving conflicts are psychological and cognitive processes, that go beyond the important, yet simplistic, serotonin theory."

Some of the psychiatrists scratched their heads. They had never thought about this matter before. Dr. Anthony and Dr. Mario abandoned their formality and applauded Marco Polo.

Dr. Paul was trapped. He had always been an excellent researcher, but unfortunately he had allowed himself to be seduced by money. During his conference, he had advertised a new antidepressant medication whose commercial name was Venthax. He mentioned having participated in the clinical research to verify its efficiency and was very encouraged with the results.

No one new this, but the illustrious professor had secretly received a million dollars from the powerful laboratory that had synthesized the drug to advertise it at this convention, as well as in his respected scientific articles published in the main specialized magazines.

In the pharmaceutical industry, after being accepted by the medical community, a single drug is capable of providing huge profits, more than most products in the capitalistic world.

Venthax was really therapeutically efficient, but its important side effects were minimized by Dr. Paul. It could affect the liver, expand the risks of heart attacks and, in certain patients, induce aggressiveness and increase suicide rates.

Dr. Wilson, the commercial director of the laboratory that produced this new antidepressant, was present in the audience. He hated Marco Polo's ideas. The debate had diverted the audiences' attention from the new drug. Dr. Wilson had hoped to leverage the international release of Venthax at this convention. He projected sales of over five billion dollars a year. But he was disappointed with the direction the conference was taking. Seeing that Dr. Wilson was completely unhappy in the first row, Dr. Paul said:

"Let's end this debate."

But Marco Polo still had a few things to say.

"We are children playing science in the theater of existence. I am a proud person too, sometimes I'm even stupid; but I am learning that in this theater, the weak use pride as their strength, the strong use humility as their strength."

Dr. Paul was paralyzed and the audience was silent. They realized that everyone is capable of making mistakes in this delicate field. Marco Polo did not impose his ideas. He exposed them.

"I am not proud. I'm realistic!" said Dr Paul.

"Then tell me, professor, did the new drug you lectured about, Venthax, have its clinical efficiency compared with placebos, which are false medication or chemical lies?"

Dr. Paul's voice trembled. He did not want to discuss this matter.

"Of course! We conducted double-blind testing. We took two groups of depressed patients. We gave the new drug to one group and a placebo to the other. Neither group knew which type of substance they were taking. But I have already mentioned all this in my lecture." "But you didn't provide us with data. What is the efficiency percentage of one and the other?"

"Venthax had a 62% rate of efficiency and the placebo had a 46% rate."

The psychology students looked at each other. They did not know that a chemical lie, the placebo, had had an efficiency rate about as good as the psychoactive drug. They had never discussed this fundamental subject at school.

With this, Marco Polo struck a fatal blow to the great master's absolutism and arrogance: "Why did the placebos have such an incredible efficiency rate of 46% on depressed patients?"

Once again, knowing where Marco Polo was headed, Dr. Paul signed his enrollment as a small student in the school of existence. With a knot in his throat, he was forced to answer so as not to embarrass himself even further:

"Because they believed in the treatment. They felt comforted and trusted the doctors that treated them."

"Very well Dr. Paul, the fabulous effect of the placebos is the spectacular effect of the human mind, which has an incredible capacity of dreaming, transcending its chaos, facing its loss, picking up its pieces, reconstructing its story and reediting the film of the unconscious mind. Drugs can help a lot, but all these processes are conquered through dialogue, the intervention of the Self, self-knowledge, exchanges and social interaction. Therefore, thank you for concluding that psychology will never die!"

The future psychologists stood and applauded their friend with euphoria. Some of them were in tears. The hope of finding treasure within the rubble of those who suffer was rekindled.

Marco Polo looked closely at the audience and ended the debate with these words:

"The pharmaceutical industry invests billions of dollars in research for new drugs that act on the human brain to treat psychological disorders, but they don't invest a cent in preventive measures, in educational improvement, in the development of the art of thinking in children, in the education of self-esteem, in the diminishing of social stress and combating physical and psychological misery. Society needs to know that in the midst of mankind's psychological disorders, the pharmaceutical industry silently prepares itself to become the most powerful industry in the world, more robust even than the arms and oil industries. This industry needs an ill society to continue selling its products. By the way, never before have so many tranquilizers and antidepressants been sold! We need to rethink the future of science and reflect on the path that mankind is taking."

Marco Polo looked at the clock and calculated that they had been debating for almost an hour, so he added:

"According to statistics, during the short period that we have been discussing our ideas, over a thousand people all over the world have had depressive crises, panic attacks, psychotic episodes and psychosomatic illnesses. More than twenty people have committed suicide. Wonderful people have given up on living and have left a profuse amount of pain for their family members, which will be perpetuated for decades. We are building a society of miserable people. Doesn't this torment you, gentlemen?" "Dreamer!" was the last word the renowned lecturer said. Marco Polo, with teary eyes, also said his last phrase:

"If I stop dreaming, I'll die!" As he said this, images of the children suffering from depression and anorexia nervosa that he treated came to his mind, disorders that were rare in the past. Children who suffered from anorexia were cachectic; only skin and bones. Marco Polo's tears became visible.

Dr. Mario and Dr. Anthony walked over to him and greeted him. Several psychiatrists were enthusiastic with Marco Polo's ideas. They were profound and affectionate. They completely agreed that psychiatry couldn't be strictly curative; it should be redirected towards prevention. While the young psychiatrist walked across the auditorium, he was greeted by many of the participants.

Anna was waiting for him outside. She had a dubious sentiment of joy and anguish. Joy, because Marco Polo's ideas had aired the alleys of her emotions, making her realize that she was not programmed to be depressed. Anguish, because his last words had guided her to an immersion into her childhood; the secrets that had made her become a chronically unhappy young woman.

When she saw him, she gave him a tender kiss on the cheek. Surprised, he did not understand her reaction, nor tried to. The debating psychiatrist took a step back and the human being emerged. He only wished to feel that moment. He allowed emotions to overcome reason.

They left the amphitheater together. They walked aimlessly, trying to find each other.

Chapter 22

Anna and Marco Polo found a pleasant place to exchange their worlds: a beautiful, spacious and flowery park. The leaves danced to the orchestra of the wind. Anna's hair was softly blown, covering her eyes.

Marco Polo knew that park well. It had been there that he had rethought his life, made speeches, composed poems with Falcon and took the first steps towards becoming a thinker. He remembered the tree he liked to hug.

Anna, without hesitating, surprised him by saying:

"I'm depressive!"

Marco Polo had not been aware of this fact.

"Anna! You're not depressive. You are a human being who is going through a depression."

"Human being? You don't know how many times I've felt like the scum of society!" Marco Polo was impressed. "What causes had led such a lovely person and a future psychologist to feel so small?" he thought. Her illness had devastated her story. Still under the influence of Marco Polo's words in the bubbly debate, Anna added:

"I intend to stop taking my antidepressant."

He calmly said to her:

"No, Anna. Don't stop taking your medication until you learn how to navigate, without fear, the beautiful and turbulent ocean of emotions!"

"But I need to do something. Your ideas and your courage at the debate have given me the motivation to do so."

"Good. Take action, but you should know that there are no heroes in the territory of emotion, only people who practice their strength one day a time. Remember what I said: Equip your 'Self' to be the leading actress in your treatment, work through the causes that are the foundation of your depressive mood, confront your disturbing thoughts. By doing this you will become the director of your life's script."

Anna was fascinated with Marco Polo's use of language. He was able to talk about complex phenomena by telling stories, using a creative inspiration and a poetic language.

"I appreciate your words, but I'm tired. My life has become an unbearable burden. I have been suffering for many years."

"May I ask you three questions?" said Marco Polo, who had already reflected on some of Anna's behaviors.

"Yes, you may," she agreed delicately.

"Are you hypersensitive? When someone offends you, do you feel very hurt, does it ruin your mood, your day?"

Surprised with the question she answered: "Not only my day. A criticism or a rejection disturbs me for a week, sometimes for a month or even a whole year. I'm very sensitive."

"Are you overly preoccupied with others' opinions, what they think and say about you?"

"Yes. I'm afraid of not being accepted. My self-esteem is terrible. Any type of rejection, even with just a look, hurts me. But how do you know all this?"

"Do you think too much? Is your mind too agitated and doesn't stop thinking? Do you suffer because of problems that haven't happened yet or do you ponder frequently about anguishing situations of the past?"

Impressed with Marco Polo's sense of observation, she took a deep breath and answered: "I can't stop thinking for an instant; my mind is restless. I suffer a lot by anticipation. I suffer because of my exams, because of what is unpredictable, because of my past mistakes and because of the mistakes I still haven't made. The past haunts me and the future torments me," her eyes filled with tears.

"Anna, you have the tri-hyper syndrome."

"Tri... what? I've never heard of this syndrome in school."

"I was fortunate to discover this syndrome and unfortunate to know that it afflicts millions of people and is the foundation of most emotional disorders. By analyzing innumerous patients, I was able to observe that many of them had three important over-developed personality traits, thus, tri-hyper. Those who are hypersensitive, hyper-worried with their social image and hyper-thinking, tend to develop depression, panic syndrome and psychosomatic illnesses. But there's good news too. This syndrome can be cured and it only afflicts the best people in society, those who are emotionally rich and excessively giving."

"Emotionally rich and excessively giving, what does this mean?" Anna asked in astonishment. "I have always read that depressed people are problematic and you tell me that they have a rich personality!"

"It's what I think. The fact that these three noble characteristics are overdeveloped, an enormous lack of emotional protection is created. That's why those who suffer from this syndrome are easily offended, demand too much of themselves and revolve around facts that haven't happened."

Anna was ecstatic. She had been going to psychiatrists and psychologists all her life, but for the first time she felt proud of herself. She was extremely sensitive, incapable of killing a bug. She used to give too much of herself to everyone and felt the pain of others.

The housemaids at her home adored her. She realized that she wasn't a fragile, inferior and despicable person, but a human being of value who didn't know how to defend herself. Because she was very intelligent, she concluded on her own:

"That's why people like me don't adapt to the social, competitive, inhumane and insensitive world. They have an open treasure that can be easily taken by people's aggressiveness and by life's problems."

Marco Polo admired her refined analytical capacity.

"Congratulations, Anna! People with the tri-hyper syndrome are excellent for other people, but they are their own flagellators. They are ethical and affectionate but they don't have an emotional skin. Except for the cases where someone wounds us physically, any kind of offense, criticism, rejection or disappointment can only wound us if we allow it to. As I said in your class: Give of yourself, but don't expect much in return from others."

Marco Polo explained that not all three pillars of this syndrome are necessary to make people develop emotional disorders. In some cases, only one pillar is necessary. He said that the prevention of this syndrome, done through the education of emotions, could avoid millions of people from becoming ill.

Looking into Anna's sweet and teary eyes, he added:

"Don't feel inferior to anyone. You are better than me in many aspects."

Anna was moved. She had always felt small in relation to other people, especially the psychiatrists that had treated her. She sometimes thought of giving up on her profession, other times of her own life. Poetry was one of the few things that excited her. Trying to hide her tears, she asked:

"Have you read Goethe?"

"I admire his sharp sensitivity and intelligence." and he added jokingly, "but he was his mother's favorite child."

"What do you mean?" asked Anna.

"According to Freud, Goethe's intellectual brilliance began with his mother. Freud said that children who were favored and valued by their mothers become more optimistic, more successful and have more courage when facing the accidents of life."

Marco Polo did not realize that these words wounded Anna deeply. Her relationship with her mother had been marked by pain. Realizing that there was something wrong, he tried to fix it.

"I don't agree with Freud. He was also the favorite son of Amalie, his mother, but although he was an intelligent thinker, his humor wasn't irrigated with optimism. Therefore, he was always tormented with the idea that he would die before Amalie. In my opinion, mothers love all their children without distinction; they only distribute their attention in a different manner because their concerns with each one are different."

Anna could bear it no longer. She broke into tears. She tried to hide her face by sitting on the bench.

Marco Polo was confused. He realized that something serious had happened between Anna and her mother. He had no intention of invading her privacy. He placed his right arm around her shoulders and respected her anguish.

The sun was setting and its rays passed through the flower petals and revealed the beautiful spring. The outside atmosphere contrasted with Anna's world. After a few moments of silence, he said:

"I'm sorry if I hurt you."

She suddenly rose and said:

"I have to go."

In truth, she was hesitating between leaving and the desire to be close to him.

"Can I see you tomorrow?" Marco Polo asked feeling insecure.

"I don't think so."

"Why not?"

Temporarily blocking out Marco Polo's words, which had encouraged her to rescue her self-esteem and to fight against her illness, she turned back into the epicenter of her conflict and said:

"You won't like me. I'm a difficult person. Even I don't understand myself."

"We're alike! I don't understand myself sometimes either," he said with a smile.

So, on one of those rare opportunities, she opened the map to her dramatic story and sobbing she cried out loud:

"They stole my joy! They destroyed my childhood without asking for my permission. Can't you see that I'm a source of sadness? What do you want from me?"

The sudden rescue of the past generated a volume of tension that obstructed Anna's flow of ideas. Marco Polo immersed himself in silence. He waited until she could recompose herself and continue.

"I was an only child and thought that my mother loved and valued me more than everything in life. But when I was eight years old, I heard a sound that has never left my mind. I heard a gunshot coming from her room. I ran there and saw my mother, lying on her bed, covered in blood. I tried to help her but I was too little. All I could do was scream: Mommy! Mommy! Don't leave me! She died physically and I died emotionally. We both died."

Rarely had anyone suffered as much as little Anna. Antoinette, her mother, had had severe depressive crises, but despite all that, she tried to give her daughter as much attention and love as she could. In between crises, she played with Anna and said that she was the best daughter in the world. However, the episodes increased and her hypersensitive mother had periods when she would withdraw. Antoinette sometimes told the maids, in the presence of Anna, that she could no longer bear to live. Anna would cry and was constantly tormented.

Her father, Lucius Fernandez, was a wealthy industrialist. He had never understood or given support to his wife. There was often quarrelling between the couple, sometimes with Anna present. Lucius understood financial mathematics very well and absolutely nothing about emotional arithmetic.

Unlike Anna and Antoinette who were hypersensitive, Lucius was a cold, calculating and irritable man who did not know how to put himself in others' shoes. He had not matured in accordance with his graying hair. He kept repeating the same mistakes. He was incapable of seeing his wife's anguish. To him, depression was a weakness; an attitude of those who had nothing better to do.

He really disliked psychiatrists. He thought they were the greatest charlatans in society. In truth, he was afraid of looking at his own being. He only entered a psychiatrist's office once in his wife's company. He left saying that the psychiatrist was crazy.

Lucius Fernandez was a man of many women. His infidelity added to his aggressiveness and his self-centered posture contributed to irrigate his wife's low self-esteem and increase her depression. He never remarried after Antoinette's death; the millionaire was afraid of sharing his money.

Anna nourished a deep resentment towards her father, not only because of his lack of affection, but because, as she grew, she began to understand that he had done very little to prevent her mother's suicide. A disturbing thought suffocated her: her father had facilitated her mother's suicide. Antoinette had killed herself with a gun that was kept in the nightstand next to the couple's bed. Deep down, Anna knew that her father kept a gun in the nightstand and another one in his car because he was suspicious and insecure. He had a paranoid personality.

"I once told my father that mother talked about dying. With an arrogant air, he categorically affirmed that I could relax because those who threaten to do something never do it. He was incapable of hearing my mother's clamors behind her sad mood."

Marco Polo, through his fine capacity of seeing what images do not show and hearing what the visible behaviors do not reveal, asked Anna a question – one that led her to penetrate the core of her emotional chaos.

"Are you mad at your mother?"

Anna felt resentment towards her father, but the resentment she nourished towards her mother was much greater. However, she denied this feeling. Her resentment was secretly hidden in the basement of her unconscious mind and had never come up in her psychotherapy sessions. Her therapists hadn't detected this dramatic sentiment, either because of Anna's resistance in talking about her mother's suicide or because they were afraid of entering this arid terrain and not being able to control her crisis. After all, Anna talked about going to sleep and never awakening again, of giving up on everything.

Besides the hidden resentment towards her mother, she felt involved in a haze of guilt. Her mother had indicated that she wanted to die and she felt she had failed to protect her. Nothing is as stifling to a fragile child's emotions as feeling guilty for their parents' actions. These conflicts marked the development of her personality. Anna became insecure, fragile, with chronically sad moods, afraid to face life and confront her own feelings. She was selfpunitive and tolerated the mistakes of others but was relentless with her own mistakes.

She had always demonstrated to her therapists that she felt compassion for her mother. For the first time she had had the courage to say that she felt anger and not pity for her. In reality, her feelings were mixed.

"Yes. Sometimes I'm angry at her. Why did she abandon me? The love she felt for me was less than her desire to live. I was all alone. I lost everything. I lost my pleasure in living," she said, still unable to accept it. And she added, "Didn't you say in your debate that those who commit suicide leave a profuse amount of pain that perpetuates for decades? I'm a living example of your arguments. To me, those who kill themselves are extremely selfish. They end their problem and create another one for others. Have you ever felt this lonely?" She was still crying. Anna had lost what she loved the most, there weren't any pieces left from her loss. She did not have anything to pick up. Marco Polo was deeply touched by her story. In her childhood, she should have chased birds, played with her dolls and walked through the alleys of existence without being afraid, but the sound of the gunfire and the image of her mother lying still on her bed were a vile play that kept being repeated on the stage of her mind, contaminating the entire structure of her unconscious mind.

Marco Polo knew that in certain cases, the development of the trihyper syndrome had genetic influences. He believed that depressed parents didn't transmit their depression to their children. In reality, what was actually transmitted was a tendency to develop the trihyper syndrome, which in some cases, if not corrected through education and the action of the 'self' as the author of one's own story, may facilitate the onset of depression and other illnesses.

He believed that social and psychological causes, such as loss and frustration, were much more important in the development of this syndrome than genetics. The causes did not necessarily have to be intense. In Anna's case, her causes were more evident. A whirlwind had destroyed the most important phase of her life.

After her mother's suicide, she had never again believed that people could truly love her, and, as a result, she had an enormous difficulty in lowering her guard. The fear of another loss was an ever-present ghost.

She felt like she was the loneliest person in the world. Marco Polo reacted to her question:

"I've never felt the loneliness that you've had to face, but I'm convinced of one thing: when the world abandons us, loneliness is bearable, but when we abandon ourselves, loneliness is intolerable. You have abandoned yourself."

Anna was shaken by this phrase. She had expected Marco Polo to pity her, that he would be paralyzed in the face of her emotional misery. Although he felt her pain deeply, he instigated her intelligence by guiding her to conclude that she had really abandoned herself. She had stopped loving herself. Her loneliness had become unbearable. However, she had raised a barrier as if she could not overcome her past.

"How can I invest in life and love it if, the one who has created me committed suicide?" The moment had come for Marco Polo to help Anna in a profound way. His concept of suicide confronted the current thought of psychiatry and psychology. He slowly raised her face, looked into her eyes and said solemnly:

"Anna, suicides don't exist!"

Perplexed, she immediately argued:

"What are you saying? For years I have tried to understand why my mother died and why people give up on living and now you tell me that suicides don't exist? Don't toy with my feelings."

"I'm serious! Depressed people have a hunger and a thirst for life," he affirmed incisively. Then, she touched a subject that was considered taboo.

"Don't say that. I have also tried to take my own life once. I overdosed on medication. What do you think I did? Didn't I want to kill myself?" she said shaking.

"No! You wanted to kill your pain and not your life. Just like your mother didn't wish to die. Actually, her desire was to destroy her sadness, the anguish that suffocated her."

"No psychiatrist has ever told me that!" Anna exclaimed.

"The concept of suicide needs to be corrected by psychiatry and society in general. The awareness of the end of existence is always a manifestation of existence itself. Every notion of death is homage to life, for only life can think. Every idea of death isn't an omnipotent attitude of human beings tracing their destiny, but a desperate attitude of trying to destroy the emotional drama that they cannot overcome. Thus, the pure notion of suicide doesn't exist. Every time a person thinks about killing oneself, they don't take into consideration the awareness of existential nothingness. Their thought is a reaction, not to eliminate their life but to amputate their pain. Suicide attempts, therefore, don't reveal a wish to die, but a desperate hunger to live."

Anna did not fully understand the psychological dimension of Marco Polo's ideas, but the little she did understand was enough to shock her, relieve her and make her look inwardly. Once again, her intelligence manifested itself:

"When I thought of taking my own life, a feeling strangled my being. I felt as if I was in a cubicle and couldn't breathe. A tempting idea went through my mind, demonstrating how easy it would be to end it all. But in reality, I struggled within myself to break free from the shackles of my imprisonment. I wanted to be free, breathe and love, I didn't want to die."

After this conclusion, Anna immersed herself even deeper within the core of her being and opened the spillways of her remote past. As if she had come out of a dark place and entered a completely illuminated room, she recalled images that had been hidden for years inside of her ruins.

She remembered pleasant moments when her mother would hide behind the couch and the curtains, playing hide-and-seek with her. She recalled when her mother played the piano while she sat at her feet completely enchanted. She remembered that, influenced by her mother, she had learned to appreciate poetry and Goethe. She also recalled a phrase that she had never rescued before: "Sweetheart, I love you. I will never abandon you."

For the first time she realized that her mother had not been selfish, but rather a prisoner of her own pain. She never wanted to kill herself. She wanted to eliminate her emotional misery. The anger she once felt, dissipated. The feeling of having been abandoned crumbled at that moment. She had rescued the love her mother had for her. Then, something sublime happened.

Sobbing, Anna exclaimed:

"Mother, I understand you and forgive you... Mother, I love you! You were wonderful."

She turned to Marco Polo and said:

"Thank you, Marco Polo! A weight has been lifted from my soul."

She embraced him softly and deeply. She held him tight in her arms and with serenity said: "If people who contemplate suicide knew how they hunger and thirst to live, they wouldn't kill themselves. They would use their hunger and thirst to tenaciously fight against their loss, disappointments and anguish. The contemplation of suicide reveals a desperate hunger to live and not a desire to die. These words need to be cried out and underlined all over the world." "The worst prison in the world is the prison of emotions, but no one is enslaved when they decide to be free. By looking at suicide from this angle, several of my patients have escaped this prison and extracted courage from their weaknesses and once again believed in life."

Rarely had two people talked so lightly about a subject that strangles tranquility. Since the air between them was light and pleasant, Marco Polo decided to show another side of his personality, his irreverent side. Raising his voice he said:

"Don't be afraid of pain, my princess, live life vibrantly."

"I'm very complicated," she said openly.

"The most complicated women are the most interesting," he said jokingly.

She disheveled his hair and tickled him. Smiling, he added:

"Be careful! You're the one who's taking a chance by being with me."

"What do you mean?" Anna asked surprised.

"I have the blood of an adventurer, the irreverence of a philosopher and the renunciation of a poet. Remember that I am Marco Polo, a traveler on the soil of life. I'm an explorer of worlds and now, of your beautiful world.

"I don't understand!"

Instead of giving her an answer, Marco Polo stood on the park bench and, disregarding the passersby, recited a poem with his arms wide open and by a vibrant voice. He remembered the good times.

My sweet damsel!
Face the night storm as birds do.
At dawn, even though their nests have fallen,
They sing without a stage or audience!
To them, life is a great party!

My dear princess!
Don't be afraid of life,
Be afraid of not living.
Don't be afraid of falling,
Be afraid of not walking.
Open up your heart; give in,
Allow this adventurer to discover you!

A small crowd had gathered to listen to the poet. Anna blushed. She had always avoided any public exposure. After he finished the poem, Marco Polo sat back down and gave her a long kiss. She trembled and gave in. After he kissed her, several people applauded.

A few elderly women were euphoric with the romantic scene. One of them, an eightyyear-old woman, said tenderly:

"Hold on to this prince, my dear. Men like him are hard to find!"

She got the message and this time she took the initiative. She kissed him passionately.

Chapter 23

Anna and Marco Polo got together a couple of times over the following week. Her love for him grew. Days later, she participated in a seminar at college on the panic syndrome. She did not know most of the participants of the seminar.

A professor said something she did not approve. He said that those who suffer with panic syndrome are emotionally fragile, have no self-control, are suspicious of their doctor's opinion and revolve around their own insecurity. Because of their fragility, each panic attack causes the world to come crashing down on them.

Her contact with Marco Polo had made Anna have a deeper perception of psychological disorders. She disagreed with the professor's pessimistic and deterministic point of view. He had been incapable of exalting the most beautiful characteristics of these patients and of showing the emotional drama they go through during a crisis. So, she bravely raised her hand to question him. The few friends who knew her admired her boldness. They had never seen her raise her hand to ask a question before.

"Could it be that these patients are not hypersensitive at all and that because they have an above-average awareness of the limitations of life and the end of existence, they're prone to having panic attacks? When these patients are suspicious of the doctors who affirm that their health is excellent; is that a sign of weakness or is it a desperate cry from someone who thirsts to live and wishes to ward off the ghost of death?"

Anna was relieved for having asked the question. She wanted her arguments to be at least respected. Her ideas made everyone reflect, but the professor didn't appreciate being contradicted. Instead of debating her arguments he chose to be ironic."

You are here to study psychology and not philosophy."

The audience enjoyed his answer. Marco Polo knew how to defend himself when he was criticized or mocked. It sharpened his thinking. Anna did not have such a defense; she had not reedited the movie of her unconscious mind; she was still a hypersensitive person who was hyper-worried about her social image. She had always made an enormous effort not to make mistakes in front of others, let alone an audience. Now that she had expressed herself in front of an audience, she was being humiliated.

Everyone was expecting her to react to the professor's contempt. But her voice became constrained and she was unable to counter argue. She was so shocked that she became paralyzed. The laughter reverberated in her mind. She got up and left the class. She left in defeat.

The next day, as expected, she didn't show up for class. She didn't leave her house or get out of bed. She kept punishing herself. She couldn't stop thinking about her humiliation in public. She kept repeating the scene in her mind. She was angry with her professor and even angrier with herself for not having been able to react. She gave in to a new crisis.

Marco Polo tried to find her at school, but she was nowhere to be found. She had been absent for several days now. He tried to call her but Anna was incommunicable, she did not want to talk to anyone. The maids, familiar with her crises, had express orders from her father not to disturb her. Marco Polo was intrigued, "What's happening? Why does she refuse to talk to me? Should I disappear from her life?"

Meanwhile, he wrote Falcon a letter. He told him about his relationship with Anna and her difficulties. Falcon replied with a few, but significant words:

Dear friend Marco Polo,

If you love a woman, fight for her. But be aware that women are marvelously incomprehensible. The day you understand a woman's soul, doubt your own gender...

As he read the note Marco Polo nodded with joy. The next day, he summoned his courage and went to visit Anna. When he arrived at her house, he was astonished with the ten-thousand-square-foot colonial palace. She was so simple, sweet and down to earth. He had no idea of how wealthy she was. There were ten suites, a ballroom, a movie theater and countless other rooms. The palace occupied an entire block.

The gates were tall, made of cast iron with spear points, all the windows were arched and the green panes were sandblasted. The yard was immense. There were lots of flowers to hide such a sad young woman.

Two maids, two cooks, two gardeners and a cleaning lady took care of the house and two drivers served Anna and her father. There were security guards inside and outside the house. Most of Anna's friends did not know that a professional undercover bodyguard took care of her safety at school.

After contacting a guard, Carlos, the butler, was called. He was tall, bald and always wore a white suit jacket. Carlos was in charge of the staff. His demeanor was grave, distant and suspicious. The butler was like an iceberg, harsh, cold and impenetrable.

"I'd like to talk to Anna."

From the palace's stairway Carlos shouted: "Have you made an appointment?"

"No. But I'm her friend."

"Anna only sees people who have an appointment."

"Please, talk to her. She will probably see me."

The butler reluctantly left. He announced the visit to Lucius Fernandez, her father. He was a man who had no respect for women and felt that all men wanted to take advantage of his daughter. He told the butler to tell him that she had gone out. Marco Polo suspected that the butler was lying and that he hadn't even given her the message.

"Sir, tell her that I won't be long, I only wish to speak to her for a few minutes."

"Please leave, sir!"

Noticing the young man's insistence from a window, Lucius opened the front door, walked over to Carlos and exclaimed: "Leave my daughter alone!"

"I'm sorry sir, but perhaps your daughter needs me."

"How arrogant! Who do you think you are to affirm such a thing?"

"I'm a friend."

"Anna has classmates, not friends."

"But I insist. I'm her friend."

"What's your name?"

"Marco Polo."

"What do you do?"

Marco Polo hesitated but was honest and said: "I'm a psychiatrist."

"A psychiatrist? That's all I needed, a psychiatrist trying to seduce my daughter....! No one invited you here."

"I'm here as a friend and not as a psychiatrist,' said Marco Polo feeling irritated.

"This is unethical. Leave!"

"Your daughter is in a cocoon. She needs to be sociable. She needs to free herself and be happy."

The arrogant businessman did not like this.

"A lousy shrink passing out moral judgment. Beat it before I call the police!" he said forcefully and went back in without saying goodbye.

"And don't you come back!" added Colonel Carlos. Both guards approached Marco Polo menacingly.

It was as if everyone there, with the exception of Anna, was living in an army regiment.

The young man left feeling upset. He felt that Anna was quite healthy, considering that she lived in military barracks. It was impossible not to be ill in such a place. He wondered if investing in this romance would be worthwhile.

He had dated other women. The last one had been extremely controlling and jealous. He couldn't breathe without her taking notice of it. Anna, on the other hand, was alienated and traded him for her own conflicts. Marco Polo experienced the old existential dilemma: his reason told him to back off but his emotions told him to insist. He had to see her one more time before giving up.

He went back to Anna's house the next day; he called beforehand to make sure that her father wasn't there. He still had to get past Colonel Carlos. Just as he had done in the past, but not as ridiculously, he disguised himself. He wore a black goatee and dark glasses. He looked like a crazed rocker. Carlos appeared after the guard's insistence.

Before he could say anything, Marco Polo said in a high-pitched voice:

"How are you doing, Carlos?"

"How do you know my name?"

"Well, Lucius told me. I believe you know me," he shouted.

"No, sir." Replied the butler, feeling unsure because of the stranger's shrieky voice.

"You've never seen this nice figure in the papers?" "No."

"That's absurd! Don't butlers read the papers anymore? Get Lucius here immediately." "Master Lucius isn't here, sir." "What? He's not here? There's good parenting for you. Come on, I have an urgent medical examination to perform."

"What examination, sir?"

"I have to examine Lucius' daughter. He begged me to come over. I'm a specialist in intestinal disorders."

"I'm sorry but he didn't tell me."

"And does he have to? The great Lucius no longer runs this house! If you don't open this door right now, I'll leave. And if his daughter worsens, you will be held accountable." Carlos was confused and Marco Polo added:

"By the way, you look kind of pale. Look at that skin rash on your face. Let me take a closer look."

Despite being authoritarian, Carlos was a hypochondriac and was obsessed with diseases. He blushed. Ran his hand over his face and his bald head began to sweat.

"This looks serious. You are currently being treated for this, are you not?"

"No sir. I haven't treated this. But what do you think it is?" the butler asked timidly.

Marco Polo took his stethoscope and listened to Carlos' stomach and just to tease him, listened to his head and said: "Hmm! Huh! Don't worry; this disease won't kill you. Take this pill now. I'll talk to you after I take a look at Anna."

He had given the butler a laxative. Marco Polo went to Anna's room while the dictator headed for the bathroom.

Her room was enormous, but it was cold and dark. It was approximately two hundred square feet in size. Anna was awake, lying in bed. Marco Polo removed his disguise and slowly walked towards the bed.

He sat next to her. She was startled when she heard the young man's voice, but she didn't get up or greet him. He tried to cheer her up.

"Anna, what's going on with you?"

She remained silent.

"I'm your friend. Talk to me!"

She covered her head with a pillow.

"Alright, Anna. You have the right not to talk to me. If that is what you want, I will disappear from your life."

He got up to leave. When he was halfway to the door she cried out:

"I told you I was complicated."

Instead of sparing her he said:

"Anna, the problem isn't that you're complicated, the problem is that you complicate life."

"Forget about me. It's the best you can do."

Filled with indignation, he shook her with a cutting phrase:

"The problem isn't the disease of those who are ill, but those who are ill because of the disease."

She took the pillow off her face and asked: "What do you mean by that?"

"The problem is with your 'self', your capacity to decide and not your illness. You've had reasons to be depressed but you insist on being ill."

"I don't wish to be ill."

"Not consciously, but unconsciously you wish to stay in the audience, you don't have the courage to go on stage and direct the play of your life. Anna, you are strong and magnificent, abandon your self-pity."

"I don't pity myself."

Marco Polo blended praise with positive criticism, for he was fully aware that defeating psychological disorders wasn't easy. He knew that empty advice did no good; it was necessary to be an artisan of the psyche.

"So, why are you always expecting people to give you approval or to pity you? I heard that you were brilliant at the seminar but couldn't take being confronted."

Anna was silent, so he went on: "You are intelligent but self-punitive; you don't allow failing, being mocked or criticized. Schopenhauer said that our happiness shouldn't be based on the opinion of others. You have forgotten that you shouldn't expect the applause of others to be free!"

Anna was shocked with these words. She couldn't escape them.

"I'm an idiot!" "Sometimes I'm an idiot too. But you should fight for you psychological health.

Remember! You have a hunger to live! Don't give in."

"There's something that gags and suffocates my soul. I know I need to fight but I can't."

Marco Polo then, quoted a famous author:

"Knowing is not enough; we must apply. Willing is not enough; we must do."

"Goethe!" she recognized cheerfully.

"Yes. Goethe. Reading him isn't enough; we must also apply his ideas."

Anna felt awkward. Every time she had a crisis, her father, instead of encouraging her to face her problems, told her to run away from them. He asked her to stay home from school when she was upset, he told her to forget her friends when they disappointed her and to leave when an environment disturbed her. He was overprotective. He wanted to compensate for her mother's absence, but his protection was unhealthy, it nourished the young woman's weaknesses, destroying her self-esteem.

Marco Polo's words made her realize that she had always made the worst choice: hiding. Noticing her introspection, he added:

"Turn your back to your problems or they will become the predators and you will become the prey. Turn this relationship around. Remember the poem, 'Don't be afraid of life; be afraid of not living. Don't be afraid of falling; be afraid of not walking.' You are a brave person; you've already begun to fight in class," he said, teasing her. He ended his arguments by saying, "no one is worthy of being emotionally secure if they don't use their weaknesses to achieve it."

Anna suddenly sat up and said: "Wait for me outside."

Surprised, he left.

She combed her hair, put on some makeup, put on a beautiful light-blue dress with a V neck. After an extremely long half an hour, she came out. Marco Polo could not believe what he saw. He was dumbfounded. She looked beautiful, charming and sensual. He asked, curious:

"Are you going to a party?"

"Life is a party!" she said cheerfully.

From that moment on, Anna took a huge leap towards her freedom. She was forever changed. She would still go through difficult times, many times she would cry and was sometimes depressed, but she never submitted to her inner prison. She learned how to turn her low moments and her failures into opportunities to grow. She decided to face life openly.

Marco Polo took her by the arm to leave. As they were opening the door, Carlos called out: "Doctor…! Doctor…!"

To Anna's amazement, he quickly put on his fake goatee, the dark glasses and disheveled his hair.

"Yes, Carlos!"

"I have a terrible case of diarrhea doctor!" he said, looking very pale.

"That's excellent news! You are eliminating all of your worms."

"What worms?"

"*Proudus lumbricoides*. Your head…, I mean…, your intestines are full of *Proudus lumbricoides*."

Anna was laughing uncontrollably.

"Is it serious, doctor?" The butler asked rubbing his belly and ready to head back to the bathroom again.

"No! Drink lots of fluids. Sit humbly on the toilet, concentrate and you will see that your worms will soon leave you."

They left and Carlos felt very happy. As they left the house, Marco Polo said:

"Someday I'll have to explain myself to Carlos and apologize."

"Don't worry. The staff detests him. I wish Carlos' *Proudus* would actually be eliminated." The evening was just beginning with the promise of being one of the most enchanting ones. Always repressing her behavior, Anna had never run on the street or played hide-and- seek in public.

Marco Polo insisted on breaking her routine. He wanted to liberate her spontaneity; free the child hidden within her and that had never been able to breathe. They raced each other and played like teenagers in the middle of the crowd. She got caught up in the moment and no longer minded the looks from the passersby. It was her story, all hers, she had to live it intensely.

He did not have a camera, but pretending to take pictures of her, asked her to pose for him. He clicked away with his imaginary camera. People bumped into one another watching them have fun. She ran into Marco Polo's arms and he twirled with her. Anna then understood that true freedom comes from within...

Chapter 24

The relationship between Marco Polo and Lucius Fernandez was bearable at most. The millionaire avoided any contact. He hoped that the relationship with his daughter would not go forward. He even took some measures to force Anna to break off the romance. He shouted, pressured and blackmailed to no success. The romance continued. However, Lucius Fernandez did not give up.

The relationship between Marco Polo and Anna gradually strengthened, and became too solid to be shaken by manipulations. It was woven with happiness, joy, long conversations and behaviors that were not commonplace.

After a few months, Anna had reedited a significant part of the conflicts archived in her unconscious. She had gradually stopped living the pain of others and excessively expecting anything in return from them. She became good-humored, stable, protected, resolute and capable of fighting for her dreams. Social conviviality was no longer a source of fear and frustration. Thus, she felt confident enough to interrupt the use of antidepressants.

Anna graduated in psychology and began to work as an intern at a large cardiology hospital, whose director was one of her father's friends. Anna and the other psychologists attended patients who had undergone heart surgery, and especially the candidates for a heart transplant.

Marco Polo frequently surprised her with a gesture, a compliment or an unexpected attitude. Sometimes, he'd bring her flowers and gave them to her in the hospital hallway. He would kiss her, say a few words to her and leave. He would transform a minute into eternal affection. To them, small gestures had a great impact.

Once, early in her internship, a few of Anna's colleagues saw Marco Polo expressing his love for her while holding a red rose in his hand. They were surprised with his attitude because they thought this kind of romantic gesture had been lost in modern times. One of her friends, feeling jealous, rudely said: "Your boyfriend is a little strange. He doesn't seem very normal."

"It's impossible to be normal when you're in love", Anna replied.

A nurse who had relationships issues and always got involved with authoritarian and dominating men, asked, "Isn't giving flowers so early in the day something a neurotic person would do?"

"I don't know. But I know that he takes care of many..." They did not understand what she meant.

"Don't you know who Anna's boyfriend is?" asked a psychologist who knew him.

"No!"

"He's the famous Marco Polo. Perhaps the most intelligent person I've ever met."

They walked into the immense building in silence. They didn't understand that intelligence and professional success could and should be combined with sensitivity and lightness.

Anna became dear to all during her first few weeks at the cardiology hospital. She had learned with Marco Polo to cheerfully greet the employees, especially the lowly ones, to joke with the patients and to fearlessly enter the epicenter of their insecurity. She learned how to be a seller of dreams and hope in an environment where the possibility of death contaminated people.

The couple went out very often and every date was special, but one of them was unforgettable. One evening, Marco Polo said that he intended to give her a special present. He left town and took her to the countryside. He stopped the car and asked her to get out.

He took her hands and they walked down the road. While they walked, he called Anna's attention to the harmony of nature.

"Every day the flowers exhale perfume, the breeze touches the leaves, the clouds float obscurely but we never pay attention to them. Listen to the serenade of crickets! It's a magnificent endless concert."

Observing his simple manner of looking at life, she asked, "What is happiness to you?". Surprising her, he frightened her by saying, "Happiness doesn't exist Anna…"

Apprehensive, she suddenly asked, "You frighten me! What hope do those who live in emotional misery have? What can I expect from life if I had so much exterior wealth but so little inside me?"

Marco Polo added, "Happiness doesn't exist in a readymade form, it's not inherited genetically, it's not the privilege of a social class. Happiness is an eternal construction". Letting out a sigh of relief, she asked, "How is it built?"

Like a storyteller who dwells in psychology, he looked her in the eyes and said: "Kings tried to capture happiness with their power, but it didn't allow itself to be captured.

Millionaires tried to buy it, but it wasn't for sale. Celebrities tried to seduce it, but it resisted stardom. Smiling, happiness whispered into the ear of each human being: 'Hey! Look for me within disappointments and difficulties and especially, find me within the anonymous things of existence'. But most people did not hear her voice and those who did, gave little credit to it."

"That's beautiful! Tell me more about what happiness is, my unpredictable poet." "Happiness is being able to say, 'I was wrong', it is having the sensitivity to say, 'I need you', it is having the boldness to say, 'I love you'".

Remembering her father, she said sorrowfully, "Many parents die without ever having the courage to say these words to their children. They forget the anonymous things." "That's true. We trip over small pebbles and not over big mountains."

Looking at him with tender love, she told him about a few real fears, which weren't the fruit of her illness. Since she loved poetry, she also used her inspiration. "Thank you for existing. But I'm afraid that our love will evaporate like the dew in the heat of the sun." "Sometimes I will disappoint you; other times, you will frustrate me, but if we have enough courage to recognize our mistakes, ability to dream together and the capacity to cry and restart as many times as we have to, then our love will be immortal."

"I love you like I've never loved anyone else!" she said, trying to move closer to kiss him. Marco Polo suddenly took a step back and raised the tone of his voice. "Now wait just a minute, young lady! You subtly entered into my life, occupied it and without even asking, invaded my heart. Therefore..." (He took a long pause).

"Come on! I'm anxious."

"Will you marry me, princess?" he asked her with a smile and lowering his head in reverence.

They kissed each other. Two worlds, two stories, finally crossed their paths. Lovingly, he covered her eyes, her forehead and her chin with small kisses.

He then wanted to give her something powerful, unique and unforgettable that would mark that moment. Something that would be capable of symbolizing everything he felt for her and also reveal the kind of man she had found. An unusual man had to give her an unusual gift.

The sky was clear and there was a quarter moon out. Opening his arms he asked her, "Anna, look at the sky. Observe the incomprehensible theater of the universe. What do you see?"

"I see beautiful stars." She replied feeling curious.

"Pick one."

She smiled. There were thousands of stars invading the pupil of her eyes. Anna chose a brilliant star towards the left side of the firmament. "I choose that one." She said pointing to it.

"From now on, this star will be yours. Even when your sky is overcast with storms, this star will be shinning within you, showing the paths you should follow and revealing my love for you."

Anna was walking on clouds. She had already gotten expensive presents, an emerald necklace, diamond rings, brand new cars, stock shares and apartments, but she would never forget that she had gotten a star. She clearly realized that the most important things in life cannot be bought. She was extremely wealthy but she had always lived in misery.

She kept the significance of the star that Marco Polo had given her hidden within. Those who have a star inside of them do not need the sunlight to guide them.

Marco Polo had the depth of a thinker and the sensitivity of a child. He didn't know it, but he would also need an internal star. His ideas would reach the whole world. He would fight for human rights, disturb environments and societies, he would go through valleys and plateaus and the skies would come tumbling down over him. To survive, he would need to see with the eyes of the heart.

Chapter 25

Anna told her father that she intended to marry Marco Polo. Lucius tried everything to stop her. He tried to get her to fall in love with someone of the same social and financial class as theirs but to no avail. "Imagine a psychiatrist in my family, watching my every step. I will not stand it. I need someone who will multiply my wealth and not keep pointing out my problems.", he thought.

He tried to entice her once again, "Honey, it's not because of the money, but there are sons of bankers and businessmen who are fascinated with you. They come from the same background as we do. You won't feel out of place. Give them a chance."

"I've dated a few of them and my emptiness only increased." "What emptiness? What's so special about this one?"

"Marco Polo truly loves me! Besides, he loves human beings, he cares about mankind."

"Don't be naïve, honey! People only care about their own pockets."

"Too bad you feel that way, father. Those who live for themselves can only see ulterior intentions in others."

He grumbled but before he could reply, she asked him, "Have you ever been in love with anyone?" Lucius faltered. He had never had an affectionate explosion, not even for Anna's mother. Lately, he was only seen with women much younger than himself, some of them were even famous, but he did not love anyone. Increasing his great fortune was the only thing that drove his emotions. Hesitating he answered, "Well, I don't know. I think I have." "Those who love don't think they have loved. Love is the only certainty of existence, father. If you've never loved someone, not even my mother, then you will never understand how I feel."

Lucius left feeling awkward. Anna really was a changed woman. He had lost his control over her. Days later, he tried again. He said he was buying a house in England and that he had managed to get her a job at an excellent hospital there. It was a great opportunity for her to get her doctorate at Cambridge.

"You don't have to end your romance with Marco Polo." He said cunningly. "It will be good for your own future if you continue your studies and be better prepared professionally."

She did not accept it. "Father, I've waited all my life for you to really care about me and that we could talk about our lives."

"I work for you, honey. I've done everything I can in order to make you happy. I give you the best clothes. You travel twice a year overseas, first-class. Your international credit card limit is of $ 100.000,00. And who at your age has a convertible Mercedes in the garage and a driver at your beck and call?"

"You've given me many things, father, but you forgot the most important thing."

"What is it?" (He was outraged).

"You forgot to give me you. I know nothing about your dreams, your fears or your tears. We are two strangers living in the same house" - she said with tears in her eyes.

Shaken, he tried to avoid the emotional scene. "Sweetheart, you are the queen of this house."

"What's the use of being a queen imprisoned inside a palace, watched by guards and with a father who lives to work?"

Lucius was silent. He did not know how to reply to these truths. Then, Anna touched a subject that she had never talked about with her father.

"Father, we've never talked about mom. Those who don't talk about their past, never truly bury it and keep their wounds alive. Mother's death is an open grave in our hearts. You've never had the courage to talk to me about her illness and the causes that made her take her own life."

Lucius was paralyzed and could not react. He could not organize his ideas. This subject was taboo. In Fernandez' house, even the maids were forbidden to talk about it. The bedroom where the couple had slept in had been locked up and, once a week was opened to be cleaned. Lucius had thought about moving, but his palace was beautiful, a unique mansion, despite its sadness. He settled for changing bedrooms.

Since her father did not say anything, Anna, remembering the fatal question that Marco Polo had asked her about her mother, made the same fatal question to her impenetrable father. She wished to help him. "Do you feel guilty about my mother's death, father?"

"Guilty? Me? That's absurd. Don't accuse me!"

"I'm not accusing you, father, I'm only asking. I need you to take a look into yourself. Don't be afraid."

Lucius' sudden and eloquent reactions indicated that the question had touched the dungeons of his mind. Desperately trying to avoid contact with the mirror of his soul, he looked at his watch and said: "I have an important meeting. I have to go."

Realizing that he had entered the unknown terrain of his own sensitivity, she insisted, "Wait! Father, even great men cry…"

His eyes filled with tears, something rare for someone who had never allowed himself the sweet and relieving experience of crying. He suffered a lot, he had insomnia and periods of anguish, but he denied the pain. His tears had always been buried under his rude behavior.

When he realized that they had secretly appeared and came onto the stage of his eyes, he quickly tried to conceal them. He would not admit a spectator contemplating his frailty, because only glory could be admired. The iceberg of his emotions was melting, but before the feeling was able to irrigate his intelligence with affection, he avoided it. "We'll talk later about great men..." and he hurried out without showing his face and without giving his daughter a chance to continue the conversation.

Lucius Fernandez avoided all conversations and situations related to internalizations, he did not allow himself to grow. He had never recognized a mistake; he had never apologized or asked for emotional help. He was a sick man who contributed to form sick people.

He had certain respectable characteristics as long as the subject was numbers and money. He was enterprising, bold and shrewd. He knew how to invest in new projects and had a knack for knowing which way the world economy was headed, but he had no idea of where his quality of life was headed.

Lucius was the major shareholder of eight companies. Together, they employed eleven thousand people. Among his companies there were a bank, a computer manufacturer, an orange juice plant and more recently a pharmaceutical lab. He also invested in the stock market; he bought shares from high tech companies, which had become the global market's rising stars. He was almost always right.

He was listed in Great Fortunes magazine as the 83rd richest man on the planet. He was the 42nd one in his country. His fortune was estimated to be more than four billion dollars. Every year, Lucius' greatest pleasure was to improve his rating on both lists. The power and prestige generated by those lists became his drug. He obsessively thought about them yearround.

Marco Polo had no idea of how wealthy his future father-in-law was. Anna did not know that either, for she did not care about money. They had never mentioned Lucius' fortune.

Because he stood on park benches and recited poetry, having an emotional explosion with the simple things, taking care of those with wounded souls, breaking paradigms and confronting prejudice, Marco Polo felt that Lucius' money could be a problem for Anna and him. He only wished to be wealthy on the inside. He rejected being standardized by the social system.

He wished to transform his story into a unique and exultant experience, in which every day would be a new day. He wanted to include Anna in this existential project, but he was worried about the difficulties she would have to go through by his side. And he was right. So he asked her: "Anna, human suffering disturbs me. One day, I'm going to abandon my practice and dedicate myself to the great social themes. Since my first year in medical school, I have been driven by this desire. Living with me might be very unstable. I fear for you. With your father you run no risks."

"But there will be no adventure!"

"But with him you'll be protected."

"But I won't have inner peace."

"With him you'll have a better standard of living."

"But I'll have no comfort."

The young man was pensive. And before he could say anything else, she added: "Marco Polo, sometimes I think that I know you very little, but the little I know gives me the certainty that you are the one I choose. I feel that being by your side, my tomorrows will be unpredictable. But tomorrows don't exist." She said with a smile.

They kissed. And as she separated her lips from his, she tilted her head and teased, "But please, break our routine a little less and create fewer problems."

"I can't.", he said cheerfully. And he couldn't.

A week later, Anna and Marco Polo came to see the powerful Lucius to set their wedding date. Trouble was inevitable. "You're being precipitated. You should wait a while longer.", her father said.

"There's no reason to wait, we love each other." - Marco Polo insisted.

So, indelicately, Lucius said: "Love! Love is a disguised self-interest."

"Father, please don't talk like that! I love Marco Polo!"

Since there was no way of stopping the marriage, Lucius tried to radically block any attempt by Marco Polo to gain access to his fortune. "I'll only accept this marriage if you sign a pre-nuptial agreement."

Indignant, Anna replied, "I'm the one who decides this father!"

Intrepid, Marco Polo interfered by saying, "Well, I'll only marry your daughter if I get your entire fortune!"

Anna was astonished. Lucius stood feeling angry at his petulance. He shouted, "You see, Anna? I told you that this young man was ambitious. Now he's showing his true self! Get out while there's still time!" Then, he looked at Marco Polo and added, "You will never touch my fortune. I have a battalion of lawyers who have their eye on you."

Anna was shocked with the direction the conversation was heading. Marco Polo stood and confirmed, "Yes! I am ambitious. I will only get married if I can take your entire fortune because to me, your only fortune is Anna. The rest is worthless. I don't want a cent from you."

Anna was dazzled. She had never been given so much value. Her unreasonable father had fallen from the pinnacle of his pride. Their wedding was set for three months from then. They planned to have a public civil ceremony and later a private religious wedding. The religious service would be ecumenical and only for a few friends, especially God's friend, Falcon.

Marco Polo's parents, Rudolph and Elisabeth, lived in a neighboring state and were happy with their son's marriage. Rudolph was always in financial difficulties. He was a shop owner who liked to help people but he was unable to collect what they owed him. He was sociable, affectionate, good-humored and enjoyed having long talks with his friends.

Elisabeth came from a wealthy family. Her grandparents had been landowners and owned vast extensions of land. Her parents had lived luxuriously. They'd had the best cars, the best houses and the most beautiful clothes. Elisabeth had lived a regal life in her youth. But her parents, as well as her relatives, had squandered their inheritance. The money was gone, along with the jewels, but the affectation remained. She was a quiet woman, with constrained gestures and few friends. Despite her ambition, she was a strong hard-working woman.

Marco Polo's parents didn't have the means to contribute to the wedding party. Lucius Fernandez stepped in. He said that he insisted on throwing a huge party for Anna. The young couple refused the luxury. Lucius then said that it would be a simple affair to match the lifestyle of the newlyweds. He lied. He secretly hired the best catering service in town. He hired the hall of the most magnificent five-star hotel, which he partly owned and had it richly decorated.

The party was not for the bride, it was for her father. Under Carlos' supervision, and the help of a dozen employees from Lucius' companies, not only did they prepare the party in secret, but also organized the enormous guest list. Most of the guests had no affinity with Anna.

Lucius invited important businessmen, celebrities, congressmen, senators, the state governor, secretaries of state and the president. The billionaire was an influential man.

He spent more than half a million dollars on the event, a small sum for such a rich man. What was to be a simple affair had become the greatest event of the year. Magazine and newspaper columnists were invited to cover the event. Busy with their intense work schedule, Marco Polo and Anna were oblivious to the wedding preparations. Carlos and his team were highly efficient.

The magnitude of the party wasn't only to satisfy Lucius' ego or to display his megalomania by using his financial power to enchant people. He truly wished to treasure his daughter. He loved her in his own way. Besides, he was trying to diminish the enormous debt he carried in his conscience. During rare moments of lucidity, he tormented himself with the idea of having abandoned the two women of his life: his wife and daughter.

He wanted to compensate Anna for the mistakes he had made and for her depressing past. Since he hadn't learned the language of emotion, he used the only language he knew, the language of money. He thought that a memorable party might redeem him.

Chapter 26

The wedding day had finally arrived. Marco Polo showed up at the hall an hour before Anna and was amazed at the presence of so many strange people. He was surprised and thought he had come to the wrong place. There were five security guards dressed in uniform identifying the guests and checking the list.

Carlos had told the guards that there was an official list, made by Lucius, and another list with the names of a few other guests invited by Marco Polo and Anna, who would be the only ones required to show their invitation and be identified. The guards thought it was strange that there were two lists, but orders are orders. Marco Polo identified himself and was recognized by name. "Congratulations on the grand party!" the guards said.

The young man nodded thanking them and went inside. The shiny chandeliers, the Persian carpets spread all over the floor, the dozens of flower bouquets distributed throughout multiple places invaded his eyes. There were more than 250 tables, all of them richly decorated with French crystal glasses. The best wines would be served. Lucius' parties were famous; he went to extreme lengths to please his guests. But this one was unique.

The psychiatrist who was a thinker, a poet, abnegated and who had a heart of a wanderer was embarrassed. Marco Polo could not believe his eyes. What astonished him the most were all the strangers who had been invited. There were more than 700 guests and he knew less than 10% of them. He greeted everyone with a nod but no one greeted him back. They did not know him and did not know he was the groom. They were not there because of him. There were more than 60 waiters frenetically serving the guests. A team of 30 security guards, dressed in dark-blue suits, walked around the room.

When he saw Lucius, he preferred silence to words. He knew that any criticism would result in an argument, which would ruin the sublime moment. He merely thought, "This man really doesn't like me!" He knew Anna was oblivious of what her father had done.

Lucius personally greeted some of the special guests and took Marco Polo with him.

He allowed himself to be led.

"Mr. Governor, first lady. This is your party." He said radiantly.

"Oh, this is my future son-in-law." Lucius introduced him without much spontaneity.

Thus, both greeted close to twenty prominent people, among them were wealthy industrial barons and bankers who were also listed in the great fortune list. There was a respect among the businessmen and an apparent scorn for this classification, but deep down, several were seduced by it. Envy and competition corroded the soul of many.

It occurred to Marco Polo that the wedding guests' fortunes added up came to one hundred and fifty billion dollars, more than the GNP of the thirty poorest countries in the world, including the African sub-Saharan countries, whose population surpassed three hundred and fifty million. But no one was worried about the misery of others. All that mattered was the party.

Marco Polo, who had learned how to think with a beggar and had lived among the poor, was now among multimillionaires. The party, which should have been a source of joy, would become a source of concern. However, he had always said that there are no rich or poor, famous or anonymous people; we are all human beings with similar internal needs.

He collected himself after he remembered this. A thought came to his mind and he calmed his restless emotions, "It's not the atmosphere that makes my mood, my mood makes the atmosphere. I'll be happy." He preferred to relax. Anna deserved it.

The police commissioner, Mr. Cleber, was also present. Since he was a personal friend of Lucius', he did him a favor and had a police battalion cover the area and had fifty members of the hostage elite division disguised as guests. The goal was to protect the important businessmen and politicians from possible attacks.

Marco Polo tried in vain to find his friends: they were scattered among the crowd of strangers. His mother was ecstatic, euphoric with the luxury of the party. It was everything she had dreamt for her son. She recalled the glorious times of a wealthy life.

There was a piano and a string quartet that made the atmosphere festive. The judge was anxious to begin the ceremony. He was astonished with the party's magnificence; he had never opened his mouth to speak to such illustrious people. Anna was finishing getting ready.

Suddenly, there was a commotion at the door. A few security guards had barred about fifteen people from getting in. They were badly dressed and behaved bizarrely, with quirks and involuntary head movements. Some of them hadn't brought any ID or an invitation and said they had forgotten to. But even those who had an invitation had been barred from the party. The guards imagined, "I can't believe that a millionaire would mix with such people."

The group began to shout insisting on getting in, creating a commotion at the entrance and getting in the way of the noble guests who were still arriving. Some of them asked the guards, "What are these people doing at Lucius' party?"

"We don't know sir, but we are throwing them out."

The group tried to force their way in, but the guards, more and more aggressively, pushed them back outside. The head of security, hired by Lucius, went over to see what was happening. Informed of the situation, he observed the mutineers and whispered to the other guards, "These people are definitely trying to crash this party. We will lose our jobs if we let them in. We can't disturb the authorities and the financial elite. Send them away, but avoid scandals."

The group resisted and the turmoil increased. Lucius was informed about the confusion and was visibly disturbed. He talked to the police commissioner, who sent his special security to investigate imagining that criminals might be present.

When Mr. Cleber got there, the head of security told him, "These people seem to have come from a mental hospital. They say that they are friends of the host. How is this possible?"

Observing them, the police commissioner said in a low voice, "Be careful! They might be terrorists or kidnappers in disguise!"

Next, with a glance, he signaled the anti-terrorism squad to move into action. The strongly built police officers took James, Ali Ramadan, Vidigal, Romero, Claudia, Sara, Mary and the kind and elderly Mr. Bonny by their fragile arms and began to frisk them and take them outside.

They had come to the party because Marco Polo had made them feel like human beings, unique stars on the stage of life, even if it was on a stage without an audience. They had to thank their wise and dear friend. Now they were being treated like social garbage again.

Isaac had brought them. Isaac was wealthier than many of the guests at the party. He got dressed in such a simple manner that he didn't appear to have a company with 900 employees. Isaac had broadened the horizons of his existential views. He had no need for ostentation.

His illness had weakened him but it hadn't eliminated his daring, his drive and his creativity. He had become a businessman who only saw meaning in walking the grounds of capitalism and conquering greater financial space if they were contributing towards the wellbeing of his employees and society in general. He had always legally employed Chinese, Arabic, Indian and Latin immigrants. He knew, from his own experience, what it was like to experience the loneliness of living in a strange land. After he overcame his mental illness, he also began to hire employees who had been released from psychiatric hospitals. He created his own social inclusion. His employees loved him.

Since Claudia did not have money to afford a new outfit, she chose a long red gown and a black jacket. Her clothes were over twenty years old and were the best she had. Her clothes did not match and they contrasted with the luxury of the other women's gowns.

Claudia felt that it was more important to feel comfortable on the inside and to show Marco Polo that, through him, she had learned how to rescue her meaning of life and to be useful for society. She also didn't have the means to buy him a gift but she wanted to turn her presence into an unforgettable gift.

Everyone noticed the group. Normally, patients who have depression, panic syndrome and other emotional disorders go unnoticed to the eyes of society, but Marco Polo's friends suffered from serious and chronic emotional disorders. Some of them frequently rubbed their hands over their face and chest. Others, such as James, had side effects because of the medication they had taken over the years. They had repetitive muscle spasms, which were similar to Parkinson's disease. To those filled with prejudice, it wasn't a pretty sight.

Some of the guests looked at them in disgust. They didn't look like they belonged to the world of the mortals. Sarah delicately said to one of them, "I don't bite, madam! I'm a person too."

In the midst of this confusion, the wife of an important senator looked with disgust and amazement at Claudia who looked at her as if she knew her. "Didn't you take dance lessons with me when you were a child?"

Disturbed, the woman exclaimed, "Miss Claudia?" "Yes. It's me."

"It's so good to see you again." She said hurrying away.

The police officers were losing their patience. Since pushing did no good, they began to drag them. Some said: "Get out or you will be arrested!"

Others added: "Don't disturb, you party crashers! This party is not for you."

Fragile, because of their psychiatric disease and the prolonged usage of medication, some of them began to stumble and cry. James suddenly shouted, "Marco Polo! Marco Polo!" His friends joined in the chant.

The din echoed into the ballroom. Marco Polo, who had been unaware of the commotion, was startled. He recognized those voices. He headed quickly towards the entrance. He had invited his friends and had hoped they would come but he knew that some of them sought isolation; they didn't like to be in strange social environments because they noticed the discriminatory glances. Ignoring the risks, they had gone to the party to show their gesture of love.

Suddenly, Ali Ramadan was violently pushed and he fell. His expression of pain and his tears made Isaac break free from the guards that held him to rescue his friend. They were not Palestinian and Jewish, they were two human beings helping each other. Isaac carefully helped his friend up and asked a police officer, "Who do you think you are, you brute?"

The guards and police officers did not like his attitude and also pushed him violently. Chaos took over. Meanwhile, Marco Polo arrived and demanded, "Stop it! Stop it!"

Seeing the groom, the guards and police officers calmed down. To the amazement of all, the groom exclaimed, "Claudia, my dear, it's so good to see you! James, you came, what a pleasure! Isaac, Ali, my dear friends!" And he hugged them and kissed their faces and foreheads.

Mr. Bonny timidly said: "Marco Polo, they wouldn't let us into the party!"

"What do you mean, Mr. Bonny? You are the most expected guests of the party, at least to Anna and me".

The police commissioner was perplexed. Many years ago, when he was only a detective, he had had the same feeling with a young man dressed as a beggar who had showed up at his precinct.

Suddenly, Marco Polo's eyes met the police commissioner's. Marco Polo was holding Claudia but he said: "Big brain! What are you doing here?"

The police commissioner was astonished, "It's that beggar, but now he's dressed as the groom! This is impossible!"

"Are you still a police chief?" "Now, I'm the police commissioner and a friend of your father-in-law." He said proudly. And added: "I've come a long way in my career. And you helped me. I've never forgotten that you said that my brain was big."

Marco Polo gasped. He thought again about the power of praise, which is capable of stimulating people's self-confidence. At the same time, he reflected on how the power of rejection, even when kidding without any intention to harm, can cause damage to the personality of others. "I'm glad that the detective never discovered that I jokingly decreased the number of his neurons.", he thought.

Marco Polo was concerned with the prejudice his friends had suffered at the entrance of the hall. Such a rejection might pulverize their self-esteem. He needed to repair this injustice. The police commissioner was scratching his head and observing them. "Congratulations, commissioner! You have really come a long way."

"Congratulations to both of us! Life is ironic. Now you are the center of attentions and I am at the center of your party's security."

Marco Polo then remedied the misunderstanding. Just to leave no doubt, he proclaimed in a loud voice so everyone could hear, "These people are my special guests! They are some of my best friends!"

Some of the guests were shocked. They told one another that they had come to the wrong party. On the other side, Marco Polo's friends proudly fixed up their outfits while they looked at the security guards with airs of grandeur. Ali Ramadan approached Marco Polo and asked, "Do extraterrestrials exist?"

Afraid that Ali's hallucinations were back, he repeated the old phrase, "I don't know.

But I do know that we create monsters within us."

"Look at all the aliens around us." He said pointing to the security guards with his chin. Marco Polo smiled. "They are strange, but deep down they're good people, Ali."

Claudia patted the face of one of the guards and with the naivety of a child she said: "Hey, handsome, this is our party!"

Anna knew most of Marco Polo's friends. She appreciated their simplicity, innocence and creativity. She would certainly be pleased to see them there.

Before they went into the huge ballroom, two famous movie actresses, Lucius' friends, arrived followed by a few reporters. One of them tripped on Sarah and fell. Sarah also lost her balance and was helped by Claudia. Irritated with both of them, the actress sneered at them and was startled by the bizarre gestures they made with their arms and head. She called security and asked, "Who are these strange people at Lucius' party?"

Seeing his friends were feeling humiliated again, Marco Polo told the actress, "Of all the garbage produced by society, the idolatry of celebrities is the stupidest."

Shaken by the stranger's nerve, the actress spit out, "Who do you think you are to talk to me like that? Don't you know that I'm a famous artist?"

"They are also actresses in the theater of existence. They have even received an Oscar for the drama they played!" Marco Polo replied while pointing to Sarah and Claudia. "Wow! But I don't even know them!" she said admiringly.

"Well, you should. They are fascinating."

Claudia and Sarah got into the game and told the actresses, "We'll give you autographs later, honey!"

And taking them by the arm, Marco Polo led them into the ballroom along with the rest of his friends. As they walked down the aisle where Anna would come in, the guests were paralyzed and a dead silence ensued. The musicians stopped playing. The unusual gestures and the involuntary movements of those people were shocking in the eyes of the illustrious guests. They weren't used to living with different people.

Claudia, holding Marco Polo, looked around and made faces to the guests. Romero was embarrassed and hung his head low but Vidigal, very loose, greeted all the guests. James was a little embarrassed, but he soon loosened up and kissed several flowers along the way. Ali Ramadan entered in solemn pomp. Holding a handkerchief in his right hand, twirling it over his head, he danced to Arabic music while he entered the ballroom. He was a happy Palestinian. Isaac was smiling. He owed nothing to anyone and demanded nothing for his well-being. Facing that pressure was nothing compared to the pressures he had faced.

Marco Polo observed, from a distance, a man who not only discriminated his friends but also was astonished to see him. He seemed to be trying to swallow him with his eyes. He mumbled, "Idiot!"

When he realized what the man had said, Marco Polo was perplexed. He couldn't believe that a guest would offend him at his own wedding. He thought he had imagined it, after all, it had become a stressful evening.

As they moved forward, the guests looked at one another trying to understand what was going on. Some of them, in a mocking tone said: "Lucius has prepared a circus show for us."

In reality, when Lucius saw the scene, he became furious. He wanted to be anywhere else in the world except there. "What a disgrace! What will everyone think of me?" he said to himself with a knot in his throat.

Before Marco Polo's friends sat down, Lucius was called because the bride had arrived. As the father, he would walk her down the aisle. He was in shock and he did not even look at any of the guests' faces when he left.

A few psychiatrists were also perplexed. They had never seen psychotic patients at a psychiatrist's party.

Before sitting down, James took a long look at the crowd. He saw tense and worried men and women, with rigid postures, dosing their behavior and without any manifestation of joy at the phenomenal party. Admiring his own power of observation, he tugged at the groom's arm and said: "Marco Polo. What a str...stran...strange group of people!" Analyzing his friend's comment, he had to agree, "They really are strange, James!"

Chapter 27

Anna arrived at the party. Just like Marco Polo, she also felt tense when she saw all the security. When she entered the ballroom, she was astounded. Trying to be discreet she asked in a low voice, "Father, what does all this mean?"

"You deserve it, honey. We deserve it."

She saw her loved one from afar. He gestured to calm her down as if he was saying, "What can we do about it? Just relax!"

The string quartet began to play the wedding march. It sounded so heavenly that the music seemed to run through every artery of the guests' body and penetrated the fabric of their soul.

The white silk gown, with some lace, covered Anna's body in a sensual way. It was a simple but dazzling gown. Because she was so beautiful on the inside, it was Anna who made her clothes shine and not the other way around.

Her wavy hair with golden strands flowed over her shoulders like waves on the beach. She was not wearing a veil; she was only carrying a small bouquet of white lilies in her right hand. It was her favorite flower, born in the marsh where she had once been.

Her friends from the Atlantic Hospital began to applaud her and whistle when they saw her, expressing their joy. No one joined in, only Marco Polo.

The ballroom was over eighty yards in length. While Anna and her father walked slowly, the guests, feeling emotional, greeted them with gestures and looks. Lucius felt like a king. For a few minutes he forgot the initial commotion. He thanked everyone with a nod. While he walked, he rescued images from Anna's past. His little girl had grown and had become a charming person.

As they approached Marco Polo, the protocol was broken more than once. James and Claudia, who knew Anna, unable to contain their joy, stood and went over to meet her. Lucius frowned. He only kept from offending them because the moment required discretion. Several other guests also condemned their attitude and said amongst themselves, "What an uncultured and tacky group of people."

Anna humbly hugged them without any embarrassment and kissed them, lightly smudging her makeup. One of the richest young women in the world had become enriched with fortunes that many of those who were there were in need of: naturalness and simplicity. Her gestures were a tribute in Marco Polo's eyes. Extremely happy Anna added, "Claudia, you look magnificent! James, you look so handsome!"

Ali Ramadan shouted, "Such a flower! Such a flower! May Allah bless you!" Isaac, in the same fashion, cried out, "May the God of Israel be your staff and your strength!"

Embarrassed, Lucius looked around to see the guests' reaction. In a cold sweat, he handed his daughter to the groom. He tried to move a little away from them. He didn't want to be photographed standing next to those strange people; he did not wish to be the object of mockery on the social columns.

While the judge began the ceremony, one of Lucius' guests discretely approached him and gave him some terrible news, which almost made him faint. He had been the one who had mumbled "idiot" to Marco Polo.

"Guess who the psychiatrist that exposed the side effects of Venthax is?" he said like a predator before his prey.

"The fool who made me lose one hundred million dollars in the stock market last month?" Lucius asked.

"Precisely!"

"Don't tell me that my idiotic son-in-law had the nerve to invite him? Which one is the culprit?"

"It's your own son-in-law," said the psychiatrist. And he sarcastically added, "With an inlaw like that, you don't need enemies."

"What are you saying, Dr. Wilson?" he blurted out visibly shaken.

Six months prior to the debate between Marco Polo and Dr. Paul at the psychiatry convention, Lucius had purchased 60% of the shares belonging to the laboratory that had synthesized Venthax. He already owned the company when Dr. Paul was bribed. The company promised to be a gold mine if the new drug was widely accepted by the doctors.

Marco Polo had begun to use it soon after the convention and noticed important side effects on his patients. Since he had been challenged by Dr. Paul Mello, he decided to research these side effects further. The results had been published in one of his first articles. The article had come out a month ago in a scientific magazine and had quickly gained international notice in magazines and especially on newspapers and TV shows. Lucius had cursed the article, but he had never imagined that Marco Polo was its author. Lucius obsessively repeated, "Every medication has side effects. This is persecution!" His stock had dropped 15% and was still plummeting. It was an economical disaster.

Digesting the facts that Dr. Wilson had reported, Lucius became pale, with tachycardia, breathing heavily and had cold sweats. It appeared as if he was in some kind of great danger. Marco Polo was the danger. His dislike for him turned into pure hatred.

He immediately had a guard call the police commissioner. He breathlessly told him, "We need to stop this marriage immediately!"

"Are you crazy, Lucius?" "No, but I will be."

"What's going on?"

"I just found out that my future son-in-law is my worst enemy."

"You can't be serious. He's a good person." said the distressed police commissioner.

"A good person?! This man has made me lose a hundred million dollars in a month!" The police commissioner was blown away. He could not believe what he was hearing. He had never heard such a serious accusation. The party, already filled with disturbances, turned into a warzone. During all this, the judge continued the ceremony.

"What has your son-in-law done? Has he stolen from you?"

"That's pretty much the same thing. He destroyed the image of one of my greatest companies, Montex Laboratories. I'll lose my rank on the list!" he said, unable to let it go. "What list?"

"Forget it."

Dr. Wilson explained it to the police commissioner, "The young psychiatrist told the press about the side effects of one of our most important drugs."

"Did he know that the laboratory belonged to his father-in-law?" the police commissioner asked.

Unsure of the facts, Dr. Wilson replied, "Of course he knew!"

When Lucius heard that, his breathlessness increased and he felt vertigo. The guests who were sitting closer to him were touched by the scene. They thought that he was emotional because his only daughter was getting married.

"He must be feeling lonely now that Anna will be gone and joy for seeing her turning into a woman." they imagined. They thought that he was remembering how his little girl had run around and played and now, was facing the challenges of life.

A sensitive congressman approached him to console him. "I understand, Lucius. One of my daughters is married. Relax, now you have a son."

When Lucius heard that, he felt a sudden tremor. He wanted to swallow the congressman or, at least, shout at him. His two friends contained him. The congressman had no idea of what was going on. Filled with compassion, he went back to his seat.

"A son!? I'm lost! End this wedding before it begins! Anna will understand after I expose him!" cried Lucius.

"Take it easy, Lucius!" said the police commissioner.

"Take it easy? Did you take it easy when you needed fifty thousand dollars? This guy can ruin me!"

Lucius Fernandez, like many of his friends, was not prepared to be a billionaire. He revolved around money instead of making money revolve around him. Before he became rich, he was more relaxed, serene, sociable and carefree. After he became a multimillionaire, he became controlling, authoritarian, anxious and suspicious. He needed a lot to feel a little, thus, he crushed his pleasure in living. His employees at his palace were happier than he was. Money had impoverished him.

Besides, Lucius had a paranoid personality. It was not a paranoid psychosis because he never fled from reality, but he was always tormented with ideas of being persecuted or defrauded. He was afraid of being kidnapped. He owned three armored cars and wherever he went he had an escort of four bodyguards. If that wasn't enough, he did not even trust his friends. He thought that everyone who approached him had ulterior motives.

But of all his psychological ghosts, the one about his daughter falling prey to a man who took advantage of her was the worst. Now, right before his eyes, his worst nightmare was coming true.

The police commissioner felt cornered because Lucius had revealed that he had needed his money in front of Dr. Wilson. He wanted to do what Lucius had told him to, but since it was a delicate situation, he was only able to reply, "How can we interrupt this marriage? Have you considered the scandal it would be? Look at the governor. There are more than twenty congressmen, ten senators and three federal cabinet members. Few businessmen in the country would be able to gather so many powerful people in one place."

So, Lucius finally realized that although many of the politicians needed his money to get elected, the scandal could create unpredictable consequences. He glanced at Marco Polo's friends and saw a disturbing scene. "Look at those wretches. They don't need to act. They are what they are. Damn scandal! We need an *alibi*!"

Chapter 28

The wedding ceremony commenced. The judge raised his voice and pronounced the famous words, "If you know of any reason why these two should not be married, speak now or forever hold your peace."

Lucius froze. He wanted to shout but he couldn't. After a moment of silence, someone shouted from the entrance, "The groom has abandoned his child!"

There was a mortal silence among the guests. Some people began to feel faint. The judge became silent. The accuser insisted from afar, "Why did you abandon your child?" Elisabeth could not breathe and she thought, "Jesus Christ! This has never happened in our family." The politicians and businessmen were dumbfounded. A cabinet member said in a low voice, "The event of the year will surely be the scandal of the century."

The women exclaimed, "Shame! How can anyone abandon a child?" Everyone was condemning Marco Polo. Lucius suddenly stood, grabbed the commissioner by the arm and said: "This is our *alibi*! This guy has never fooled me! Get security over here. Get Anna out of here!"

"Calm down, Lucius! Wait!"

"Wait for what?"

"This might get turned into an uncontrollable agitation. The safety of the authorities might be at risk!" he said trembling.

The strange man came closer and shouted, "You left your child, crying and without breathing!" Some of the guests commented, "Murderer! This man is worthless!"

Anna felt a knot in her throat. Marco Polo anxiously tried to raise his eyes to see who was denouncing him. His friends from the Atlantic Hospital had stilled even their repetitive movements. They barely breathed. The astonished audience tried to reach the accuser with their eyes. The ballroom became too small for such indignation. The mumbling was intense. The commissioner decided to take action. He ordered twenty squad cars to be on standby around the hotel. He also positioned fifty undercover police officers. Raising his hand and suddenly lowering it would be the sign for them to move into action. He would get Anna out of there; and also protect Lucius, the most important authorities and businessmen. As he raised his hand to make that signal, another vibrant voice called out in the ballroom. It was Marco Polo, "I assume my guilt. I have abandoned my child. My professional activity and my existential worries have stolen my time. But I promise him that I will never abandon him again."

The elderly ladies said to one another, "What a sorry excuse for a father! How can he put work before his child? That's an excuse!"

"Nourish your child with wisdom and simplicity; irrigate the kid with freedom! Don't let your child die or lack education." said the strange man in an even louder voice.

"Besides being my enemy he's a terrible father. A scandal cannot be avoided. Come on, let's end this!" said Lucius to the commissioner, pushing him to get him to take action.

Sweat was running like raindrops down the commissioner's face. He knew that the confusion could be so great that people might trample each other. When he was about to give the signal once again, he saw Marco

Polo taking Anna by the hand and walk towards the accuser. He took a deep breath and told the one hundred eyes fixed on him to wait.

"Yes! I will educate my child." And looking at his bride he exclaimed, "I'll ask Anna to help me with this care."

Some people, perplexed with his nerve, said: "Irresponsible! He's had a kid and now he wants another woman to take responsibility for him."

Lucius went even further, "Scoundrel! He wants to bring his bastard child into my family. It has to be now commissioner!"

For the third time, the commissioner raised his hand. He could not go against the one who had favored him so much. When he was about to lower his hand, starting off the agitation, another voice occupied the ballroom. To everyone's perplexity, especially Lucius', a young woman who had always been fragile, timid and insecure and who never spoke in public came forward. Anna exclaimed, "I'll take care of Marco Polo's child as if it was my own kid." And looking around, added, "And those who do not allow their inner child to live will lose their spontaneity, destroy their simplicity and suffocate their creativity. They will be unhappy before God and before men. They will be transformed into wretches, even if they do live in palaces. Their intelligence will be sterile even if they are intellectuals."

The congressmen, senators, cabinet members, bankers, industrialists and their wives almost had a collective panic attack. Gasping, they rubbed their hands over their faces, scratched their heads, looked at one another and were deeply shaken.

The accuser came closer and Marco Polo said: "Falcon, my friend! You were the only one missing!" He and Anna embraced him affectionately and kissed him.

The audience went gradually from astonishment to enchantment. Only someone as irreverent as Falcon would arrive in such a manner. He had never been worried about social makeup. At this sublime moment in the life of his dear friend, formalities did not matter nor was he concerned about what others might think. He wanted to publicly give the best gift a human being can receive: one's heart.

His young friend was becoming famous and overburdened with activities. This pleased and worried Falcon at the same time. He knew that if Marco Polo, like any other person who reaches success, were not careful, he might destroy the curious, adventurous, daring inner child, who loves, dreams and is enchanted with life. He knew that the only place where aging is inadmissible is the territory of emotions.

Many of the guests had already destroyed their inner child and lived in an emotional asylum. Existence had lost its flavor. They were alive only because they breathed. They did not question themselves, they did not internalize and they did not realize that life and death are indecipherable phenomena in the theater of existence. They became part of the audience in this incomprehensible theater. They were constantly in motion, but they never got anywhere. They were considered gods, who were wealthy and famous, but also bankrupt.

Anna had met Falcon a few times. She agreed with and learned from his and Marco Polo's ideas. She had been greatly influenced by their bubbling joy, their courage to explore new things and to think differently. They helped each other. She wanted to be like them, think like an adult and feel like a child.

Falcon had also come because he wanted to thank Marco Polo for having broken his paradigms and helping him to rescue his son. Marco Polo had been disciple and master, son and father, who showed that the small can learn from the great and the great can allow themselves to learn from the small. There were no hierarchies in the territory of wisdom. Seeing his daughter and Marco Polo kiss the strange man was too much for Lucius.

He sat down and said: "This is a mirage! What's going on?"

"I have no idea!" said the commissioner wiping the sweat of his face with a handkerchief.

Some of the guests, feeling calmer now, opened their minds and exclaimed, "What a fabulous theatrical play. We've never seen anything like it. Lucius is a genius!"

Others, still in shock, found relief by drinking whiskey and vodka. There were even others, who were involved by a curtain of fear and were afraid that a shot might be fired.

Despite the distinct reactions, most of them gathered around the three characters forming a circle. Some of them stood on their seats to see the spectacle. The judge could not stop blinking, a nervous habit he had. Confused, he asked the pianist, "Are all weddings of the rich like this one?"

After embracing Marco Polo and Anna, Falcon recalled the old days in the parks. As if he was standing on a bench, in a completely public place, he proclaimed to both of them, "All love is beautiful at birth, but few resist the heat of the sun. May your love withstand the tests of existence!"

Spinning Anna with his left hand, Marco Polo cried out, "I will sail the seas of anxiety, I'll climb the mountains of fear and I'll walk over the valleys of disappointment so as not to let love die! I'll do everything I can to turn this beautiful woman into the princess of my story!"

The women, who had wanted to crucify Marco Polo earlier, now changed her opinion about him, "What a romantic young man! What a prince! This is the type of man my daughter needs."

Next, Falcon stepped back and began to sing, in his harsh voice, the song that had become the anthem of his life, *What a Wonderful World*. With his hands, he mimed the melody and pointed to the flowers. Marco Polo joined in. The piano and violins came to life. It was phenomenal.

While they sang, they put Anna between them. At the beginning of the song, they mentally apologized to Louis Armstrong and completely changed the lyrics, making up new lines for the bride. The two thinkers thought that Anna symbolized all those people who had gone through chaos during their childhood, irrecoverable loss, but despite everything, still believed that life was worth living. The fact that Anna had overcome her illness encouraged them.

"Life hasn't spared you, you withstood torment but survived," sang Marco Polo. "Thank you for existing. With you, life is sweeter" sang Falcon.

"And I think to myself...what a wonderful girl," they sang in duo.

"You've stumbled and hurt yourself, but you never gave up on your dreams." "You shine for us, you shine for the world."

"And I think to myself...what a wonderful girl."

The song penetrated the innermost fabric of Anna's psyche, it became the mind's sublime activity and her emotions soared causing delight and making her cry. The princess who had lived in a dungeon was free. While she cried, she saw a movie in her mind, beautiful images of her mother hugging her, playing the piano for her, her first date with Marco Polo and the star he had given her.

Rarely had a child gone through the deserts Anna had crossed and rarely had anyone found such a pleasant oasis. Several guests began to cry.

After the song in Anna's honor, Claudia shouted to the musicians, "Waltz!" and pulled Falcon over to dance. Smiling, he made a gesture with his open hand as if to say, "Let's go for it!". The bride and the groom also began to dance freely and happily. Marco Polo's other friends also joined in and began to revolutionize the party. Later, Claudia chose someone else to dance with. Falcon, understanding the message, also asked another lady to dance with him. She was a banker's wife who had never danced with her husband. James invited a single middle-aged woman to dance with him.

Marco Polo was dancing with Dora and Anna invited her father's friend, who she liked a lot, to dance. The musicians were euphoric, but the judge almost had a heart attack. He kept shouting, "I haven't finished the ceremony!" but no one paid attention.

Isaac did not know how to waltz. Ali Ramadan had learned with Claudia. Seeing that his friend had been left out, Ali tried to teach him. Unafraid of learning, Isaac took his first dance steps with his friend. It was the first time in history that a Palestinian and a Jew had danced the same waltz together.

Suddenly, Dr. George appeared on the dance floor. Marco Polo was intensely pleased to see his former anatomy professor. After 'hurricane' Marco Polo had gone through his life, he had reviewed his values and his strictness.

His wife had supported him heroically, but it had been worthwhile. Dr. George had learned the path to affection. He became a kind, gentle and sociable man who had rescued his inner child. He learned how to play with his two children. At their birthdays, he'd dress up as a clown to entertain them.

He also caused a turnabout in the anatomy lab. His first class was no longer about dissection techniques of blood vessels and muscles; he began to talk about existential crises and dreams of the future doctors. The master had learned how to love debating ideas and not submission. He had changed so much that he asked his students to investigate the stories of the cadavers they were about to study. If they could not find anything, they had to imagine a story for them with dreams, joys, losses and challenges and, then, write it and affix it over each table as a sign of respect for the people there.

Dr. George started a foundation called "A human being, a fascinating story". This foundation's objective was to teach students from other schools how to discover the value of life and know that to become a great doctor, it is necessary to be an explorer, like Marco Polo, who discovers great stories within those who are anonymous.

Next, Dr. Flavius, the ER chief, discretely appeared on the dance floor. He was now head of his hospital. After Marco Polo came into his life, he understood that in the face of pain and death there are no giants or heroes. He became concerned with the conflicts that are hidden behind headaches, muscle pain, chest pain, tachycardia and hypertension crises.

Dr. Flavius, moved by sensitivity, started the foundation called "The integral human being". This foundation was formed by doctors, psychologists and psychiatrists and through pamphlets and lectures, intended to make emergency health professionals talk with their patients.

He wished to train them to listen with their hearts and understand that they treated people and not disease, human beings and not organs. The success of this training decreased the number of hospitalizations, cured illnesses and prevented many suicides. His wife, who was six months pregnant, insisted on coming to Marco Polo's wedding. She wanted to thank him for the changes in her husband, although Marco Polo knew that it was Dr. Flavius who had truly changed his ways. Her husband's emotional progress had made her feel like the happiest mother-to-be in the world.

Dr. Alexander was also there. When Marco Polo saw him dancing with his wife, he slowed down and greeted him affectionately. The noble professor had understood that if one of the greatest geniuses in Mankind, Einstein, had been the victim and the agent of prejudice, then no one is free of this evil.

He did some research and detected that many people still felt that those who went to a psychiatrist were crazy. With Marco Polo's help, he set up a foundation called "Prejudice never again" in order to diminish the social stigma of psychiatric patients and to elevate their self-esteem. He began to show that deep down, each human being has some king of psychological disorder and that the disease of prejudice is the worst of them all.

A well resolved, serene, balanced and wise man, an artist of psychiatry, approached the couple from behind in an almost imperceptible way. It was Dr. Anthony. He and his wife, to whom he had been married for over forty years, danced as if they were two teenagers. The newlyweds thought, "We want to age like them", because the way they looked at each other revealed that they had transformed the phase of least muscular strength into the phase of greater emotional strength and of intimate love.

After Marco Polo had debated at that famous convention on the dictatorship of the hypothesis of serotonin, the confrontation between psychiatry and psychology, and had exposed his complex theory that the human psyche co-inhabits, co-exists and co-interferes with the brain, Dr. Anthony and several illustrious psychiatry professors had spent many sleepless nights.

They invited the young psychiatrist to set up a scientific society to study the last frontier of science: the nature of *Homo sapiens*' psyche or soul. Marco Polo, Dr. Anthony and his friends had discussions of the highest academic level. Being part of them was like having one's intelligence caressed. Besides, they debated the possibility of psychiatry becoming a specialty of psychology and not only a part of medicine.

Suddenly, from the left side of the crowd, a person in a hurry appeared. He asked people to let him through insistently. Euphoric, he walked toward the dance floor. It was Dr. Mario. When Marco Polo saw him, he stopped dancing and hugged him and his wife for a long time.

Dr. Mario, in an unusual attitude, kissed his cheek. Then, the director of the Atlantic Hospital took his wife in his arms and began to dance in the center of the dance floor. When he met Marco Polo for the first time, he was in his third marriage and about to divorce again his wife, but after the 'tornado' Marco Polo swept through his life, the walls crumbled. He abandoned his throne, was no longer a psychiatrist at home, he became humanized and a gentleman.

His three children, from his two previous marriages, were in psychotherapy. Dr. Mario had been a specialist in criticizing them, pointing out their mistakes and being a rulebook, but after he drank from the fountain of spontaneity and became a dancer in life, he started to hug them, kiss them, captivate them and listen to them.

He learned how to apologize, recognizing his failures and having the courage to say that he loved them. His children were simply perplexed with him. They discovered that they had a psychiatrist-father and not a father-psychiatrist. They quickly finished their treatment. Thus, they were no longer future guests at a psychiatric hospital.

Dr. Mario took such a huge leap in the understanding of existence that he began to give innumerous conferences both nationally and internationally, discouraging psychiatric hospitalization. He understood that psychiatric hospitalization was a blow to the unconscious. In cases where hospitalization was inevitable, the hospitals should involve patients in dance, theater and arts and crafts so that they would feel useful. He could count on Dora and the other psychiatrists to help him. Claudia was one of the most active patients and Isaac became the sponsor of this project.

Isaac and Ali Ramadan also became dreamers. They had long talks with Marco Polo to know what they could do to help the Palestinian and Jewish people to overcome their conflicts. They mourned emotionally every time there was a Palestinian terrorist attack and an Israeli retaliation. They cried, not because of their illness, but for their people. "There was less suffering and it was less disturbing to be hospitalized than it was in many Middle East places," they thought.

With Marco Polo's guidance, they understood that, unfortunately, the violence in Palestine killed some people physically and emotionally killed millions, there were no winners in this conflict; everyone was a victim. They believed that if Palestinians and Jews were convinced that they weren't two distinct races or cultures in conflicts, but human beings who belonged to the same species with similar psychological needs, the majority of their resistance and suspicion would end. The three friends would fight so that this idea would be understood and widespread.

Except for Isaac, the sum of Marco Polo's reactionary friends' financial means to run social programs was meager. The financial balance was almost in the red. Some of them had financed their cars, others had mortgaged their homes and others had bank loans to pay. But despite all these, they would begin a social revolution incomparably greater than that of the multi-millionaires at Lucius' party, whose 'emotional GNP' was one of the lowest in this beautiful blue planet.

Two months before his wedding, Marco Polo had told Anna and Falcon about something that was burning in his heart. The principle of inevitable co-responsibility continued to control him. He wanted to set up an institution called "Human beings without boundaries" (HBWB) to deal with social conflicts, racial confrontations, the educational crisis and physical and psychological miseries.

He also intended to launch a worldwide movement to pressure the pharmaceutical laboratories that produced psychotropic drugs to invest part of their profit in the prevention of psychological disorders. He would suffer grave consequences for this audacity.

Marco Polo felt that the solution for the serious human conflicts began with the youth and not adults. However, he was saddened with what the predatory capitalism was doing to human beings, especially to the children in every modern society.

It afflicted him to know that in England, 78% of the children from the age of ten and older went shopping as their favorite pastime. It's what was demonstrated in the National Consumer Counsel. They grew with chronic anxiety and dissatisfaction because they hadn't learned how to free their creativity and extract pleasure from the small everyday stimuli. In most countries, the situation was the same.

Falcon and Marco Polo were disturbed by the emotional and physical hunger in the third millennium. In the world, a child dies of hunger every five seconds and the childhood of a child is assassinated by consumerism every second. Very few people cared about these two very serious crimes against Mankind.

The two rebellious friends would fight with all their might, to the last drop of blood, so that millions of young people of all races, of all religions, of all cultures, would no longer be servants of a social system that numbs the mind, steals their identity and transforms them into mere costumers. They wanted them to engage in the HBWB project, to be passionate about mankind and to create global projects in order to transform Mankind.

They felt that youth should act on the stage of life as leading actors and not die in the audience, subjugated by an individualistic, illusory, self-destructive, dependent life, imprisoned by routine and gagged by unhealthy standards of beauty.

Marco Polo had moments of failure, precipitation and anxiety but being around him was an invitation to walk on soil that had never been walked on before. He would turn his story into a great odyssey, just as exciting as the story of the 13th century Marco Polo.

He would get into a lot of trouble; he would shake a few of the society's pillars and would suffer implacable persecution, but he would not change who he was nor would he stop hugging trees and talking to flowers.

His relationship with Anna awakened his courage even more. A couple so passionate for adventures had never been seen before. The commotion at the wedding was a reflection of the life they would have. The disorder had been so great that there was the risk that they wouldn't get married.

Marco Polo was glad to see his friends gathered there, unafraid of life. He had learned from all of them. To Lucius Fernandez's disbelief, not only Marco Polo's friends broke with the protocol. A few couples including businessmen, congressmen, senators and even a cabinet member, stopped being spectators and came onto the dance floor.

Most of the authorities, businessmen and celebrities, however, were deeply irritated with Lucius, because they had come to network both politically and socially but they found a band of lunatics. They frowned and enjoyed a moment of the old bad mood.

There were other psychiatrists present. Some thought that a collective delirium had occurred. Others relaxed and allowed themselves to enjoy everything.

Lucius became hysterical. He kept rubbing his hands over his face, grinding his teeth with trembling lips. He was a serious candidate for the Atlantic Hospital. He looked at the commissioner, his guardian and repeated, "Kidnap my daughter, take her away from here or there will be another suicide in my family!"

"You're out of your mind, Lucius!"

"I'll give you five hundred thousand dollars for the job!", he said without hesitating.

"How much?"

The commissioner faltered. A couple then bumped into him while they were dancing.

The matter was momentarily cut short.

Never again was there such a shocking episode as that one. The judge, middle-aged, had married many people, but he had never gotten married. During the confusing wedding ceremony that still had not been completed, he thought perplexedly, "It's better not to risk marriage."

It had been an irreverent event, a young woman who fell in love with a dream salesman who had influenced mutilated people who rebuilt their lives and that despite all of their limitations, had learned how to dance the waltz of life with a free mind, unafraid of being who they are and unafraid of tomorrow.

It was not a happy ending, it was a happy comma, because this story, just as life, does not end with a period, it is an endless restarting. Happiness would have to be continuously rebuilt, for they would still cry, would go through loss, challenges, anxiety and misunderstandings.

At one point, Marco Polo, Falcon, Anna, Dr. Mario, Dr. Anthony and other friends made a circle in the center of the ballroom and began to twirl with emotion. They twirled and twirled and twirled.

While they twirled, they observed the faces of the spectators closely and noticed that, to most people, modern society was becoming more and more like a huge psychiatric hospital or a society of beggars who had not abandoned their homes but who had abandoned themselves; of people who sometimes have plenty but beg for the bread of pleasure, tranquility and wisdom.

To others, however, the world became a school or a circus or a place of adventure or a dance floor or a mixture of all of these. Marco Polo and his friends did not know where people, including themselves, would be placed in the future of mankind.

All they knew was that their place would depend on each one's courage to walk the paths of their own being, open the windows of their intelligence, rethink their story and choose freely.

They stopped twirling and together shouted to the audience and to themselves,

"Welcome to the future!".

THE END

Review Request

Before you go, can I ask you for a quick favor?

Would you please leave this book an honest review on Amazon?

Your review won't take long, but it can help this book reach more readers like you.

Thank you for reading, and thank you so much for being part of the journey.

-Augusto

www.ingramcontent.com/pod-product-compliance
Lightning Source LLC
Chambersburg PA
CBHW022100090426
42743CB00008B/662